THE VOICE FROM THE WHIRLWIND

THE VOICE FROM THE WHIRLWIND

INTERPRETING THE BOOK OF JOB

Edited by
Leo G. Perdue and W. Clark Gilpin

ABINGDON PRESS
Nashville

THE VOICE FROM THE WHIRLWIND
INTERPRETING THE BOOK OF JOB

Library of Congress Cataloging-in-Publication Data

The Voice from the whirlwind : interpreting the book of Job / edited by Leo G. Perdue and W. Clark Gilpin.
    p. cm.
    Includes bibliographical references.
    ISBN 0-687-43812-8 (pbk. : alk. paper)
    1. Bible. O.T. Job—Criticism, interpretation, etc. 2. Bible. O.T. Job—Criticism, interpretation, etc.—History. 3. Bible. O.T. Job—Theology. I. Perdue, Leo G. II. Gilpin, W. Clark.
BS1415.2.V65   1991
223'.106—dc20
                              91-42391
                                  CIP

Grateful acknowledgment is made for use of excerpts from the following:

From *The Jerusalem Bible* (JB), copyright © 1966 by Darton, Longman & Todd, Ltd., and Doubleday & Co., Inc. Used by permission of the publisher.

From the Revised Standard Version of the Bible (RSV), copyright © 1946, 1952, 1971 by the Division of Christian Education of the National Council of Churches of Christ in the USA. Used by permission.

From the New Revised Standard Version of the Bible (NRSV), copyright © 1989 by the Division of Christian Education of the National Council of Churches of Christ in the USA. Used by permission.

Chapter 7, "Providence in Medieval Aristotelianism: Moses Maimonides and Thomas Aquinas on the Book of Job," has been reprinted from *Hebrew Studies* 20-21 (1979–80): 64-73. Used by permission. Chapter 2, "The God of Job: Avenger, Tyrant, or Victor?" copyright © 1991 Tryggve N. D. Mettinger. Used by permission.

MANUFACTURED IN THE UNITED STATES OF AMERICA

Editorial Board and Contributors

Judith R. Baskin is Associate Professor and Chair, Department of Judaic Studies, State University of New York at Albany.

Michael Fishbane is Nathan Cumings Professor of Jewish Studies, University of Chicago Divinity School, Chicago, Illinois.

Carole R. Fontaine is Associate Professor of Old Testament, Andover Newton Theological School, Newton Centre, Massachusetts.

Langdon Gilkey is Shailer Mathews Professor Emeritus of Theology, University of Chicago Divinity School, Chicago, Illinois.

W. Clark Gilpin is Dean and Associate Professor of the History of Christianity, University of Chicago Divinity School, Chicago, Illinois.

René Girard is Andrew B. Hammond Professor of French Language, Literature, and Civilization; Professor of Comparative Literature; and Professor of Religious Studies (by courtesy), Stanford University, Stanford, California.

Edwin M. Good is Professor of Old Testament, Stanford University, Palo Alto, California.

James M. Gustafson is Henry R. Luce Professor of Humanities and Comparative Studies, Emory University, Atlanta, Georgia.

Norman C. Habel is Professor of Old Testament, University of South Australia, Underdale, South Australia.

Stuart Lasine is Associate Professor of Religion, Wichita State University, Wichita, Kansas.

Tryggve N. D. Mettinger is Professor of Old Testament in the Department of Biblical Studies, the Theologicum, Lund University, Lund, Sweden.

Carol A. Newsom is Associate Professor of Old Testament, Candler School of Theology, Emory University, Atlanta, Georgia.

Leo G. Perdue is Dean and Professor of Hebrew Bible, Brite Divinity School, Texas Christian University, Fort Worth, Texas.

Susan E. Schreiner is Assistant Professor of Historical Theology, University of Chicago Divinity School, Chicago, Illinois.

James G. Williams is Professor of Bible in the Department of Religion, Syracuse University, Syracuse, New York.

Martin D. Yaffe is Associate Professor in the Department of Philosophy and Religion Studies, University of North Texas, Denton, Texas.

PREFACE

In May of 1988, six persons met at the University of Chicago to plan a symposium on the book of Job that would eventuate in publication. In addition to the two editors of this volume, these six persons were Dr. Susan Schreiner, Dr. Carol Newsom, Dr. Stuart Lasine, and Dr. James Williams. The symposium took place during the 1989 annual meeting of the Society of Biblical Literature and the American Academy of Religion, held in Anaheim, California.

The symposium and this collection of essays would not have been possible without the support and encouragement of several persons. The planning committee is especially indebted to Dr. David Lull, Executive Director of the Society of Biblical Literature, for his important role in helping to arrange the symposium; and to Rex Matthews, our Abingdon Press editor, for his keen interest and personal involvement in this project through its various stages. Finally, special thanks are due the Disciples Divinity House of the University of Chicago for supporting both the symposium and the publication of this collection through its William Henry Hoover Lectureship.

CONTENTS

INTRODUCTION

Leo G. Perdue
and
W. Clark Gilpin

The book of Job, among the most compelling works of the Jewish and Christian canons of Scripture, has become one of the classics of Western culture. The manifold influence of Job on theology, philosophy, art, and literature derives not only from its literary excellence but also from its distinctive Jewish perspective on perennial features of the human predicament: the relation of good to evil, the nature of God, the character of justice, and the enigma of suffering. The book's profundity does not arise, however, from "solving" these problems of existence. On the contrary, it does not hesitate to leave the reader with painful questions about suffering or calamity; it challenges simplistic appeals to moral order in history; it enmeshes human responsibility in fate or destiny, but without absolving the human of responsibility. From antiquity to the present, therefore, the book of Job has been a fascination, often a problem, occasionally a scandal and a danger.

By its seeming refusal to offer univocal prescriptions, the book of Job has evoked extraordinarily different readings. The history of interpretation of Job is the history of a long cultural debate, in which shifting points of tension in the history of culture refocus "the point" of the text. To be sure, the surface of the narrative remains familiar. A man of wealth and upright life is beset by catastrophic destruction of family, property, and health. Unconsoled by the advice of friends, convinced that disaster has befallen through no fault of his own, he pleads his case before God. Ultimately, family, property, and comfort are restored to him. But different readers in different contexts have reread and retold this story in ways that have

11

given it multiple and sometimes directly conflicting meanings. In the histories of Judaism and Christianity, there is not one Job but many.

This fact about the history of interpretation of the book of Job has directly influenced the following collection of essays. They are united neither by one thesis about *the* meaning of Job nor by the conviction that a single, particular point of view will yield that meaning. Instead, this collection proposes that a consideration of multiple perspectives on the book will make all of us more attentive readers. It proposes that leading contemporary scholarship can contribute to such attentive reading. It proposes that contemporary readings of Job are deepened and extended if they are aware of the history of interpretation. It invites the reader to join this cultural dialogue, to return to Job, to rethink this classic text, to reconsider its many-faceted reflections on human existence.

In a formal way, these multiple perspectives are represented in the three main divisions of the book. Each major section will introduce contemporary readers to the interpretive vantage points of different, but complementary, academic disciplines: biblical scholarship, historical scholarship, and contemporary theological, ethical, and literary reflection on the text. The essays demonstrate the ways in which new interpretive *contexts* have regularly reshaped the horizons within which the critical questions raised by the *text* of Job are understood and answered. In the remainder of this introduction, we offer some comments first on the *text* of Job and then on the *contexts* of interpretation.

The Text of Job

The book of Job underwent a rather lengthy literary history before it achieved its present canonical form. Tracing this development and assigning precise dates are difficult, but biblical scholarship, especially over the past two centuries, has made repeated efforts. While there is no consensus among scholars of Job about historical-critical questions, the following represents one possible reconstruction.

The Joban folk tale, partially preserved in chapters 1–2 and 42:7-17, is generally regarded as the oldest part of the book, originating no later than the period of the Hebrew monarchy (ca. 1000 B.C.E.–587 B.C.E.). The poetic dialogues (3–27, 29–31, 38:1–42:6) may best be traced to the social upheaval incurred by the Babylonian exile (587 B.C.E.–538 B.C.E.). Two poetic additions probably derive from the Persian period (538 B.C.E.–332 B.C.E.): the poem on the inaccessibility of wisdom (28) and the Elihu speeches (32–37). Whatever dates are assigned to the various stages of the growth of the book of Job, the present form of the book was not achieved until the fourth century B.C.E.

This literary history, encompassing several centuries and representing numerous writers and editors, has complicated the task of interpretation. As is the case with many books in the Hebrew Bible, no single author is responsible for the entire book.

The folk tale is a didactic narrative (cf. the Joseph story in Gen. 37–50) in which a hero (or antagonist) is introduced and characterized by a particular virtue or ability that is confirmed by his or her action. In the narrative of Job, the hero is a wealthy, righteous, pious man who serves God. An anti-hero, who is deceitful, then typically enters the drama of the didactic narrative and causes the hero some misfortune. This role is played by "the Satan" (a type of prosecuting attorney), who questions Job's integrity: He serves God only because of reward. The Satan, with God's approval, afflicts Job with a series of disasters. Job loses all that he has, including his health. Later the wife serves in the role of the antagonist in attempting to persuade Job to "curse God and die." While the conversation between Job and the three friends in the narrative appears to have been replaced by the poetic dialogues, it may be that they also became the antagonists of Job in the original folk tale.

As the didactic narrative proceeds, the hero demonstrates, through conflict and struggle, his or her virtue or ability. Thus, in the folk tale Job probably continued his unquestioned faith in God, though again the poetic dialogues change Job into a defiant, accusing character who attacks the justice of God. Didactic tales usually have as their climax a judgment scene that confirms the integrity of the hero and announces punishment for the antagonist. In the folk tale (42:7-17), Job is exonerated and restored to his former position, while the friends are condemned and ironically must depend on Job's intercession to escape divine punishment.

The folk tale approaches the question of the "suffering of the righteous" by means of the theory of retribution: God punishes the wicked and rewards the righteous. However, the theory of retribution is modified by postulating the belief that God tests the righteous at times to determine if they will remain faithful. If an exilic date is appropriate for the poetic dialogues (3–27, 29–31, 38:1–42:6), the crisis precipitated by the Babylonian conquest of Judah gave rise to the rewriting of the folk tale. Its theory of retribution and testing of the faith of the righteous could not adequately address the horrors of the Babylonian holocaust. In the poetic dialogues, the character of Job is transformed from a patient, long-suffering, righteous, faithful worshiper of God to an angry accuser. The Job of the dialogues is righteous though not perfect like his narrative counterpart in the folk tale. The center of concern shifts from the virtue of Job to the character of God.

Chapters 3–27 consist of three cycles of dialogue between Job and his three friends (now adversaries): 3–11, 12–20, and 21–27. The literary composition of the third cycle is in disarray. One solution to this problem is offered in the following arrangement:

21	Job
22	Eliphaz
23	Job
24	Zophar(?)
25:1-6; 26:5-14	Bildad
26:1-4; 27:1-12	Job
27:13-23	Zophar

These dialogues assume primarily the form of disputations: the address of the opponent, the accusation (indictment), the argument, and the concluding summary or counsel. On occasion, the character Job borrows from the lament genre when he invokes the deity, presents his complaint, describes his suffering, reproaches God, petitions for help, condemns his enemies, and confesses his sins or asserts his innocence. Unlike laments in the Psalter, Job does not petition God for help, acknowledge his confidence in God's willingness to help, make a vow, or thank and praise the deity for divine justice and grace. Instead, Job attacks divine justice, denies God is merciful, and indicts the Almighty for divine misrule of the cosmos. It is the injustice and caprice of God, not human sin, that resides at the problem of the suffering of the righteous. The three opponents, who are the stalwart defenders of God, intensify and eventually personalize their charges against Job, but the third cycle of disputation ends without a resolution or clear winner. The poetic dialogues then shift to a soliloquy in which Job addresses the Almighty (29–31). Job begins with contrasting his former life of well-being (29) with his present misfortune and sorrow (30). Chapter 31 is an attestation of innocence in which Job utters some twelve vows by which he legally defends his honor. At the end, Job throws down the gauntlet to God and dares the Almighty to meet him in a courtroom where justice will prevail.

The final section of the dialogues consists of two speeches of God ("the voice from the whirlwind") and two responses by Job (38:1–42:6). Most scholars of Job see this section as critical for interpreting the book. However, there is no consensus about either the meaning of the speeches or Job's two responses. Two approaches have been taken to interpreting the speeches of God. One approach focuses not on the content but rather on the theophany itself. Thus some scholars argue that God's turning to Job demonstrates divine compassion and care for the sufferer, while others think that Job's encounter with divine majesty negates the theory of retribution and makes insignificant all prior experience with its questions. Another approach attempts the more risky venture of interpreting the content of the speeches. Here, interpretations range from God's efforts to sustain justice in creation and history, in spite of the presence of chaos and evil, to God's transcending human standards of justice, to God's admission of divine culpability in distorting justice and wreaking havoc. What is common to most of these interpretations is the rejection of the validity of the doctrine of retribution.

Job's two responses also receive varied interpretations. Some scholars think Job repents of a rash and unsubstantiated attack on the justice of God. Job now turns to God in humility and trust and gives thankful praise for the Almighty's loving concern and communion with the sufferer. Several scholars think Job does not repent of his accusations against God, describing his repentance as tongue-in-cheek. Job has tricked God into disclosing divine caprice and misrule.

Two poetic additions conclude the final composition of Job: the poem on the inaccessibility of Wisdom (28) and the Elihu speeches (32–37). Chapter 28 presents an elegant poem that asks about the location of wisdom. Noting that wisdom is beyond the reach of humanity, the poem concludes with the traditional affirmation that wisdom resides with God. Subsequently, to "fear God and to turn from evil" comprise the true meaning of wisdom. Elihu's four speeches have no respondent, either God or Job. And they seem to add very little to the content of both the debate that precedes and the theophany that follows. The speeches generally have been ignored as irrelevant by most interpreters of Job.

Biblical scholars, especially since the Enlightenment, have been primarily concerned, until recently, with tracing the literary history of a biblical book and interpreting each stage of its compositional development in isolation from the others. Biblical scholarship has been largely a historical-critical enterprise. The essay by Tryggve Mettinger represents this approach. Thus the folk tale, the poetic dialogues, the poem on the inaccessibility of Wisdom, and the Elihu speeches have been treated as isolated units with their own authors, themes, dates, audiences, and social contexts. Few efforts to relate the stages and provide a uniform interpretation of the entire book have been undertaken.

However, since the 1970s, biblical scholarship has entered into the vast domain of literary theory and has used a variety of its methods to investigate the meanings of texts: new criticism, Aristotelian interpretation, comparative literature, Russian formalism, structuralism, folklore studies, and readings influenced by psychological and sociopolitical ideologies, to name some of the more important approaches. Employing new, literary approaches, some scholars have focused their attention more on the final form of the text of Job than on its literary history. The essays by Edwin Good, Norman Habel, Michael Fishbane, Carole Fontaine, Stuart Lasine, René Girard, and James Williams in this collection represent scholarship that has taken this methodological turn. This does not mean that Job does not have a lengthy literary history, but it does indicate that some scholars are attempting to give the book a single reading that focuses on its present canonical form.

Contexts of Job

Turning from the text to the interpretive contexts, it is obvious that no single volume could provide a full history of the interpretation of the book of Job. In this regard the essays are illustrative, not exhaustive. Michael Fishbane, for example, suggests how Job participates in a context of "inner-biblical discourse," in which the text alludes to symbols and rhetorical conventions found in Scripture as a whole. Appreciation of the placement of "Joban rhetoric in the full spectrum of biblical language," Fishbane argues, enhances the reader's appreciation for the argumentation of the speakers within the book itself. Just as there is literary context, so, from another point of view, there is social context. Judith R. Baskin illustrates this in her essay on interpretation of Job by the rabbinic sages. Baskin explores the rabbinic debate about whether or not Job was a Gentile in order to demonstrate that "the effort to represent Job as an Israelite, or conversely, to compare him unfavorably with Israelite exemplars because he was a Gentile, is certainly evidence of contradictory Jewish attitudes toward Gentiles in the rabbinic period." Third, the context for reading Job may be more specifically philosophical or theological. Thus the essays by Martin D. Yaffe and Susan E. Schreiner investigate the use of Job by Maimonides, Aquinas, and Calvin as a resource for exploring the powers and the limits of human wisdom. Langdon Gilkey reflects on the theological questions posed by the book of Job within a contemporary theological framework. In these and other ways, the multiplicity of historical and contemporary contexts for understanding the book of Job suggest to readers a variety of possible and compelling paths of entry into this inexhaustible book.

This employment of multiple perspectives on the book of Job is not, however, intended merely to celebrate profusion for its own sake. Joban interpretation has definite continuities. But, as suggested above, these continuities are formed more decisively by the points deemed worthy of debate than by the individual positions put forward in the course of cultural dialogue on Job. This is evident, for instance, in the perennial effort to define the character of the *dramatis personae* in the Joban drama: God, the Satan, the friends, and Job himself. Who is Job? Not only the rabbinic sages but also Franz Kafka posed that question. Who is God? In the opening essays of the collection, biblical scholars Tryggve Mettinger and Norman C. Habel explore a series of characterizations of the deity: God the Avenger, the Tyrant, the Victor, and the Sage. In the concluding essays, theological ethicist James M. Gustafson returns to these contending characterizations by asking three carefully crafted questions about the relation between God and human well-being: "Is God experienced (not simply thought) as indifferent to the well-being of humans? As providentially caring for the good of humans through the course of events? Or as being the source, but not the guarantor of the well-being of humans?" The book of Job evokes such fundamental questions from a serious reader. It resists easy answers to those questions. Perhaps the evocation of such intellectual and religious honesty is the principal source for continuities in the history of the book's interpretation.

PART I

Biblical Interpretations of Job

CHAPTER 1

IN DEFENSE OF GOD THE SAGE

Norman C. Habel

God's lyrical reply to Job from the whirlwind has long been a conundrum for biblical
interpreters.[1] Numerous questions are raised in the book of Job for
which one might expect straight answers in God's closing oration.
Few, if any, are forthcoming. The obvious specifics of Job's case
are apparently ignored. Job's demand that God specify the charges
against him seems to be bypassed. Instead God engages in a poetic
defense of the mysterious *ʿēṣâ* that informs the universe.

It is my contention in this chapter that the book of Job is as much
about God as it is about the specifics of Job's crisis. The reply of
God from the whirlwind, I would argue, is a theological defense of
God the sage. This *apologia* offers a profound alternative to the
various characterizations of God offered in the rest of the book: the
God of the prologue who intervenes directly in human lives, the God
of the friends who reacts when humans act, the violent warrior God
whom Job experiences in his affliction, and the mysterious first sage
who acquires wisdom and appears to hide it somewhere. The
apologia from the whirlwind offers a fresh defense of God as sage
that is worthy of our consideration in a time when cosmic ecology is
no longer confined to the libraries of theologians.

My approach here will be largely thematic, focusing on the
images and portrayals of God in the book of Job and relevant
wisdom materials, and taking into account those exegetical niceties
that highlight the distinctive features of God's character designa-
tions throughout the text. This thematic theological study will
confine itself primarily to the characterizations of God from the
wisdom tradition, where the poet's theology in God's reply from the
whirlwind represents a significant development.

21

The Successful Sage

Before exploring the characterization of God as sage, it seems
appropriate to consider briefly the image of the sage, which
dominates the wisdom tradition found in the prologue of Proverbs.
This work is chosen because here the link between human sages and
God the sage is made explicit. The sage in this tradition is one who
(1) acquires wisdom, (2) exercises wisdom, and, (3) anticipates the
fruits of wisdom. This sage belongs to the elite of society—honored,
educated, and successful.

The first priority of the wise is to acquire wisdom.[2] The counsel of
the sages is clear:

> Wisdom comes first. Acquire wisdom.
> With all you acquire, acquire discernment.
>   (Prov. 4:7)

Wisdom may be acquired, it seems, in three ways: by following the
instructions of those sages who know the wisdom tradition (Prov.
4:1ff.), by heeding the call of Wisdom herself and embracing her as
guide (Prov. 1:20ff.), or by receiving wisdom as a gracious gift from
the Lord (Prov. 2:6).[3] The prologue, it would appear, no longer
distinguishes sharply between these three modes nor views them as
mutually exclusive. To acquire wisdom, by whatever means, is the
commitment of all would-be sages; to embrace wisdom is their goal.

Equipped with the fear of the Lord as the appropriate attitude and
the teachings of the tradition as the accepted guidelines for traveling
the way prescribed by wisdom, the sage was ready to exercise
discipline in the search for wisdom (Prov. 4:13; 8:10). The tenets of
wisdom that were to be followed were the outcome of generations of
observation and discernment. The training of a sage involved
developing the acumen to observe, discern, and test these laws of
life distilled in the wisdom tradition. Qoheleth reports how time and
again he "observed" various things "under heaven" with an eye of
critical discernment.

Those who follow the principles of wisdom faithfully can expect
success. Wisdom herself promises that those who love her more than
longevity, wealth, or honor will enjoy precisely those rewards. This

vision held up by wisdom for her devotees may be idealized, yet it seems to reflect a basic dream of success that sages hoped to achieve:

> Blessed is the person who finds wisdom
> and the person who gains discernment.
> For the gain is better than the gain from silver
> And its profit better than gold.
> She is more precious than jewels
> And nothing you can desire can compare with her.
> Long life is in her right hand;
> In her left hand are riches and honour.
>
> (Prov. 3:13-16)

Surprisingly, this portrait of the successful sage is followed by a reference to Yahweh's creative deeds:

> By wisdom Yahweh set the earth on its foundations;
> By discernment he established the heavens.
>
> (Prov. 3:19)

Why this apparently intrusive reference to God's creating the earth by wisdom? If Crenshaw is correct in asserting that the wise "refused to reinforce their teachings by appealing to the doctrine of creation," what is the point of this allusion?[4] I would argue, in the light of the discussion that follows, that the focus here is not on God as creator but on God as sage. As the first sage, God is the prototype of all sages; God is the model of primordial success. Wisdom has worked for sages from the beginning. By exercising wisdom and discernment, God was able to achieve great things, the construction of heaven and earth. For those who follow suit, the sky would appear to be the limit.

God's Acquisition of Wisdom

In its present form, I would argue, the soliloquy of Wisdom in Proverbs 8 includes an account of how Yahweh acquired wisdom and became the first sage. This soliloquy is frequently considered a classic portrait of divine or cosmic wisdom as distinct from human wisdom.[5] It should be recognized at the outset, however, that the figure of personified wisdom associated with Yahweh in this chapter is the same figure who offers herself as the mentor of mortals and the means by which monarchs rule. The wisdom that God acquires here appears to be the same wisdom that other sages may acquire. And acquiring wisdom is the first priority of a sage. Accordingly, Yahweh the Sage first acquires wisdom. As Wisdom herself testifies:

> Yahweh acquired me first!
> His way before his works.
> From of old, from antiquity I was set up.
> From the first, from the beginnings of the earth.
> (Prov. 8:22-23)[6]

As Vawter has shown, there are no convincing linguistic or contextual grounds for depicting Yahweh as "creating" or "begetting" wisdom.[7] The verb *qānâ* is a technical term for "acquire" throughout Proverbs (4:5-7; 16:16) and the Old Testament. Yahweh acquires wisdom in the primordial domain; Yahweh is the first sage. Even the primordial deeps (*tĕhōmôt*; cf. Gen. 1:2) were not yet in existence, and the structures that order the universe were not yet in place (Prov. 8:25-29). Wisdom is preexistent. Yahweh acquires her as a first act and then functions with wisdom in a particular way to construct the universe. Clearly wisdom is depicted here not as a divine attribute but as a divine acquisition, the vehicle for Yahweh's successful design of the cosmos.

This acquisition is described as "his way [*derek*] before his works." As God's *derek,* wisdom seems to be a governing principle or design that enables Yahweh to construct the world successfully. Beyond the complexities of the visible cosmos lies a mysterious governing principle or design, depicted here as Yahweh's companion, one with whom Yahweh celebrates from the very beginning (Prov. 8:30-31). Those would-be sages who fear Yahweh, the first sage, and embrace Wisdom and follow her as the way can also expect to succeed.

The portrait of God as the sage who acquires wisdom in the primordial time represents an alternative characterization of God to that of Yahweh as the mighty warrior who acquires kingship. Like Marduk and Baal in their respective domains, Yahweh becomes a king through conquest.[8] Yahweh's victory over chaos in the primordial time (Ps. 74:12-17) is superseded and subsumed by his intervention in the historical domain. Through his conquest of the Egyptians in the Exodus event and at the battle of the Reed Sea, Yahweh is acclaimed not only as incomparable among the gods but also as the king who will reign forever (Exod. 15). As king Yahweh rules, establishes a covenant with the Israelites, and intervenes in their lives. Yahweh disposes of their enemies and expects total allegiance from all followers. Yahweh is El Gibbor, the hero king who intervenes to perform great and terrible deeds (Prov. 24:8; Deut. 17:10).

The book of Job, I would argue, challenges the adequacy of this traditional characterization of God as the warrior king, the God who acts or intervenes.

The God Who Intervenes

Job is the model of success, the perfect sage. He was not only blameless but "feared God and shunned evil" in accord with the classical counsel of the wise (Job 1:1; cf. Prov. 3:7; 9:10; 14:16; 15:33). This interpretation of the passage is confirmed by the *inclusio* that links this verse with the midpoint of the book (Job 28:28):[9]

> Behold to fear God is wisdom,
> To shun evil is discernment.

Yahweh repeats this verdict when he announces to the Satan:

> Truly there is no one like him on the earth
> a blameless and upright man,
> who fears God and shuns evil.
>
> (Job 1:8)

The challenge of the Satan, the accuser, is whether Job will fear God without the rewards of wisdom. The fear of God is the beginning of wisdom. Faith is the prerequisite of discernment. What more should Job need? Will Job still be wise if all the success that comes with following the way of wisdom is eliminated? Will Job still discern truly without the blessings he enjoys as a successful sage?

Such is the focus of our questions *if* we concentrate on the character of Job. If, however, we focus on the character of God in this prologue, we are struck by a harsh incongruity. This is not the typical God of the wisdom tradition but a deity who holds court with a celestial council, a heavenly ruler with reporting messengers. Here is a God who in one realm makes ad hoc decisions about particular people and in another intervenes to implement those decisions. Here is a God who acts, who intervenes, who interferes directly in the lives of human beings rather than following previously announced laws of divine behavior. Here is a God who is fiercely jealous about one successful mortal and allows himself, by his own admission, to be enticed into a wager with the accuser (Job 2:3). Here is a God like the God of the prophets, who makes decisions in the council on high and intervenes in the lives and history of his people. Unlike the God of the prophets, however, there is here no ''Thus says the Lord'' to explain the reason for Yahweh's act of intervention.

The second incongruity here is that God acts in a way that appears to contradict the typical *modus operandi* of God in the wisdom tradition. Job has followed the way of wisdom, feared God, shunned evil, and been successful. He is the greatest. Reward was the natural outcome of such a life. For God to intervene and erase all these successes without any provocation by Job seems not only arbitrary but totally out of character with God. God contravenes the moral laws of divine behavior upon which the traditional way of wisdom was founded. This God does not appear to be God the sage but a version of God the jealous king, who is apparently willing to violate human life to gratify personal ends. Can such a characterization of God be allowed to stand without reply? The portrait of God in the prologue, it seems, is a deliberate provocation for a fresh defense of God the sage.

The God Who Reacts

As soon as Job begins to curse his origins and accuse God of arbitrarily imprisoning him in a hedge of afflictions, the friends rise proudly to God's defense. They function broadly within the wisdom tradition, focusing forcibly on the moral character of God. God is honorable, they argue, operating strictly according to the divine principles of cosmic and moral order established from the beginning. Where humans are righteous, God blesses them; where they are wicked God chastises, afflicts, or, in the last resort, destroys them. The God of the friends is not a God who acts or interferes but a God who reacts. The pattern of the universe, with its inbuilt moral code, is already determined. Justice is a guaranteed system of reward and retribution, of God reacting to the good or ill that mortals do.

For every human action there is a corresponding divine reaction, whether directly or indirectly through the governing laws of life. Job's condition, therefore, is a reflection of God's reaction. Human observation and the canons of wisdom theology would appear to lead relentlessly to this one conclusion.

Initially Eliphaz reminds Job that "the fear of God" ought to be his enduring consolation and cites a number of proverbs to substantiate the traditional wisdom position that what sages sow they will also reap (Job 4:6-11). Eliphaz testifies to the validity of the sapiential principle that retribution is the necessary and natural consequence of human misdeeds just as reward is the natural consequence of righteousness. Job is not impressed with Eliphaz's compassion. A true friend, replies Job, is loyal even when a sufferer forsakes the fear of Shaddai and loses faith in God (6:14).[10]

The friends claim to know the valid traditions of wisdom inherited from the fathers (15:18-19; 8:8-9) and to have proved their veracity through personal observation and discernment (5:27; cf. 4:6). They accuse Job of subverting the fear of God by his arrogant claim to a superior level of knowledge. With blatant sarcasm Eliphaz asks Job if he was the first human ever born, acquired Wisdom for himself in the primordial council of God, and kept her secluded as his private companion (15:2-10). The friends dare not even contemplate the characterization of God in the prologue. According to their theology, Job must be in the wrong.

Clearly the friends are threatened by Job's challenge to their secure understanding of God. Bildad clutches at straws in his opening defense of God when he blurts out:

> Does El pervert justice?
> Does Shaddai pervert the right?

>   Your children must have sinned against him
>   And he dispatched them over to their wickedness.
>
>   (Job 8:3-4)

Zophar admits there is a mysterious side to God's wisdom in the operation of the world, but from the human side of heaven the moral principle of human action followed by divine reaction holds good. Job should consider himself fortunate that God exacted from him less than his guilt demanded (11:6). Eliphaz pushes the implication of Job's guilt to the limit. For Eliphaz God's integrity stands unassailable, even before the heroic Job. God cannot be exposed as fickle by a human sage like Job. Job's horrendous crimes have led to God's heavy reaction. There is no other conclusion. The character of their God must remain unimpeachable. There is no just world if God is not the moral God of their tradition, the God who reacts.

God the *Gibbôr*

Job was not informed why God should suddenly intervene in Job's life. Job knew within himself that by the past canons of wisdom tradition, the act was unwarranted. He intuited that God had taken the initiative and intervened for some personal end. Job felt betrayed. Accordingly Job's portrayal of the God who intervenes is less than complimentary. From Job's vantage point, this God not only intervenes in human lives but also hounds human beings as prey.

This is the mighty *gibbôr*, the hero, the warrior who attacks Jcb with poisoned arrows and seeks to overwhelm him with terror and dread (6:4). This is God the merciless hunter who watches for particular human prey to pursue (7:20-21), the violent and cruel warrior who smashes and rends Job personally (16:6-16). Violence seems to be characteristic of this God, at least in Job's experience, even though Job claims, "There is no violence in my hands and my plea is pure" (16:17). This is the warrior king who leads troops against Job, as if he were an enemy king in a walled city, and proceeds to strip him of all dignity and glory (19:6-12). For Job, God, the *gibbôr*, seems to be the "God Who Acts" gone berserk in the life of one mortal.

Given this propensity of God's, Job is stirred to challenge the character of God as sage, or more specifically the way God exercises wisdom with a heavy hand (Job 12). This God, according to Job's portrayal, promotes cosmic destruction and social disorder rather than peace, order, and stability. His *modus operandi* is an exercise in anarchy, his style fosters violence, and his governance seems to negate the very nature of wisdom as the ordering principle of the cosmos and society:

> With him [God] are wisdom and power,
> His are design and understanding.
> When he breaks down there is no rebuilding;
> When he imprisons there is no release.
> When he holds back the waters they dry up;
> When he lets them loose they overthrow the earth.
>
> (Job 12:13-15)

God exercises wisdom by demolishing what humans have constructed. In his wisdom he nullifies the efficacy of society's leaders. In the city gate, the court, and the temple, God renders community leaders impotent. He deprives trusted elders of their capacity to discern truth. Instead of promoting discernment, God blunts it; instead of promoting enlightenment, God fosters darkness; instead of stirring the human intellect, God creates morons:

> He deprives people's leaders of their minds,
> And makes them wander in a trackless waste.
> They grope in darkness with no light;
> He makes them wander like a drunkard.
>
> (Job 12:24-25)

Instead of providing people with a clear *derek* to identify their purpose and destiny in life, God activates a chaos (*tōhû*) that resembles the primordial wasteland. This violence of God apparently results from the way God consults Wisdom and monitors her design for the world. Job's experience of God as *gibbôr* seems to have influenced his exposé of God the sage. God does not exercise wisdom according to the moral code of behavior upheld by the wisdom tradition. The mysteries of God may, according to Bildad, be deeper than Sheol, but according to Job God releases darkness from the depths of Sheol to envelop the world, create disorder, and leave the universe disoriented (12:22). God is an anarchist—a violent anarchist. To call this God wise seems to be totally absurd.

God the First Sage

At the midpoint of the book of Job, after the characterization of God by the storyteller of the prologue and the speeches of the three wise friends and the distraught Job, the poet of Job offers a new portrait of God the first sage.[11] The location of this portrait seems to be a commentary on the inadequate characterizations that have preceded. The poet seems to be saying that if these are the best images of God that so-called human wisdom can discern, then Wisdom must be inaccessible and God must have hidden her in primordial seclusion. Some would argue that wisdom in Job 28 is a cosmic, divine wisdom that is quite distinct from human wisdom. The text here, as in Proverbs 8, however, speaks only of one wisdom that both mortals and God seek to acquire.

The theme of this pivotal poem is the search for wisdom. The underlying metaphor is the search for what is rare and precious. In that search three central motifs appear: the place or source of the precious item, the way or means of access to that item, and the process of discovering the item. In developing these motifs a number of polarities emerge: The capacity of humans and God to discover precious earthly items of relative value is compared with the priceless worth of wisdom. For those who would be wise, the quest for wisdom is the ultimate goal in life.

For all their capacity for penetrating to the limits of the earth for rare and precious items, humans are still faced with the ultimate question:

> Wisdom, where can she be found?
> Where is the place of discernment?
> (Job 28:12; cf. v. 20)

The process of discerning wisdom is here depicted in terms of discovery. Wisdom is to be found (*māṣāʾ*) in the midst of the search; wisdom, like other rare items, has her appropriate locus in the universe. She is embedded in the hidden depths. In the wisdom tradition of Proverbs, wisdom promises that those who seek her diligently will "find" her (Prov. 8:17, 35; cf. 1:28; 4:22; 24:14), and those who find her will enjoy life. According to Job 28, however, wisdom cannot be found by mortals employing any of the traditional means for searching the extremities of the universe (28:13). Wisdom seems to be inaccessible to treasure-hunting humans; it lies hidden in its own secret domain.

God, however, did discover wisdom and became the first sage:

> God discerned the way to her [wisdom]
> And came to know her place.
> For God looked to the ends of the earth
> And saw everything under heaven.
> When God fixed the weight of the wind
> And meted out the waters by measure,
> When God made the rule for the rain
> And a way for the thunderstorm,
> Then he saw her and appraised her,
> Established her and probed her.
>
> (Job 28:23-27)

The process of God's discovering wisdom reflects the activities of a typical sage. God looked toward the ends of the earth and, like Qoheleth the sage, "saw everything under heaven" (Eccles. 1:14). The sage "observes" reality with a critical eye and discerns all aspects of the subject under investigation. The subject of God's empirical examination is the total cosmos; the goal of God's search is the discovery of wisdom.

God, as the first sage, not only sees but also in that very act "discerns." Discerning (*bîn*) is a critical act of inquiry, an intellectual penetration of the matter in hand. God discerns the way to wisdom and her "place" in the universe. The world is a cosmos in which all entities have their divinely appointed role (*derek*) and locus (*māqôm*) in the design of things. Wisdom is not something in God but is a mystery of the cosmos. Wisdom belongs to the primordial geography of the world, which God explored in the beginning.

Wisdom is not discovered by God wandering like some

primordial explorer across the pristine cosmic landscape. Rather, God discovers wisdom in the process of creating the universe and establishing its principles of operation.[12] The world is not a haphazard collection of creations. Each part is created to fit into the cosmic design. The thunderstorm, for example, cannot just rumble endlessly and aimlessly. It too has a *derek* that determines how it functions in the cosmic complex. It is in this act of God ordering creation as a cosmos that God "discerns" wisdom.

Wisdom here seems to be viewed as the integrating design that gives the cosmos coherence, momentum, and purpose. Her presence is revealed in the process of designing creation, in the measuring, weighing, ordering, and establishing of natural laws. She is like a primordial blueprint that holds the secret to how things work in the chaos of this world. To possess wisdom is to know that secret. God as the first sage discovered this Wisdom as the hidden design of the universe and demonstrated the capacity to discern her presence in the act of creation. Wisdom was God's teacher.

Having discovered Wisdom, God, like a professional sage, proceeds to "observe," "appraise," "establish," and "probe" her.[13] These four verbs may reflect the activities of an artisan viewing Wisdom like a precious gem to discern her flawless character. More likely, however, these verbs are reflections of God's functioning as sage and creator. As a typical sage God "observes" (*rā'â*, cf. Eccles. 1:14; 3:16) and "probes" (*ḥāqar*, cf. Eccles. 12:9; Job 5:27; 32:11; Prov. 28:11) the character of Wisdom so as to know her intimately. As the creator, God "establishes" (*kûn*) Wisdom in her place as the integrating design, just as he established the heavens and the earth (Ps. 24:1-2; Jer. 10:11; 33:2; cf. Prov. 8:23). By "appraising" or "recounting" (*sāpar*) wisdom, God appears to be acting like a scribe (*sōpēr*) and confirming wisdom as an integral part of the cosmic record.

The poet's characterization of God is that of a primordial sage, the first and apparently the only sage, to discover Wisdom in person. Humans have no direct access to this mysterious cosmic secret (cf. Job 15:7-9). And one would assume that such a God is likewise remote, holding the mysteries of life as a private possession. But, as if by some theological sleight of hand, the text takes us back full circle to the opening lines of the book of Job and announces:

> Behold, to fear the Lord is wisdom;
> To shun evil is discernment.
> (Prov. 28:28)

Human beings may not be able to find wisdom by themselves, but if they fear God and have faith in the Almighty, like Job, they may acquire wisdom and enjoy life in abundance. And the cycle of Job's dilemma would presumably begin all over again.[14]

God's Defense

If the God of the prologue is too arbitrary and selfish, intervening at will in human lives; if the God of the friends is too mechanical, reacting according to a rigid code of reward and retribution; if the God of Job in his anguish is too violent, harassing humans and creating anarchy; and if the God of the poet's commentary in Job 28 is too remote and inaccessible, does God's poetic defense from the whirlwind offer a genuine alternative characterization or approach to the theology of God as sage? Some would argue that the speeches of Yahweh are a huge bluff, an intimidating display of power or a catalogue of conundrums that cannot be taken seriously as a theological defense.[15] I would argue that the structure of the book seems to demand that God's answer be taken as a profound *apologia* from God himself. This speech is God talking about God. God's own God talk is not thetical or even proverbial in form. God the sage offers a poetic reply in the form of challenge questions. The starting point of theology is a vast array of questions posed by God about the cosmos and God's role in that cosmos.

Initially any audience, like Job, might be nonplussed, feel small, and believe that God alone has the answers to the riddles posed since God alone is the primordial sage who discerned wisdom in the design of the cosmos at the beginning. The grand oration of Yahweh does appear to be an apologetic overkill, especially when God waxes lyrical about Leviathan. But after repeated hearing—and after all, the text was meant to be heard by more than Job—the challenge questions[16] that God poses so dramatically reveal clues about the character of God, the functioning of the cosmos, and the nature of wisdom. And the question form, like God the sage, keeps the wise seeking and learning in the search for theological wisdom. Theology, like wisdom, is discerning in the search.

The pivotal concept in God's theological self-defense is the term *ʿēṣâ*, God's design of the cosmos (38:2). This design is the wisdom of God expressed in the plan of creation, as discrete from any history-oriented plan of salvation. Job is accused by God of obscuring that design with his ignorant portrayals of reality. If Job's challenge did indeed obfuscate God's wisdom and design, and Job after all spoke more correctly than the others (42:7), then the defense of God would seem to offer a corrective to the other characterizations of God in the book, especially Job's.

To acquire wisdom and discernment, it seems, demands placing oneself in the domain of the primordial, the context of origins, there to reflect on how and by whom reality is designed and constructed. Admittedly God's opening challenge question to Job may be tongue-in-cheek when he begins:

> Where were you when I laid earth's foundations?
> Tell me if you have gained discernment.

Yet entering the creation scene, the context of origins, where God himself acquired wisdom in the beginning, seems to be the latent directive for those who would discern this cosmic design. And the questions God poses hold further clues to the discovery process. To understand God the sage, one must go back to the beginning via the cosmic structures that now exist. One must reach beyond exterior constructions of the universe to contemplate the first sage designing existence as a planned cosmos.

God commences his defense by pointing to the primordial structures of the universe, which reflect its cosmic design (38:4-7). The earth is a stable edifice with a blueprint, exact measurements, and solid foundations. Wisdom is required for an artisan to construct a house, and "discernment for those who establish it" (Prov. 24:3). God becomes the wise artisan of the cosmos, the architect of a universe hailed by the court of heaven as a finished masterpiece (cf. Zech. 4:7). Here is a God concerned about stability and precision, not anarchy and disorder.

Not only is the earth firmly fixed and secure, but also the sea, with its propensity to revert to chaos, is governed by a law (*ḥōq*) that limits and contains its destructive potential (38:8-11). Chaos is not eliminated but kept within bounds like a child in its playpen, like a baby monster in its pool. Leviathan and Behemoth, the classic representatives of primordial chaos, are likewise kept in check (40:15–41:26).[17] These limits are for the good of the cosmic community, not unfair impositions of the innocent as Job alleges (3:23; 7:12). The design of the cosmos does not eliminate the natural raging of the sea but fixes its boundaries. The designer of this world is not a sage who promotes violence but one who contains it. This is not God the *gibbôr* who attacks life on earth but the God who has subdued and organized chaos to enable the existence of the living world without threat of extinction. God does not foster destructive chaos, as Job had maintained (ch. 12), but channels it for constructive patterns and purposes.

Within this cosmic edifice there is a pattern of governing rhythms, hidden depths, appointed loci, and functional laws that interact with, or relate to, human existence. Morning is on standing orders to make a regular appearance and keep the wicked in check. Death, which may eventually claim all mortals, has gates that regulate the flow of life to the underworld. With each dawn the wicked are exposed for what they are. In such a scene there is no necessary divine reaction or divine act of intervention to punish or annihilate the wicked. Their presence is evident with the dawn, and their evil activities are thereby limited. The cosmic design has a way of preventing evil from becoming an all-consuming force in the world.

Significantly, both light and darkness have an appointed locus in the cosmic design. The earth is not flooded with constant brilliance, as is the presence of God's throne, nor is it overwhelmed by darkness, as in the face of Sheol. God does not unleash "deep gloom" from the underworld to confuse mortals, as Job suggests (12:22). Opposites have their place in the rhythm of nature. God the sage constructed a world in balance, with polarities and play, with patterns and paradoxes, with yin and yang. Here is not a God who intervenes or reacts, but one who modulates and constrains. Job's efforts to expunge one day from the cosmic calendar or invoke the powers of darkness for his own ends are therefore futile. Yahweh's appearance to Job is not to disrupt the grand design of things but to point Job precisely to that design.

Even the meteorological phenomena of the heavens are regulated
by the same wisdom principles and have their individually appointed
destinies. They are not, as Job implied, agents of rampant violence
and unrestrained destruction. The fierce thunderstorm, too, has its
own *derek* and showers blessings even on the uninhabited
wastelands. Every corner of the cosmos is embraced in this
providential design, however mysterious some of the processes of
preservation may be. After all, how does hoarfrost happen?

Clouds, it seems, presented one of the most fascinating enigmas
of the celestial design. Clouds, in their constantly changing
formation, have an inbuilt wisdom, a discernment of how to move
and change with the weather. If God the sage built this wisdom into
the clouds, is there not a similar capacity accessible to mortals who
observe the clouds in operation? Wisdom seeks to grasp wisdom.
God the sage knows the wisdom planted in the universe and by
which the universe operates. The human, it seems, who wants to
comprehend or acquire this wisdom must enter the world of God's
design to explore these mysteries. A supreme test, perhaps
suggested tongue-in-cheek, would be to appraise or count the
passing clouds, just as God appraised Wisdom herself in the very
beginning (Job 28:27). (Ironically, the new science of chaos is
seeking to do something similar.) The profundity of God's design is,
however, never plumbed; beyond each mystery discerned there lies
another to be solved.

According to God's defense, in Job 38–41, all realms of the
universe, including the animal kingdom, illustrate the character of
God the sage in action. Wild creatures no less than humans depend
on God for their sustenance and habitation. Job, who had accused
God of hunting him down like a lion, is challenged to hunt food for
lions to sustain the ecology of the wild. The lion is not the target of
divine retribution as the friends maintained (4:10-11) but the object
of God's sustaining search. The shy creatures of the wild, especially
at perilous times such as gestation or birth, are also given divine
protection. God is their unseen midwife. God is present at transition
points in the life cycle of all beings. These designated times in the
natural cycle of things are indicators of God's design and concern.
Here is no hunter of animals or humans, no intervening *gibbôr*. Here
we meet the lord of the animals and their life cycles. If this is the

delicate ecology of life that God sustains in the wild, humans ought to be able to discern similar patterns in human life cycles. The mysteries of nature reveal enough to demonstrate that God the sage is at work and inviting humans to discern God's design and wisdom. Even the wild ass has its appointed place in God's providential plan. The wild ass is to be envied because it is free to enjoy the wilds. Each animal is created to fit its environment, each has the wisdom to function in its world, each has the discernment to soar, discover, or display its character as appropriate. All, that is, except the ostrich. And such comic anomalies are taken care of by a separate clause in God's primordial contract with nature. God watches over some creatures in a personal way, not as a spy, as Job asserts, but as the moderator of excesses and the protector of the helpless. The human who would know God's wisdom must explore the world of the wild where God both hunts for lions and hides ostrich eggs.

Conclusion

God's appearance in the theophany may indeed have been a personally meaningful experience of the numinous for Job, but God the sage who speaks in that theophany offers no immediate consolation for Job in his suffering. God's whirlwind response to Job's challenge to appear in court probably means that Job can assume his innocence and that his integrity has been recognized, but God the sage does not hail him as a "hero of righteousness." The comment of Yahweh after the storm, that Job spoke more appropriately than his three friends, may ease Job's mind somewhat, but God the sage makes it abundantly clear that Job has not yet grasped the principles of wisdom that inform the universe. However much we may appreciate that Job found meaning in "seeing God" in the whirlwind experience, the theology of the whirlwind is not about consolation, justification, or validation. Nor does Yahweh's speech seek to answer in simple terms the eternal questions of why there is evil in the world, why the innocent suffer, or why God does not seem to implement justice. In the world of the wise there are no absolute solutions to the open-ended questions of life.

The speeches of God are the defense of a sage to a community of critics who would be wise in the ways of God. God offers a defense by challenging Job, and any who would listen, to discern God as the sage who designed a world of rhythms and paradoxes, of balanced opposites and controlled extremes, of mysterious order and ever-changing patterns, of freedom and limits, of life and death. Within this complex universe God functions freely to monitor the intricacies of the system, to modulate its ebb and flow and to balance its conflicting needs. Here there is no El Gibbor, no hero king performing mighty acts of intervention, no swift administration of justice. To know this God is to live in the cosmic system, discern its flow, and explore its governing principles. This God is no indulgent father but a shrewd sage who confronts Job with tough questions and tantalizing clues that will exercise the mind and test the spirit of all those who would be wise. God's cosmic design is to be explored, not obscured. After all, being hit by a theophany is only the beginning of wisdom.

CHAPTER 2

THE GOD OF JOB: AVENGER, TYRANT, OR VICTOR?

Tryggve N. D. Mettinger

The author of the book of Job was nothing less than a literary genius. When we consider the magnitude of such an artistic achievement, T. S. Eliot's humbling appraisal of the works of Shakespeare comes to mind: "About anyone so great," Eliot says, "it is probable, that we can never be right; and if we are never right, it is better from time to time we should change our way of being wrong." The research into the book of Job undertaken during the last decade has indeed "changed our way of being wrong" and perhaps even moved us a bit in the right direction. Contributions such as those of Gordis, Keel, Kubina, and Habel have been of special importance.

However we define the theme of the book of Job (and various attempts have been made to do this) it is clear that the issue of God—to be more exact, God in his relation to evil and suffering—is the basic concern of the author. What does the God with whom suffering Job ultimately stands face to face look like? What I want to do in this essay is to give a presentation of the God notions in Job that take their cue from new advances in research. In doing this it must be remembered that in ancient Israel questions about the nature of God were *ipso facto* also questions about the origin and nature of the world. Concepts of God and of world view—what in German are called *Gottesverständnis* and *Weltverständnis*—belong together.

It may be assumed that the author of Job, in wrestling with the problem of theodicy, had prima facie three different possible models of reality: He could lean (1) toward a dualistic understanding in which existence is predicated upon polarities that cannot be deduced from each other, (2) toward a monistic understanding in which a single cause is the ultimate ground of both good and evil, or, again (3), toward an understanding that God is *jenseits von Gut und Böse* ("beyond good and evil"), which boils down to saying that the notion of theodicy itself is somehow irrelevant.[1]

This leads us to the two chief questions to be addressed here: First, does the author propagate a theology whose God is morally neutral, an amoral God? Second, does he present a God who is responsible for both good and evil,[2] a monistic concept of God, or does he end up with a more dualistic view of matters?

Regarding the first issue, Gordis argues that the author is making use of an extended analogy: Just as the natural world possesses order and beauty, so the moral universe of man possesses order and meaning.[3] Tsevat argues in a completely different way: The book of Job demoralizes the world, in the sense that it makes it amoral. What God obliquely says to Job is "You were not present when the universe was created. . . . What, then, makes you assume that it is justice which is its foundation?"[4] "Only the elimination of the principle of retribution can solve the problem of the book," says Tsevat.[5] Tsevat's study has had some effect on the subsequent discussion. Preuss, for example, understands the book as an expression of the crisis of act consequence theology. Wisdom and its basic dogma (the idea of divine retribution) are summoned to court, says Preuss. The God speeches show us creation-faith that has been developed into criticism against wisdom. They expressly repudiate the idea that there is in creation an inherent order.[6] Habel, too, follows Tsevat's lead: The natural order is amoral. The principle of retributive justice as a mechanical law of the cosmos is repudiated in the book; the world is not run according to the moral principle that Job and his friends had espoused. "The food for the lion and the kill for the raven are innocent creatures who no more deserve to die than any others."[7]

Keel has chosen a different path altogether. On the basis of an iconographical analysis of comparative materials from Mesopotamia and Egypt, which brings the mythological background of the God speeches to the fore, he argues that the God speeches depict YHWH as the God who protects his creation and who annihilates evil.[8]

On the second issue, whether the book tends toward a monistic or a dualistic understanding of God, one can in recent research find two opposite tendencies. On the one hand, Brenner speaks explicitly of "the two-sided Godhead" and says that "God is considered the ultimate source of both good and evil." Behemoth and Leviathan are symbols of evil subdued but at the same time created by God.[9] Similarly, Habel speaks of "the unexpected dark side of God" and suggests that "Job finally understood that 'the Lord gives and the Lord takes away'" (1:21).[10] On the other hand, scholars who emphasize the mythological material in the God speeches tend toward a more dualistic understanding of their message: God mounts a battle against the evil forces. Here one can mention Keel, Lindström, and Gibson.[11]

Let us now turn to the text itself. What we find in the book are no less than three different understandings of God, which all compete with one another: the God of the friends, the God of Job (in the Job speeches), and the God of the whirlwind (in the God speeches).

The God of the Friends

We can be very brief about the God of the friends. God is the engineer of the mechanisms of retribution. This teaching about act and consequence may be termed "the theology of the natural man."[12] The friends illustrate this principle as the law of sowing and reaping (4:8). The part played by this teaching in the argument of the friends is transparent. To begin with they refer to it in order to comfort Job: The Lord of retribution punishes the sinner but rewards the righteous (4:6-8). The argument moves from cause (Job's piety) to effect (his final success). But as Clines has demonstrated, there is a difference between the standpoints of each of the three friends.[13] As the argument proceeds, the perspective is reoriented so that the argument goes from effect (Job's suffering) to cause (his alleged sins).

It is quite clear then that the God of retributive justice is the great avenger. For the friends, there is one single principle of causality permeating human existence, namely, divine retribution. God punishes evil; evil does not come from God. If we are allowed to revocalize the verb in 5:7, it reads *kî 'ādām lĕ'āmāl yôlid*, "for humanity engenders evil'' (author's trans.; cf. Job 15:35; Isa. 59:4).[14]

The God of Job

Let us now turn to the speeches of Job. Here we meet an understanding of God that amounts to nothing less than a nihilistic credo. As to the first of our two questions, it is clear that Job speaks of a God who is not amoral but actively immoral. We have two main observations in this connection. In the first place Job labels God a criminal. For Job, his suffering indicates that God has taken some sort of legal action against him (''Let me know your suit against me,'' 10:2). Like his friends, Job assumes that the act and consequence pattern ought to function (6:24; 13:23). For the friends, Job's suffering alone is sufficient evidence to conclude that Job is a sinner worthy of punishment. To Job the same logic leads to the conclusion that God is a criminal. Therefore, Job indicts God for injustice:

> I am blameless! . . .
> It is all the same. Therefore, I would say:
> ''Guiltless and guilty, he destroys both!
> When a scourge brings sudden death
> He mocks the despair of the innocent.
> The earth is controlled by a criminal [*rāšā'*]
> who covers the face of her judges.
> If not he, then who is guilty?''
>
> (Job 9:21-24)[15]

That criminal charges are being brought against God is made probable by other formulations in Job.[16] Job himself is aware that he is on the verge of blasphemy, as we learn from chapter 13 where he says:

> . . . let come on me what may.
> I will take my flesh in my teeth,
>   and put my [*nepeš* ''life-force''] in my hand.
>
> (Job 13:13-14 RSV)

Pope is probably right that we have here the counterpart of Akaadian *napishtam lapātum,* "to touch one's throat," "to seize one's neck," an expression of self-cursing.[17] Job makes the gesture of self-imprecation. He touches his throat; he is prepared to speak even at the cost of his life.

In the second place, Job depicts God as a God who created a world void of meaning. To Job's friends the world is characterized by order and meaning, dominated by the principle of divine recompense, with its close, almost causal connection between act and consequence. To Job, creation conforms to no moral pattern, and existence itself has no structure. This is especially clear in two passages. In Job 3 the sufferer curses the day of his birth. The formulation in verse 4, "That day! Let it be darkness," *yĕhî hōšek,* is an inversion of the words in the creation narrative, "let there be light," *yĕhî 'ôr.* Fishbane rightly describes Job 3 as "a counter-cosmic incantation."[18] The other passage is Job 12:7-25 ("ask *bĕhēmôt*"), which contains a satirical doxology on God's wisdom and counsel (*'ēṣâ*) in verses 13-25. God withholds the waters, causing drought, and then sends a deluge, wreaking havoc on the earth (v. 15); God makes nations great and destroys them (v. 23). To God belong both the misled and the misleaders (v. 16). There are no indications that God's disastrous acts are acts of punishment. They are rather expressions of the fickle temperament of a God who is seen as the omnipotent tyrant.

This satirical doxology is one of the striking examples in the Job speeches of the use of perverted hymnic praise to point up the issue. This literary technique has a counterpart in the inversion of the chaos battle tradition. In place of the chaos monster as the target of God's assaults in hymnic praise, the Job speeches put the innocent sufferer: "Am I *yām* or *tannîn,* that thou settest a guard over me?" (7:12 RSV).[19] The ambiguous formulation in 9:17 may refer to God's assaults on Job with the tempest, *śĕ'ārâ,* a well-known weapon of the deity of the chaos battle.[20] Neither should we overlook the use of the verb *bāla',* "to swallow," "to destroy," in "your hands fashioned and made me altogether—yet now you destroy me."[21] That Death or Sheol is a swallower is a well-known concept.[22] In the Apocalypse of Isaiah it is God who swallows Death (Isa. 25:8). It could well be that Job 10:8 is an ironic allusion to this idea: Instead of swallowing the chaos monster, God here is said to swallow his

own creation, innocent Job (cf. Job 2:3). The use of the verb *pārar*
(16:12) to describe God's attacks on Job (*šālēw hāyîtî waypar-*
pĕrēnî) may have the same background since it occurs in the Psalms
in a chaos battle context (Ps. 74:13: *'attâ pôrartā bĕ'āzzĕkā yām*).
The Job speeches depict a God who is not merely amoral but
actively immoral, the omnipotent tyrant, the cosmic thug. Then
what about our second question? In 9:22-24 we already found the
idea expressed that the evil in the world derives from God himself.
"If not he, then who?" The satire on God's *'ēṣâ* in 12:13-25 shows
similar leanings toward a monistic view of God: He withholds the
waters and sends them out to overthrow; he multiplies and
annihilates; to him belong both misled and misleaders.

The God of the Whirlwind

Let us leave for the time being the matter of the concept of God in
the speeches of Job and turn our attention to the speeches of God.
We will first survey the material and then revert to our two basic
questions.

When God speaks to Job "out of the whirlwind," the very
formulation implies that the text is describing a theophany. But what
we have here is by no means a case of education through
overwhelming. As Kubina[23] has convincingly demonstrated, the
God speeches are part of a structure pervading the book as a whole, a
structure characterized by the legal metaphor. For Job, suffering
implies a divine accusation (10:2), but, he argues, a trial in court
would acquit him, and he even formulates a set of accusations
against God. It is now of fundamental importance to note that God
does in fact defend himself against Job's accusations. The speeches
of God are part of the book's intellectual wrestling with ultimate
questions. In the introduction to each speech of God we find God
formulating a counterchallenge.

In the first speech God's challenge is *mî zeh maḥšîk*, "Who is
this who clouds my design in darkness?" (Job 38:2). The obvious
reference is to Job's satirical doxology in chapter 12 (note God's
'ēṣâ in v. 13). But in a wider sense all that Job had said about

creation as void and meaningless, especially in chapter 3, is here challenged by God. In the second speech, again, God's challenge is formulated: "Would you pervert my justice, would you declare me a *rāšā'* in order that you may be justified?" (Job 40:8, author's trans.).[24] The Hiphil *taršî'ēnî* has a declarative sense. The obvious reference is to Job's accusation in chapter 9 where he says that God is nothing but a *rāšā'*, a "criminal" (9:24). These two thematic challenges are important hermeneutical keys to the two speeches of God.

Thus in his first speech God defends his *'ēṣâ*. God defends himself against Job's accusation that he is arbitrary and that creation conforms to no moral pattern. The emphasis on the limitations of Job's knowledge is in line with this.[25] What Job is not aware of is the nature of God's activity in manifesting the divine "counsel" or "design." God refers to the very architecture of creation (38:4-7), to his protection of the cosmos by damming up the waters of chaos (vv. 8-11), to his taking action against sinners at the dawning of every day (vv. 12-15). The recesses of the sea and the gates of death are not beyond his reach (vv. 16-21). The second part of the first speech presents YHWH in the role of the "Lord of the Animals," if Keel is right.[26]

In the second speech God defends his righteousness; he is no *rāšā'* (40:8). The introduction contains a passage (vv. 9-14) that should not be overlooked. It contains a series of summons to Job to do certain things if he has an arm like God's (vv. 9, 14): "Look upon the proud and humble them! . . . Crush the wicked where they stand! Hide them in the dust together!" (vv. 11-13).[27]

Brenner took this passage to contain a partial admission of divine failure.[28] This is hardly correct. On the contrary, the author here sets the subsequent presentation of Behemoth and Leviathan into perspective. What Job is *unable* to do God *is* doing in his dealings with these beasts. Behemoth and Leviathan are thus to be seen as typological representatives of "the proud" and "the wicked." The author has here used two zoological specimens to serve his purposes, namely, the hippopotamus and the crocodile. It is clear, however, that his main interest does not lie in the zoological details, however interesting they might be in their own right. Leviathan is well known from Old Testament passages about the chaos monster (Isa. 27:1; Pss. 74:14; 104:26; Job 3:8), and this gives us some clues as to the direction the speech is taking. Ruprecht, Keel, and Kubina have taken us quite a bit further in their investigations of the imagery of the God speeches.[29] I am in agreement with these scholars and believe that the use of the hippopotamus and the crocodile in Job reflects a similar usage of these animals in Egyptian mythology, where we find the evil god Seth, the enemy of the god Horus, taking the shape of a hippopotamus or a crocodile. The battle between Horus and Seth is well attested in Papyrus Chester Beatty no. I (twelfth century B.C.E.)[30] and in the temple of Edfu, with its eleven wall reliefs and accompanying texts.[31] In Edfu the cultic drama was performed on the sacred lake. Horus harpooned Seth, who was represented for cultic purposes by a hippopotamus-shaped cake. Among the reliefs from Edfu one mirror scene is especially revealing. On one side of a relief we see a hippopotamus, on its "reflection" a crocodile. Incidentally, it is interesting to note that the version in Papyrus Beatty I is presented as a trial at court before the tribunal of the gods.

The idea that the second speech of God in the book of Job reflects an Egyptian version of the chaos battle myth is supported by Job 40:18. Here Behemoth has "limbs like bars of iron." As Lang has pointed out, there was an Egyptian designation of iron as "bones of Seth."[32]

Seen against this background, Behemoth and Leviathan refer to one and the same chaos power that is the enemy of the creator God. It is then important to note that each description in Job contains a reference to God's supreme power in subjugating the chaotic forces. We cannot go into details here; it suffices to say that Habel has made a good case for understanding 40:23–24 in this way ("El takes him by the mouth with rings, he pierces his nose with hooks")[33] and that Rowold has managed to make sense of 41:2-3 in a similar manner.[34]

There is thus in each of God's speeches a profound connection between the thematic challenge in the respective introductions (darkening God's design and declaring God a criminal) and the contents of the corresponding God speech. Interpretations that take Behemoth and Leviathan to be merely didactic images for Job that demonstrate the futility of Job's challenging God[35] hardly do justice to these connective elements. The very point of the second speech is that God is not a criminal and that his way of dealing with evil clearly demonstrates this. His supremacy over the chaotic forces is pointed up with formulations marked by Hebrew humor: The chaotic waters are described as a child in her swaddling bands (38:8-11), and Leviathan as a pet animal (40:29; cf. Ps. 104:26).

God As Victor

Let us now return to our two basic questions. First, does the author of Job invite his readers to faith in an amoral God? Our review of the speeches of God gives some clear indications to the contrary. God's second speech is, in fact, a reply directed against Job's accusation that God is a *rāšāʿ* (40:8). Furthermore, Behemoth and Leviathan are presented as illustrations of the proud and the wicked whom Job would be able to subdue if he had an arm equal to God's (40:9-14). They are suggestive symbols of the anti-divine powers. God contends that he is the Creator who actively cares for his creation by subjugating the evil in the world.

In the first speech we find another relevant passage, 38:12-15, where God commands the morning and assigns the dawn its place; he takes hold of the skirts of the earth and shakes the wicked from it. The motif here, ''God's help at dawn,''[36] is one with deep roots in the ancient Near East, as Janowski has demonstrated in a recent study.[37] The dawn is the time for the epiphany of the sun god, who is the supreme judge, taking action against all evil in all its cosmic-mythic dimensions (demons, Apophis, etc.) and its historical manifestations (criminals and sinners). This is the background of the Israelite idea of God's judgment at dawn (Zeph. 3:5; Ps. 5:4).[38] Indeed, the formulation in Job 38:15 on the arm of the sinner anticipates what is said in 40:9-14 on the arm of God. In the second major part of the first speech of God (38:39–39:30), it is hard to find any emphasis on the idea that God is amoral. On the contrary, this whole section is designed to emphasize God's care and protection.

Our second major question was whether the book of Job exhibits tendencies toward a dualistic or a monistic theology. It seems clear that since the speeches of God offer an elaborate *Auseinanderset-zung* ("opposition") to what precedes, one cannot without further ado extract the author's theology from formulations in the prologue or in the dialogue between Job and the friends. This has been made especially clear by Lindström in his study of "alleged monistic evidence."[39] We are indeed left with the speeches of God.

Perhaps we should after all avoid the simplistic alternatives of dualism and monism to describe the theology of the God speeches. In his discussion of "the symbolism of evil," Paul Ricoeur sketches a typology of the myths of the beginning and the end of evil. On one hand we have the drama of creation with the chaos battle, on the other hand the Adamic myth. In the first type the origin of evil is related to the origin of things; in the second it is related to the fall of humanity.[40] What we have in Mesopotamia is a theodicy of the first type. In Israel we find a continuum. At one end there is Psalm 74 with the full-fledged combat myth of creation (vv. 12-17), at the other end Genesis 1–11 with the idea of creation through the unchallenged word of God and with only vestigial traces of the suppressed battle myth but including the story of the fall of humanity. It is important to note that Psalm 104 (vv. 5-9, 26) and the God speeches in Job place themselves somewhere between these two extremes, as Levenson has pointed out.[41] Behemoth and Leviathan represent ultimate evil and are subdued by God. At the same time it is said that God created them (40:15, 19; 41:25).

Here much depends on the depth of intention in these formulations. It seems to me that within the overall perspective of the book, the main emphasis of the God speeches is on an antagonistic theology.[42] The God of the author of the book is neither avenger, nor tyrant, but victor! When Job accuses God of placing him in the position of Yam and Tannin (7:12), God defends himself, saying that he throws himself into the fray, engaging in a trial of strength with the truly sinister forces and subduing and imprisoning them. It seems that the idea of God as the preserver and protector of his creation has a more important place in the author's agenda than the question of the ultimate origin of evil.[43]

While the author of Job is apparently acquainted with the *Urgeschichte* ("primeval history") of Genesis and even with the story of the fall of humanity,[44] it is clear that the author does not take recourse to the story of the fall in the theodicy he presents. However, there are formulations about the creation of Behemoth and Leviathan. Does the author of Job include his antagonistic theology within an overall perspective that is ultimately monistic? We simply do not know. *Ignoramus—et ignorabimus!*[45]

CHAPTER 3

THE PROBLEM OF EVIL
IN THE BOOK OF JOB

Edwin M. Good

I am convinced that the purpose of the book of Job is to solve the problem of evil. Even if it is, I think the book does not actually solve it. Toward the end, it suggests a view of the world in which evil ceases to be the same problem that it is in most of the book. That the author of Job sets out to resolve that issue seems to be in doubt, for two reasons: First, we cannot, in my opinion, know anything at all about the author of Job; second, I fail to see that in fact the book answers the problem.

What is the problem of evil in the book of Job? It is the same problem that the rest of the Hebrew Bible sees in evil, namely, the difficulty of reconciling pain, suffering, and defeat with the doings of a deity (1) who created the entire world and pronounced it not merely "good" but, as Genesis 1:31 quotes him, "very good," and (2) who tells the Chosen People many times over that if they obey the law and observe all other divine demands upon them, they will receive a good, secure life.[1] The latter point is made again and again not only in the deuteronomic ambit of the Bible (e.g., Joshua–Kings) but also in the classical prophets.

That makes the problem clear enough. If the world conforms to the design of a creator who is both good and omnipotent,[2] evil must be excluded. If any evil is to be found there, the creator is either not powerful enough to exclude it or is not good after all. Evil must be hidden inside a god who engineers a universe that contains either the actuality or the possibility of evil. Indeed, if the deity possesses some evil, it is no surprise to encounter the divine claim that the world is "very good."

50

The problem of evil, then, is the question of whether the creator of the universe is really in charge or not. A creator who is in charge must have the power to make the universe work as he wants, so that people can live in it in accord with his expressed wishes. If something about the universe does not cohere with the expectations the deity gives people to assume, then we have to ask whether the god is good or not.[3] Power and goodness collide somewhere out there, and it is almost impossible to combine them in a single idea of a single god. Archibald MacLeish quotes a popular bit of religious doggerel in his Job drama, *J.B.*:

> If God is God, he is not good.
> If God is good, he is not God.[4]

This presents a very interesting problem. The power of an "Almighty God" sometimes overrides perfect justice. The goodness of an all-just deity sometimes fails to provide everything that people need. Goodness or power: It seems that you can have one of them to the utmost degree in one deity, but it is very difficult to conceive the matter in such a way that you can have both. The Western cultural tradition not only allows us to *want* both of them but also claims that we *have* both. But the philosophical and theological laborers in the vineyards have not yet successfully shown how we can have both.

The Problem of Evil: The Prologue

The problem is quite visible in Job. In chapter 2 he has been assaulted by that dreadful malady, whatever it may be (and there is no way to know). His wife urges him to "curse [*bārēk*] Elohim and die!" (v. 9). He responds, "You're talking like a fool. We receive good from Elohim, and we do not receive evil" (v. 10).[5] The deity is only good and cannot do evil. If Job has received evil, it has either come from somewhere else than the god and cannot be blamed on him, or it only seems evil. If the evil is only a seeming one, then there is no "problem" of evil. I doubt that we can take that position with Job. The first two chapters hinge on the irony that, left to his own devices, Job has succeeded in "avoiding" evil (see below), but with the dispute between Yahweh and the Prosecutor,[6] he receives evil, which is the reason given in 2:11 for the three friends' visit. The entire surrounding of this passage seems testimony against the idea that evil is only a mirage.

As an indicative sentence, Job's reply to his wife implies that evil lies outside of the god's activity or control. On this account, the deity is good but is not in complete charge, is not responsible for everything that happens.

Most other translations of Job's sentence read it as a question: "Do we receive good from Elohim, and do we not receive evil?" Though the Hebrew does not have an interrogative particle, many apparently indicative sentences in the Bible seem best understood as questions, and this is a plausibly correct translation. On this reading, humans can get both good things and bad ones from the god and should not be surprised at either. The god is in charge, but we cannot expect everything that happens to be only good. Job's sentence in 2:10 can be read, then, to say both that the deity is good but not all-powerful and that he is all-powerful but not only good. Indeed, because we cannot definitively pronounce either the indicative or the interrogative form of the sentence as the only correct one, the sentence makes those two opposite statements simultaneously. Not only can it be read to say both things, but there is also no way to decide that one is right and the other wrong.[7]

The occasion for Job's remark is the arrangement between Yahweh and that other character in the heavenly court, whose title I translate as the Prosecutor, whom others call the Adversary, and whom the Hebrew text calls "the satan" (*haśśāṭān*), not a proper name but a title. As described here and in Zechariah 3:1-5, the *śāṭān* is a member of the divine court, and I take him to be a sort of divine district attorney, poking his nose here and there through the world in order to bring wicked people to the bar of divine justice. Far from being the god's adversary, he is the divine law-and-order officer. He is not the principle of evil, however much he became so in later Jewish and Christian mythologies, but on the contrary, in Job, is a principle of good, of justice.

Yahweh brags to him about Job: "There's no one like him on earth, a scrupulously moral man, religious, one who avoids evil" (1:8). And there is our very word: evil (*rāʿ*). *Job has no "problem of* evil,'' because he assiduously avoids coming into contact with it. The Prosecutor can explain that: ''Is Job religious for nothing?'' he asks with some heat. No wonder Job is religious. Yahweh has ''hedged him around,'' protected him from danger and threat so that Job has become immensely rich. Anyone would be religious if it paid so well. But now, the Prosecutor proposes, damage his goods, and you'll see how religious he is.

The Prosecutor then says something that I have again translated differently from the way others do. Most versions have ''He will surely curse you to your face,'' a strong statement. I wish to be relatively literal: ''If he does not curse you to your face—'' (*'im-lō' 'al-pāneykā yebārăkekkā*)[8] says the Prosecutor, and that is all he says. The sentence is incomplete, in Hebrew and in English.

I have gone into this sentence in some detail in my book, *In Turns of Tempest.*[9] In essence I argue that the sentence is rhetorically a formula of curse upon the speaker. Like most curses in the Hebrew Bible, it omits the result clause:[10] ''If he does not 'curse' you to your face, [may something awful happen to me].'' The sentence has usually been read as a very strong assertion. ''If he does not curse you to your face—'' means ''He certainly will.'' I am perfectly willing to grant that that outcome is assumed by the curse, though the conditional first clause leaves Job some space of freedom. But I think that something is gained and nothing is lost by perceiving a curse statement. What is gained, in fact, is the realization that the statement is a formula of *self*-curse: The result is to happen to the speaker. The Prosecutor calls down an unstated catastrophe on himself.[11]

It is not a curse on Job: ''If he does not curse you to your face, may his skin be torn off by lions.'' That would make no sense, since we would expect the deity to prefer that Job not curse him. It is not a test: ''Let's give him some grief and see whether he does not curse you to your face.'' For that we might expect another clause beginning ''And if he does—'' (*wĕ'im* . . .). It is not what a major part of the tradition has made it, namely, a wager: ''If he does not curse you to your face, I'll buy you a good ham sandwich.''[12] The Prosecutor is laying himself drastically on the line. We do not know what catastrophe he has in mind if the outcome goes awry, but the fact that we hear no more of him after chapter 2 at least suggests that whatever the curse was, it came about and put the Prosecutor out of commission. Perhaps that is why he became the Devil; he had no place to go but down. We could make up quite a good new myth of the fallen angel from that idea.

Losing his entire fortune and family in chapter 1 and touched with pain in his own body in chapter 2, Job succeeds in both situations. At the end of the first episode, the story says, "Job did not sin" (1:22), and in 2:10, "Job did not sin with his lips."[13] But we are told why the three friends came to see Job: "Three of Job's friends heard about all the evil that had come upon him" (2:11). At the beginning, Job is praised because he "avoids evil"; now "evil" has come. But the story has certified that Job is free of "sin."

That differentiation of sin from evil is important, I think. Job avoids sin by what he says and does in response to his troubles. But several times he is praised because he "avoids evil," and he says in 2:10 that we do not receive evil from the god (if my reading is right). Yet in 2:11 he has received "evil." Sin is, it seems, an action (or inaction), evil an event, and here the term points to Job's suffering. The story implies that evil is not a moral category. The Prosecutor's self-curse would uphold that idea. Curses, as the ancient world thought of them, had no moral entailments. They were in one sense pure magic—statements that, simply by being made, caused things to happen.[14] Job's troubles in the story, then, reflect neither on his morality nor on Yahweh's.

The Problem of Evil: The Poetic Speeches

Where is the problem of evil in Job? We will get there. First, we need to notice that several things change as chapter 3 begins. For one thing, we begin the poetic speeches. For another, Yahweh takes no part in the deliberations until his dramatic entry at chapter 38. For still another, the Prosecutor disappears, and we see no more of him.[15] Another thing that changes at chapter 3 is Job's tone of voice. James's famous remark, "You have heard of the patience of Job" (James 5:11) has become a cliché, sometimes the only thing people are aware of about Job. As chapter 3 begins, Job emphatically ceases to be patient. Perhaps James never read beyond chapter 2.

At chapter 3 Job does some cursing of his own, calling down a curse on his birthday and his conception, and in effect putting a curse on the whole creation. Job wants it all undone, wiped away. He wonders why he had to be born, why anyone has to be born, and he wishes he were dead. But he does not wonder why he is suffering. The suffering is most unpleasant, but he does not ask, "Why is this happening to me?"

That subject is dropped into the conversation by Eliphaz. Eliphaz compliments Job on helping people in trouble, but the compliments mask something:

> Is not your religion your confidence,
> your hope, and the integrity of your ways?
> Think, who that was innocent has perished,
> and where have moral people been destroyed?
> As I have seen, those who plow iniquity
> and sow toil, harvest it too.
> They perish by Eloah's breath,
> are finished by his nostril's wind.
>
> (4:6-9)

Eliphaz connects what the story in chapters 1–2 carefully distinguished. He identifies religion with moral innocence and contrasts them to sin, and he rounds out his picture of the world by saying that the actions of good people—the "innocent," the "moral"—avert destruction, while the sinful actions of bad people destroy them. Eliphaz collapses sin into evil, as if there were no difference, and he proposes the claim that bad things do not happen to good people.

He assumes both that the god is in charge and that he is good. Therefore, everything that happens in the world reflects divine justice. Suffering and pain, like happiness and health, are part of the system of justice. Deserving makes the world run. The deity treats everyone according to approval or disapproval, rewarding with health, prosperity, and good things those whom he approves, punishing with pain, failure, and death those he disapproves.

In such a structure, evil is problematic if someone who deserves good treatment suffers. Job is suffering. By Eliphaz's logic, the deity must disapprove of him. Yet we know from chapters 1–2 that Yahweh emphatically approved of Job: "There's certainly no one like him on earth" (1:8). While that sentence in itself might be mildly ambiguous, the unconditioned praise about his moral scrupulosity, religiousness, etc., that immediately follows seems to prevent our supposing that Yahweh thinks Job is without peer on earth in wickedness.

Eliphaz, to be sure, assures Job that the disapproval may be temporary:

> Ah, happy the man whom Eloah corrects;
> do not despise Shaddai's discipline.
> for he wounds, and he binds up;
> pierces, and his hands heal.
> In six troubles he will rescue you,
> in seven, evil will not touch you.
>
> (5:17-19)

There is the word again, "evil." But evil *has* touched Job, as we know from 2:11, when its touching him was the motivation for the friends to visit. For Eliphaz, the deity can be expected to protect against evil, but wounds and troubles may be a way of exerting discipline. But Eliphaz is having some difficulty with his idea, and he apparently distinguishes not between evil and sin but between this discipline and the destruction that comes on those who "plow iniquity and sow toil." Yet he makes no effort to fathom why Job is being disciplined.

It is a while before Job echoes Eliphaz. At the start, he only wishes he were dead, and the pain is only pain, not yet punishment. In his next speech, the thought is beginning to take hold:

> Instruct me, and I'll be quiet.
> How have I erred? Make me understand.
>
> (6:24)

Job is kicking against the thought that the suffering is his own fault. If he has sinned, it does not affect the deity, and he suggested immediate forgiveness:

> Why not lift my guilt,
> carry away my iniquity?
> For now I lie down in the dust;
> you'll search for me, but I won't be there.
>
> (7:20-21)

The question of the relation of guilt and innocence to evil has arisen by virtue of Eliphaz's suggestion. Job picks it up and leads into the wish for a trial, so that his guilt can be decided objectively. That desire must stem from Job's assumption that he is being punished for something, and he would like to know what it is. Before he leaps into the language of trial, he ponders some problems about it, especially in chapter 9.

The main problem is whether power is consistent with justice, and Job begins by doubting that it is:

> If I summoned [a legal term] and he answered me,
> I wouldn't believe he was hearing my voice,
> he who tramples me down with a whirlwind,
> enlarges my wounds for no reason.
>
> (9:16-17)

A trial is problematic because the judge is unfairly attacking Job. Justice will be so badly skewed that he could not get fair treatment:

> If I'm innocent, my own mouth condemns me;
> if I'm perfect, he'll do me fraud.
>
> (9:20)

Those are strong words. Power—even divine power—is not justice. Job uses stronger words in 9:24:

> Earth is given over to a wicked hand;
> he covers its judges' face—
> if not, then who is it?

The "wicked hand" belongs to the god, and Job is sure that it prevents justice from being done.

> For he's not a man like me whom I could answer,
> come together with him to trial.
> There's no arbiter between us
> to lay his hand on us both,
> to take his rod off my back,
> tell dread of him not to terrify me.
>
> (9:32-33)

Remarkable! Job brings up the thought of an "arbiter" who would intervene with authority between himself and the deity, but he drops the thought as soon as he has it: "There's no arbiter between us" (*lō' yēš-bênênû môkîaḥ*).[16] He ends the first cycle of speeches with a reversion to his death wish:

> Are not my days few enough?
> Stop, stand off from me,
> and I might cheer up a bit
> before I go and don't return,
> to the land of deepest dark,
> land of gloom, like dusk,
> deep shadow, all disordered,
> which shines like dusk.
>
> (10:20-22)

Job now doubts that the god is both powerful and just. He knows the power, feels it on his body, but precisely for that reason he cannot affirm the justice. Supposing that suffering is divine retribution for sin, he knows he has done nothing to deserve this treatment. And of course, since neither Job nor the friends have the slightest clue about the Prosecutor, they assume that the deity has direct responsibility.

I will not pause over everything Job and the friends say; I do that in *In Turns of Tempest*. I want to call attention to some places where Job modifies the argument that his suffering is punishment for something he has not done. He wants to prove his innocence of the accusations, the details of which he cannot find out. The friends do not help him at all. They are sure that, because Job suffers, he is bad.[17] Not only does the god punish those whom he disapproves with suffering and pain; you can also tell whom the god disapproves by noticing who is suffering. They know no more than Job what he has done, but he must have done something. If Eliphaz wrongly charges him with crushing orphans' arms (22:9), he certainly thinks that Job has done something equally unconscionable. Job, on the other hand, thinking as the friends do that deserving runs the world, knows he has done nothing to deserve his pain.

In the second cycle, he conceives new ideas of help that might be available to him against this arbitrary governance. He vividly describes how the deity attacks him:

> His troops surround me;
> he splits open my guts without pity,
> pours my gall on the ground,
> breaches me, breach upon breach,
> runs against me like a warrior.
>
> (16:13-14)

Then Job proposes that he has a friend in high places, a "witness" ('*ēd*) as he calls him, who can somehow turn the legal decision in his favor:

> Even now, Ah! my witness is in heaven,[18]
> my supporter is on high,
> my interpreter, my friend, to Eloah—
> my eyes are sleepless—
> and he[19] will decide for a hero against Eloah,
> between[20] Adam and his friend.
>
> (16:19-21)

That is a difficult, bitterly disputed passage. I take it that the "witness," who can decide in Job's favor against ('*im*) the god, is an advance on the "arbiter" (*môkîaḥ*), whose existence Job denied or wistfully doubted in 9:33. He is at least sure that the witness is up there to help him.

In chapter 19, the sense of alienation from every supportive human contact deepens. Though the friends have at least stayed there, they have stopped being friendly:

> Pity me, O pity me, you my friends,
> for Eloah's hand has touched me.
> Why do you pursue me, like El,
> not satisfied with my flesh?
>
> (19:21-22)

The pitch of emotion rises even higher:

> Would that my words were written,
> would that they were engraved in an inscription,
> with an iron stylus and lead
> forever in rock they were incised.
>
> (19:23-24)

It is the only reference to writing in Job, and the quatrain progresses from simple writing (*ktb*) to "engraving" (*ḥqq*) to the even deeper "incising" (*ḥṣb*) with an iron tool, the letters filled with lead.[21] The spoken word dissipates into air, the word written on perishable leather or wood can disintegrate, but what is cut or dug into rock may permit the complaint to stand visible forever.[22]

But then Job takes still another step beyond the "arbiter" and the "witness": "As for me, I know my avenger lives" (v. 25). Unfortunately, I can go no further with Job's statement. He goes on for six more lines, in which I can read each word, but they do not combine into sentences that make sense to me.[23]

I have called this character not a "redeemer" but an "avenger," taking the cue from the *gōʾēl haddām* of Numbers 35:12, 19-27 rather than the kinsman (*gōʾēl*) of Ruth 3:9, etcetera. The former sense of *gōʾēl* seems to me to match better Job's bitter alienation from everyone (19:13-21) and the divine pursuit of him (v. 22) than the more amiable example of Boaz. Those who prefer a kinder, gentler assistant to Job are welcome to it. Job claims that the god is murdering him, and out of his pain he postulates a powerful character who will take vengeance for the murder. Job has ascribed the power to "decide" (*ykḥ*) in a legal sense to the witness (16:19), but the *gōʾēl*, especially on the analogy of Numbers 35, has the strength to overpower the deity.

With these two powerful allies, Job has moved from the thought of the god as the doubtfully just judge in a trial, through the thought of a supporting witness who can decide a legal case, to the thought of an avenging warrior who solves the problem of the evil in Job's life by removing its cause.

Job has some further changes of mind. Most fascinating is the movement in chapter 21. Earlier, Job doubted that he could get a fair trial, because he was sure the god was powerful and not sure he was just, though he ought to be. Therefore, Job began to desire more overt action on his behalf by other powers. We may perhaps wonder whether he realizes how hypothetical the ideas of the "witness" and the "avenger" are, though he never repudiates them. If so, we might understand why he begins to rethink the structure of his universe.

Job's assumptions about how the world works do not differ significantly from those of the friends. He still thinks that the deity rewards the people who please him and punishes those who do not. From that premise, and certain that the god is displeased with him, he draws a new conclusion:

> Why do the wicked live,
> mature, and increase strength,
> their progeny established,
> their people before them,
> their offspring in their sight?
>
> (21:7-8)

He does not ask *whether* the wicked live and prosper but *why* they do. All the good things happen to them that do not happen to Job—"their offspring in their sight" where Job's are buried under the rubble of that fallen house. But Job knows where his problem lies:

> As for me, is my complaint with humans?
> Why shouldn't my breath be short?
> Face me and be appalled,
> lay your hands on your mouths.
>
> (21:4-5)

The responsibility for the good life wicked people enjoy is to be placed upon the god:

How often is the beacon of the wicked snuffed out,
does their calamity come upon them,
does he apportion destruction in anger?

(21:17)

"He" can be no one but the god. And there is Job's own answer to
his prior question, "Why do the wicked live?" It is because the god
approves of them. Job and the friends have had their priorities all
wrong. It is not that bad things happen to bad people; quite the
contrary. And Job himself is the prime demonstration that good
things do not happen to good people. Job has just figured out the
puzzle: The deity rewards those who please him, and it is the wicked
who please him. It is no wonder that Job is being punished; he insists
on being good.

In chapter 23, Job reverts, against all reason it seems, to the wish
for a trial. It is baffling that he should want one, in view of the
position to which he has come. But he cannot find the judge:

Ah, I go east, and he's not there,
west, and I don't discern him,
north where he works, and don't perceive him;
he hides in the south, and I cannot see him.
Because he knows the way I'm on;
he'll test me, I shall emerge as gold.

(23:8-10)

The combination of "hides" and "because" is telling. Job cannot
get a trial because the deity hides to prevent it, knowing that if the
trial has even a semblance of justice, Job will win.

Job shows, then, that his case turns the standard notion of
retributive justice on its head. Far from running the world so that
justice wins and injustice loses, so that righteous people have it good
and wicked people have it bad, the god rewards those who by human
standards are wicked and punishes those who by human standards
(and, according to 1:8, divine standards as well) are moral. In
21:29-30 Job even proposes that everyone knows this:

Have you not asked those who pass on the road,
and do you not mistake their signs
that on a calamitous day, a wretch is spared,[24]
on a day when fury is led forth?

The idea exactly opposes the Prosecutor's argument in chapter 1, that Job is religious because it pays, and Yahweh had rewarded him for goodness with wealth and happiness. Job, to be sure, knows nothing of that debate, but he now sees that the governance of the world is the opposite of what he had thought. He is punished not in spite of being moral but *because* he is moral.

But he insists that he must stick by it. He even takes an oath on the deity's life:

> As El lives, who has turned away my case,
> Shaddai, who has embittered my soul,
> as long as I still have breath,
> Eloah's wind in my nostrils,
> if my lips speak viciousness,
> my tongue, if it utter deceit—
>
> (27:2-4)

Job leaves unsaid the catastrophe that will fall on him if he speaks falsely, continuing to be "scrupulously moral" all the way. He turns to the friends:

> I'm damned if I'll say you are right;
> until I perish, I'll not turn away my integrity.
> To my rightness I hold fast, will not weaken it;
> my heart finds nothing from my days to taunt.
>
> (27:5-6)

Let the god do his worst, Job will not abandon his sense of being right. Together with what follows, this is a quite explicit claim, I think, that Job is the deity's moral superior:

> Let my enemy be considered wicked,
> the one who rises against me, vicious.
>
> (27:7)

The "enemy," "the one who rises against" Job, can be no one but the god, and the god is therefore to be considered just what Job has sworn solemnly never to be: "vicious" (*ʿawwāl*, cf. *ʿawlâ*, v. 4). The problem of evil is suddenly reversed. If the deity is wicked, the entire system of justice in the world is skewed and corrupted. More than that, when the deity commands people to be good, he lures them to destruction by false promises.[25]

The Problem of Evil: The Summation Speech

Job's summation speech in chapters 29–31 begins with the description of how pleasant his life used to be (ch. 29) and how terrible it is now by contrast (ch. 30) and concludes with a long series of curses upon himself as preparation for the trial (ch. 31).[26] Now—astonishingly—Job falls back on the old understanding of reward and punishment:

> What is Eloah's portion from above,
> Shaddai's inheritance from on high?
> Is it not disaster for the vicious,
> calamity for evildoers?
> Does he not see my ways,
> number all my steps?
>
> (31:2-4)

That was not the way he talked in chapter 21, when he said that the god brought disaster on the righteous, not on the vicious, or in 27:7, when he described the god himself by the very word "vicious." Here he seems on the face of it to revert to the old saw: The deity rewards the good and punishes the bad, and Job, under the deity's careful surveillance, will receive the reward he deserves. The series of oath-curses in the rest of chapter 31 then sets out the grounds of that deserving.

If Job has not returned in 31:2-4 to the prior understanding, he enunciates the amazing idea that "Eloah's portion" and "Shaddai's inheritance" will deal disaster to the deity himself. If Job still defines the god as "vicious," as he did in 27:7, the god's own work will end in his own dissolution and disaster. Otherwise, we must see that Job has abandoned the ground he occupied in chapter 27 and has rejoined the friends on the ramparts of the standard retributive theory, from which they have been shooting darts at him all this time.

Either way of reading 31:2-4 seems to me possible. Reversion to the old, comfortable ways of thinking about good and justice might stem from Job's recollections in chapter 29 of just how pleasant (to him at least) his former life-style was. Clearly he got to that place in life by assiduous attention to the deity's rules as he understood them, and perhaps he can regain the lost ground by taking up the old patterns once again. The radical application of the meaning of "vicious" in 27:7 to 31:3 is a bit more difficult. In that case, the series of curses in the rest of chapter 31 are feisty statements of Job's position about himself, and in the penultimate one in verses 35-37, challenging his persecutor to proceed with the trial, Job thumbs his nose at the deity and proclaims, against all his other expectations, that justice *will* win out in the universe, even if it entails the dethroning of the god. The chapter permits both of those readings,[27] and I now see no way of deciding that one is right and the other wrong.

The Problem of Evil: The Yahweh Speeches and the Responses of Job

The next voice we hear is that of Elihu (chs. 32–37), but in this article I do not propose to listen to Elihu.[28] Finally Yahweh answers Job "out of the whirlwind." And what an answer it is! Many interpreters have noticed that Yahweh says nothing about Job's problems about goodness and justice, let alone about evil and suffering. Not everyone is impressed. "A sublime irreverence," says one commentator;[29] "empty and worthless," says another, "a three-hour lecture on natural science," yet another.[30] The vision of the universe is grand, from

> when the morning stars sang together,
> and all the sons of Elohim shouted
>
> (38:7)

to Leviathan, that astonishing monster, whose

> sneezes flash with light,
> his eyes are like dawn's eyelids,

from his mouth come flares,
fiery sparks fly out.

(41:18-19)

The speech presents its cosmology, its animals, and its monsters
as a challenge to Job, questioning whether he is a deity and inviting
him to try it.

> During your days have you commanded morn-
>   ing,
> instructed dawn of its place?
> . . . .
> Have you entered Sea's springs,
> walked around in the Deep's recesses?
> . . . .
> If you have an arm like El's,
> and with a voice like his you thunder,
> deck yourself with pride and puissance,
> with glory and grandeur clothe yourself.
> Strew about the furies of your anger,
> see everyone proud, bring them low,
> see everyone proud, humiliate them,
> and trample guilty people where they stand.
>   (38:12, 16; 40:9-12)

In the entire speech, Yahweh asks if Job knows what no human
could pretend to know and invites him to do things no human could
do. In the last passage quoted, he specifically invites him to govern
the world in accord with the retributive principle. There is an
element of arrogant sarcasm in the speech, and we must wonder
about its effect on Job. Does it strike him with awe of the divine
power, which can do so much that he himself cannot do, so that he
forgets about the problem of the divine justice? Does it make him
cower before the divine power and abandon all thought of receiving,
let alone demanding, divine justice? The power implicit and explicit
in Yahweh's presentation of himself in these speeches is the most
obvious characteristic of the deity. Yet Job always knew that the god
was powerful. It is not clear that he has learned anything new,
except that the god can also be arrogantly sarcastic.

I think there is a point where Yahweh shifts the issue. The first speech ends (40:2) by challenging Job to get one of his helpers to do something for him—interestingly enough, the *môkîah*, the one whom Job denied or postulated most tentatively in 9:33. Job's reply in 40:4-5 is a noncommittal refusal to say anything. That is not good enough, and in 40:8 Yahweh asks the question that shifts the issue:

> Would you even annul my order [*mišpaṭ*],
> treat me as guilty so you may be innocent?

I will not traverse all the possible changes to be rung on that very subtle rhetorical question.[31] It is often read (taking *mišpaṭ* as "justice" or "judgment") as the frontal challenge to Job's entire being, declaring him simply wrong and with no right to demand anything. That reading is surely consistent with the rest of Yahweh's portrait, nor does it shift the issue at all. I should prefer to see "order" as meaning something different from what Job had thought. The question may propose that Job's insistence on his structures of guilt and innocence, his demand that either he or the god be found right and the other wrong, undoes the whole world order. Job is wrong, yes, but wrong in thinking that order rests on morality. Deserving does not run the world; justice (*mišpaṭ*) in the narrow sense is not the order in the broad sense. If it were, the world would have to revolve entirely around human action and divine response to it, and no space would be left for such marvelously uncontrollable monsters as Leviathan.

The implication is that when bad things happen, they do not at once reveal human (or divine) moral failure. Job did not begin with that misconstruction of the world (there is no trace of it in chs. 1–2), but he was seduced to it first by Eliphaz and then by the other friends. He let himself be snookered into thinking that the problem of evil has something to do with sin and human (or divine) moral deserving. The entire discussion of Job and the friends, resting on the supposition that the god punishes by suffering and that the sufferer is the sinner, turns out to have been a tangent, a wrong turn that led nowhere but to more suffering.

We could spend a great deal of time on the response.[32] Job had not understood what he was talking about (42:3), but he now both hears and sees Yahweh (v. 5).[33] He closes with this remarkable couplet:

> Therefore I despise and repent
> of dust and ashes.
>
> (42:6)[34]

Turning away from the Christian translations, which tend to see this as Job's acknowledgment of guilt and his repentance (so RSV)—just what the friends consistently advised—and from the translations agreeing with the Jewish Publication Society version, that Job's change of mind comes from his realization not that he is wrong but that he is insignificant ("being but dust and ashes"), I see something else. I take 40:8 to signify that the issue has ceased to be guilt and innocence at all, and I see the phrase "dust and ashes" as a metonymy for the entire religious structure of guilt and repentance. Job supposed that his pain was punishment of guilt and asserted his innocence against it. Now he thinks that it was the wrong question. Suffering has no connection with sin, and the world is not run by deserving. He "repents of dust and ashes," gives up the entire structure of the world as mirroring moral retribution. He repents of repentance, even, perhaps, of religion.[35]

The Problem of Evil: The Final Tale

In the final tale Job gets everything back twice over. Is that reward for his goodness? Do good things after all happen to good people? There may be ways to twist the story around to avoid that, but 42:10 makes it hard to succeed: "Yahweh reversed Job's fortune when he prayed for his friends, and he increased Job's holdings twofold." Having renounced repentance, Job's praying for his friends is surrogate for their repentance, and having prayed for them, he receives double his former wealth. The syntax of verse 10 makes it clear that that is not a mere temporal sequence. Still, if the issue has been shifted, and what happens is not proof of people's spiritual standing with the deity, then the doubling of fortune is nothing more than doubling of fortune, even when done by Yahweh. But the sequence still does not look like a mere temporal sequence.

No book of any depth speaks with a single voice. Every one contradicts itself somewhere along the line, and so no book provides the definitive answer to anything—unless, to be sure, the question is banal and superficial. Job does not deal with superficial questions, and I think we see in the book several different, and incompatible, answers to the same profound questions.

But we do not see a solution to the problem of evil, unless denying that moral quality is an index to external circumstance is a solution. And if it is, the solution simply consists of saying that the problem has become a nonproblem, that the world is a place in which moral quality and external circumstance are unrelated.

Yet there is a solution to the problem of evil in this closing tale that, curiously, has been overlooked. "All his brothers and sisters and acquaintances came to see him and ate a meal with him in his house. They consoled and comforted him about all the evil that Yahweh had brought upon him, and each gave him one *qĕśîṭâ* and one gold ring" (42:11). Those are very substantial gifts, enough by themselves to make Job wealthy again. More important is the comfort and consolation. Eliphaz, Bildad, and Zophar had come "to console and comfort" Job (2:11), and he called them, among other things, "troublesome comforters" (16:2) and said, "How you console me with empty air" (21:34). Now his relatives and friends succeed in what the three failed in, for their consoling and comforting is narrated in finite verb forms (*wayyānûdû lô wayĕnahǎmû ᾿ōtô*), whereas the three friends' consoling and comforting is detailed in infinitives (*lānûd-lô ûlĕnahǎmô*).

The comfort of the close human community, not debate and doctrinal instruction, solves the problem of "all the evil that Yahweh had brought upon him." The problem of evil that has a solution is not the abstract problem of the relation between power and goodness but is Job's own problem of suffering and alienation.

CHAPTER 4

WOUNDED HERO ON A SHAMAN'S QUEST

JOB IN THE CONTEXT OF FOLK LITERATURE

Carole R. Fontaine

Few biblical books are as difficult as the book of Job. Whether the topic under consideration is the vocabulary, literary structure, date, author's intent, or interpretation of the content, Job has always stumped the experts. Linguistically, the book shows strong Aramaic influence in sections, hapax legomena abound, and in terms of literary usage, the author (or authors; the singular will be used in the following for simplicity's sake, but the possibility of multiple authorship should be borne in mind) "copies hardly at all and imitates only rarely."[1] A man named Job is given as a proverbial example of goodness in Ezekiel 14:12-23, along with a Dan'el (of the Ugaritic Epic) and Noah, implying that such a legendary character was known at the time of that prophet's ministry during the Exile. Dates for the book range all the way from the patriarchal era (2100–1500 B.C.E.), based on parallel texts from the ancient Near East, to the last postexilic period (third century B.C.E.).[2] Whatever its date, the work never seems to lose its relevance for readers, or stop raising critical theological questions for its successive audiences. It is the opinion of this interpreter that it is precisely the uncertainty that surrounds so many aspects of this work that contributes decisively to the "pleasures of the text." With Job, we are free to engage in some of the more playful aspects of the game of interpretation because so little about Job can be "fixed."

Given the general uncertainty about the date of the book, and hence about the life-setting out of which it grew and the intentions of the author, it is not surprising that the content of the work should prove enigmatic as well. Just what is this book about? one might ask. Is it about the riddle of righteous suffering? How to speak faithfully of God in the midst of suffering?[3] Is it about the surfacing of the "scapegoat mechanism" in ancient Israel,[4] or perhaps the inability of humans to know and understand the divine plan?[5] It seems that there will be as many answers to the questions of content, function, and form in Job as there are interpreters.

Certainly, Job presents us with many anomalies in its relation to the shape of the mainstream tradition as it is usually understood. Given the God known from the rest of the Hebrew Bible, are readers really expected to believe that this same Yahweh is behind the afflictions besetting Job, and for no better reason than a "wager," at that? (Job, who is unaware of the wager, certainly has trouble with this reading of divine causality!) If a late date for the book is accepted, how does the dualism suggested by the machinations of "the Satan" or "Adversary" fit into the well-developed monotheism of Second Isaiah and others? Why does God's "answer" to Job seem to be so little to the point? It is not only the behavior of Yahweh that is puzzling, but that of the hero and his comforters as well. Why does Job, who laments about the failure of cultic redress for his wrongs, disprove his own statement by taking an oath in chapter 31 that leads—as cultic religion proclaimed it would—to the resolution of his complaint in a confrontation with God? Why do the friends give such poor comfort, if that is indeed their aim?

Job and the Structure of Tales

Many of these difficulties become less troubling when we analyze the book from the perspective of genre, and the present writer has argued in another place that the book in its entirety may be understood as a "poeticized folktale."[6] Using the "formalist" analytic model developed by Vladimir Propp in his *Morphology of the Folktale*[7] for the study of Russian fairy tales, those findings suggested that the prose and poetic portions of Job exist in a far more intimate relationship to each other than is usually noted by commentators. The prologue and epilogue, rather than being disposable appendages that take second place to the existentialist grandeur of the poetic speeches, are of primary importance not simply for the establishment of the setting and action but also for the structuring of the poetic sections as well. Though the prose of Job clearly defines the work as existing in the world of the ''tale,'' it too is not without the qualities of ''high'' poetic art demonstrated in the dialogues, showing the marks of fine crafting, and perhaps even an epical substratum.[8] Together, prose and poetry exhibit a profound symbiosis, each partaking of aspects of the other. Hence, a closer look at the mode of action and characterization found in tales from diverse cultures and historical epochs becomes invaluable for interpretation of the text. Before embarking on a description of what might be gleaned after such a reaping, it might be helpful to mention some of the limits and liabilities of the use of Propp's model.

There are, of course, a number of criticisms that have been leveled at the importation and deployment of Propp's model on literature outside the European fairy tale corpus, as well as certain logical, internal problems with method. Pamela J. Milne's work, *Vladimir Propp and the Study of Structure in Hebrew Biblical Narrative*,[9] admirably sets out some of the difficulties and advantages of the method and is a valuable bibliographic resource for studies in this area. We need not review here what she has done so well there, since space does not permit a full exploration of the matter. Instead, I will simply gesture toward some of the problems that seem particularly relevant to any attempt to apply the model to the surface structure of Job. First, what kind of presuppositions and conclusions support the search for a universal narrative structure, which is what some of those using Propp's method seem to be doing? Is it assumed that structural variants of these narratives arise spontaneously throughout historical periods and across geographical boundaries, and if so, what features in a society and/or author/teller serve as prerequisites for these unrelated replications? Are those who use this method suggesting a basic identity, at least for the production of imaginative literature if nowhere else, among the disparate cultures that contain structural variants, even where one culture might be preindustrial and another postmodern? In other words, while there may be no difficulty accepting the structural similarities between the Joban tale and, for example, the Egyptian

"Tale of the Eloquent Peasant," since they generally share time, place, and world view, accounting for the occurrence of shared motifs in the Egyptian "Tale of the Doomed Prince" and the European fairy tale of Rapunzel may be more problematic—at least until one traces the basic Rapunzel tale back to its diffusion from the Greek islands. Those who do not choose to answer such questions by viewing variants as the product of cultural migration and "contamination" must give some accounting for the existence of the manifold replications in the materials they study. Usually, the allegedly "common" features noted by developmental and Jungian psychology in the process of ego individuation within the family are considered the basis for the "polygenesis" of similar tales.[10] As Max Luthi, a noted interpreter of tales in all their forms, writes, "Fairy tales are unreal, but they are not untrue; they reflect essential developments and conditions of man's existence."[11] He elsewhere continues, "One feels that fairy tales are concerned with portraying essential processes in life. Testing, threatening danger, destruction—and salvation, development, and maturation—are portrayed before our mind's eye in images which are unreal, but for that reason fascinating."[12]

In fact, Luthi is correct when he links the genesis of tales to the conditions of *"man's* existence" (emphasis mine), though it is doubtful that he considered his words from a feminist perspective. The experience from which psychologists work and that they have elevated to the status of "normative" human experience is in fact the experience of men. One may well ask, as some feminists in folklore studies are doing, about the relevance of such a model when applied to female heroes ("heras" or "sheroes," as they have been called). Although females predominate as characters in and tellers of European folk tales, worldwide men predominate as actors in and makers of tales and myths[13]—no doubt filling the leisure hours created by their nonengagement in food preparation and child care. Since this was probably the case in ancient Israel, the unconscious, androcentric bias incorporated into Propp's method and the work of its interpreters does not rule out its applicability for the book of Job.

Second, is it in fact appropriate to apply Propp's model, derived as it was from a corpus of European heroic fairy tales, to tales of other genres and times? Does the interpreter not run the risk of

attempting to force ancient texts into models they were never made
to fit? Obviously, critics who seek to perform such analysis must do
so warily, privileging the integrity of their own texts over the
demands of the model. Propp's model *has* been used successfully, at
least in this author's opinion, as a first step for the description of the
surface structure of tales that, while they may not be heroic, still
bear some family likeness to the kinds of materials Propp
catalogued. Those using Propp's model outside of the European
corpus seem to succeed best when they are sensitive to the
differences between their corpus and the one Propp used, and feel
free to fit the model to the text, rather than the reverse. Further, no
analysis should stop with the successful employment of Propp's
categories, since it reads primarily the syntagmatic or "horizontal"
axis of the tale's structure. It is a preliminary step only, not an end in
itself. This, of course, is one of Lèvi-Strauss's great criticisms of
Propp's work,[14] and the enterprise of narrative study is indeed
enhanced when paradigmatic analysis that aims at understanding the
"vertical" dimensions of the text is also conducted. Texts make
their "meanings" by the unfolding of the syntagmatic axis, but
communities make meaning when they read and interpret that text
"paradigmatically" in the context of their history and social values.

Finally, one internal problem with Propp's contentions about his
model was specificially validated in the work on Job. Numerous
critics have taken exception to Propp's statement that the
"functions" or actions that link a tale together always occurred in
the same invariant sequence. Propp himself allowed for the
incursion or replication of sets of sequences of functions within his
model, so that the actual surface structure of a tale might in fact
deviate from that expected if a tale's sequence simply ran from
function 1 through 31. That is, a tale's surface might be represented
by 1 2 3 4 *5 6 7 5 6 7* . . . 29 30 31, rather than proceeding by
functions 1 2 3 4 5 6 7 8 . . . 29 30 31 and so on. In the preliminary
comparative work conducted on Egyptian, Anatolian, and Meso-
potamian myths with tale-like structures, it was found that "donor
tests" in particular—that is, the challenge of the hero by a donor and
the subsequent transfer to the hero of needed implements or
information—tended to occur within the preparatory sections of the
narrative rather than in the location where Propp's model expected

them.[15] Hence, flexibility in the application of models to ancient Near Eastern texts certainly seems warranted. Having said all this, let us now turn to the insights about folk narratives such as tale and myth drawn from folkloristic analysis, with special reference to their application to Job.

Folktales are not unlike myths in many respects. Rather than categorizing these narrative forms as "false stories" as moderns often do, structural analysis has shown that both tales and myths aim at the resolution of conflict and the fulfillment of "lacks" and has confirmed the structural relationship between the two genres.[16] Myths operate at the social level: Things that took place in the distant past between deities and humans still affect human society and nature in the audience's "now." Tales, however, address themselves to the individual level—they are the "success stories" of a given culture and tend to mirror the psychological development of its (male) individuals.[17]

Interestingly, in the tale as understood through the Propp model, action takes precedence over character. (Indeed, the neglect of characterization in analysis caused by this preference for action constitutes one of the major critiques of literary methods based on the Proppian model.) That is, for Propp the heart of the tale is hidden within the sequence of set actions performed in a certain order; the identity and personal characteristics of the actors are of secondary importance.[18] Thus characters appear to be more examples of ideal types who fill certain roles in the tale action rather than the realistic, "flesh and blood" creations familiar to us from modern prose. This probably reflects the genre's origin as oral literature, composed during performance from "stock" elements known to the storyteller. This process of composition in part accounts for the striking similarity among tales around the world and across time boundaries. The tales extant from the ancient Near East are obviously literary versions of oral tales, but the compositional characteristics of the genre still live within these artistic "daughters" of the oral tale.[19]

Common to the world of tale characters is a certain fluidity or ambivalence of behavior. Heroes may behave like villains as they attempt to achieve their aims. One might think here of the questionable behavior of the patriarch Jacob in his quest for blessing and bride, the advance given to Ruth by Naomi for securing a *gō'ēl,* or the trickery in the actions of the Hittite goddess Inaras as she arranges the defeat of a family of dragons in the Early Bronze Age "Myth of Illuyankas" found at the ancient capital of Hattuša in Turkey.[20] A similar situation is found in the Egyptian myth called "The God and His Unknown Name of Power" from a manuscript from the Nineteenth Dynasty. There the goddess Isis takes the villain's part as she tricks the sun god Re into revealing his secret name, thus filling her lack of knowledge, and issuing in a magical procedure for treating snakebite.[21] If the scathing, nearly blasphemous quality of Job's speeches scandalized pious audiences of the past and present, their tone and seemingly abrupt "reversal" from the "patience" of Job's first responses to adversity (Job 1:20-22; 2:7-10) are fully in keeping with the shifting characterization of tale heroes.

Other tale characters are apt to show similar reverses of behavior as they move to fill new roles or are "revealed" to be something other than what they appeared to be when first introduced. False villains may perform typically villainous actions at the outset of the story that cause the hero to set out on a quest or be driven away from home, but in the end, unlike real villains who receive punishment, they atone for their deeds, restoring "double" to their returning hero.[22] Such a movement occurs in the epilogue in Job, where Yahweh punishes the friends and rewards Job. False heroes make heroic claims, but at the tale's end they are revealed as imposters when the real hero is recognized and restored. Job's friends, with their "standard" retribution theology, claim to understand the workings of God, but in the end, Yahweh affirms that it is Job who has "spoken of me what is right" (42:7, 8).

Helpers and donors (those who give the hero needed assistance, information, or magical items), roles also played by Job's wife and friends, often act in ways that seem distinctly unusual or unhelpful. In the Nineteenth Dynasty mythological "Tale of Two Brothers" from Egypt, the god Anubis, attendant of Osiris in the underworld, is older brother to the hero Bata. As might be expected of a god connected with judgment of the dead, Anubis fills roles that are both judgmental and helpful with respect to his heroic brother. In an episode that is a structural forerunner of the famous incident of Potiphar's wife in the Joseph cycle (Gen. 39), Anubis believes his villainous wife's allegations of sexual misconduct by Bata and attempts to murder his brother. Later in the tale, however, Anubis goes on a quest to magically revive his now-dead brother, thus filling the roles of seeker-hero and helper.[23]

It is quite common to find heroes receiving much-needed help in remarkable forms from unusual sources. In the same tale, Bata receives information about his brother's murderous intentions from animal donors, marvelous talking cows who warn the innocent brother. In the Sumerian "Descent of Inanna," the goddess is aided in her search for her mate Dumuzi by "holy flies," whom she rewards with the perpetual right to inhabit taverns and annoy beer drinkers, while listening to wise speech and joyous songs.[24] That such animal helpers are connected to the numinous is underscored in a Sumerian lament composed by the great poet Enheduanna, daughter of Sargon of Akkad. In line 91 of the *Nin-me-sar-ra* (known as the "Exaltation of Inanna") she raises her voice in supplication to that goddess, who is styled as "my divine impetuous wild cow."[25] The perplexing parade of creatures in Yahweh's answer to Job in 38:39–41:34 is not so out of place or irrelevant as is often assumed by commentators, once placed in the context of tale helpers and donors. They are there to convey information to Job that will help him complete his quest for meaning.[26] Living illustrations of the mystery of creation, these animal helpers allow Job to place the suffering of human beings in a less parochial, more cosmic perspective.

Use of the folktale model similarly makes sense out of what some have considered the unexpected disappearance of the Satan and Elihu from the epilogue, where we might have wished to see all the narrative's loose ends tied up when the friends receive their comeuppance. Propp's model provides for the reappearance of sequences of functions or "moves," and in this reading Elihu is not a false hero but a helper who replicates the function of FG, "receipt of a magical agent" (= F), here the rather unmagical helper Elihu, and "guidance" as this out-of-the-blue helper directly foreshadows Job's upcoming struggle with Yahweh (= G).[27] Since Elihu is a helper and not a false hero, his absence from the epilogue is not surprising. The same is true for the disappearance of the Satan, the villain of what Propp calls the "Complication," those preparatory functions that serve to set the hero on his adventures. In complex tales of intertwined sequences such as Job, normally only the most recent antagonists of the hero, in this case the friends as false heroes, are punished in the denouement.[28]

Perhaps one of the most central features of any tale is the various kinds of tests—the great deed to be done, the debate to be won, the river to be crossed—that prove the main character worthy of help. Often, testing appears in triple form: The same test is repeated three times, with the hero finally succeeding on the third trial, or three successive tests occur, each more difficult than the last.[29] Other variations include those where the hero succeeds at passing the test after two companions have failed. Post-Proppian research on the nature of the folktale test has been particularly helpful, dividing these functions into three groups:

1. preliminary tests (donor tests)
2. basic tests (the hero's struggle with the villain)
3. supplementary tests (exposure of false heroes)

E. Meletinsky notes that each test successfully passed plows energy back into the hero's actions, energy needed to overcome the "entropy" caused by the villainous acts.[30]

The Joban prologue gives us a clear presentation of tests after the first two complications of villainy visited upon Job. In the first villainous act, his children and goods are taken from him (1:6-22); in the next, he suffers personal harm (2:1-10). (The Egyptian "Tale of the Eloquent Peasant" begins, by the way, with exactly the same structure of repeated villainies, which are used as they are in Job to set up a series of dialogues on the meaning of suffering and justice between the peasant and the local magistrate.)[31] Leaving home—one of the hero's most significant acts—to sit upon his ash-heap, a symbol of squandered mortality, Job's preliminary (i.e., donor) test is administered by his wife in 2:9. Job's hostile reply to her inquiry about the role of his notion of personal integrity in the prolongation of his misery ensures that he must undergo more intensive donor testing before he can find his way out of his dilemma. After the expected mediating lament of Job 3, donor testing resumes, but now in the form of poetic disputations among Job and his three friends, dialogues that are themselves constructed in triads of escalating hostility. Even though we have moved from prose into poetry, the author continues to use the structure of the tale as the skeleton upon which to flesh out in the poetry the psychological and theological conflicts implied by the prose tale.

The third cycle is, of course, problematic, but even there some reference to tale structure helps make sense out of the progress of the debate. It is exactly in the third dialogue of the third poetic donor test that we would expect to see the greatest triumph, and that is precisely where the textual integrity of the dialogues break down. However, something new from the tale's repertoire may be observed in this garbled cycle as Job begins to make "avowals of innocence," first in reply to Eliphaz in Job 23:10-12, then in response to Bildad (27:2-6), and culminating in his great "oath of innocence" in chapter 31, where we might have expected a reply to Zophar. In this analysis, these oaths act as more traditional magical aids do in that they allow Job to reaffirm to himself his own sense of his integrity, a sense that prepares him for the upcoming basic test of struggle with Yahweh in chapters 38–42. In this reading, the Hymn to Wisdom in Job 28 fulfills Propp's functions F, "provision or receipt of a magical agent," and G, "the hero is transferred, delivered, or led to the whereabouts of an object of search," where "the object of search is located in 'another' or 'different' kingdom."[32] Elusive wisdom, which cannot be found in the furthest boundaries of the tale universe, can be located in human actions—"Behold, the fear of the Lord, that is wisdom; and to depart from evil is understanding" (28:28 RSV). For Job, Wisdom acts as a magical helper who encourages him to take the oath of innocence of chapter 31. Here I stand with some important "precritical" interpreters: Though the vocabulary of 28:28 may strike us as suspicious, especially when placed in Job's mouth, this verse represents the heart of the book in its final form and may not be brushed aside.

Folkloristic studies of the art of storytelling have emphasized the impact of interaction between the teller and the audience on the composition and performance of any given tale.[33] When dealing with ancient texts, such dimensions are, alas, lost to modern critics, but we may infer that the poetic dialogues are not simply an instance of individual artistic brilliance but equally as much a response to the needs of the author's audience. The "Tale of Job" continues to be told by psychologists and artists, by "survivors" of the terrors of the modern world, by commentators on the ancient text. I would like to offer now another reading of Job's journey, a reading originally suggested by folkloric and anthropological material on animal helpers and their relation to human illness.

Job: A Shaman's Tale

In the wealth of folkloric materials and anthropological studies on the meaning, interpretation, and responses to illness by the human community, there arises a consistent theme—that of the shamanic journeys undertaken by the "wounded healers" of other-than-literate societies. The general pattern found in the descriptions of a person's entry into the shamanic world is one that strikes chords of resonance with Job's story. Often, a perfectly normal person who may be either completely enmeshed or marginalized in his or her world is seized by a dread disease. The meaning of the disease may be interpreted in a variety of ways by the culture involved. The spirit of the sick person may have been stolen by evil ones, or it may have strayed during sleep; sorcery may be involved, or perhaps a dislocation is felt in the social organization of which the sick person is a part.[34] At any rate, action must be taken to reincorporate the sufferer into the community and to ready the community for the reception of the newly healed member.

In hunting and gathering cultures, the magical abilities of the shamanic healer were called upon to correct and assist in this liminal situation, since illness means danger not simply to the sufferer but also to the community as well. Often the dread illness functions in the literature as a sort of ad hoc initiation, as the afflicted soul is sent wandering away from its body to return eventually in possession of the secrets of life and healing. The symbolic death of the sufferer—that is, the illness—is not the period put to the sentence of life but rather a threshold into new levels of awareness and social integration. The sufferer becomes the healer, returning from the underworld exile of illness as the bearer of health for all. Barbara Myerhoff writes of the shaman:

> The shaman is above all a connecting figure, bridging several worlds for his people, traveling between this world, the underworld, and the heavens. He transforms himself into an animal and talks with ghosts, the dead, the deities, the ancestors. He dies and revives. He brings back knowledge from the shadow realm, thus linking his people to the spirits and places which were once mythically accessible to all. It is the special responsibility of the shaman to return to *illud tempus* on behalf of his people, to make his ecstatic journey through the assistance of animal tutelary spirits, to bring back information of the other realms to ordinary mortals. [35]

Well and good, but how exactly does a shaman effect a cure, and what relation does such a process have to the pattern of activity portrayed in the book of Job? Modern persons usually find themselves obliged to disregard reports of the shamans themselves as to how they do what they do and search instead for some healing mechanism, usually psychological or social, that is triggered by the shaman's symbolic activity. That shamanic activity is aimed at psychosocial conflict resolution is clear, [36] and the proposals as to how shamans go about this are varied, ranging from the suggestion that ritual symbolic healings act through inducing the release of endorphins in the brain to the invocation of such time-honored explanations as suggestion, catharsis, or social restructuring. [37] In fact, current studies in psychoneuroimmunology suggest a model that can account for a variety of types of symbolic healing. Much simplified, imagery and emotions processed in the right hemisphere of the brain act on the limbic system, or primitive brain, and there produce direct effects on the autonomic nervous system, hypothalamus, and pituitary gland. This activation directly stimulates the immunological systems of the body. [38] In fact, laughter and joy *can* heal, and terrifying images and feelings of grief *can* slay. The nightmare image of the divine warrior that haunts Job both expresses his disease and perpetuates it. J. Gerald Janzen is quite right when he pinpoints what he calls Job's "imaginative outreach" (Job 3; 9:33-35; 14:13-17; 16:18-22; 19:23-27) as the beginning of movement toward healing. He writes, "The *fact* of Job's imaginative outreach, as an act of solitary and thoroughly awakened consciousness, is perhaps more significant than its *content* and *tendency*. For now, it signals his awakening from the 'dogmatic slumbers' in which he had formerly lived in creatural piety."[39] In general, students of shamanism agree that the role of the folk healer is to dramatize the conflict felt by the client or social group, attaching it to shared mythical symbols and images that can then be successfully manipulated toward health and conflict resolution.[40] As part of the therapeutic encounter, the shaman may choose to enact this dramatic restructuring of the problem through the vehicle of his or her own body, engaging in magical flight, trance, or other forms of ecstatic consciousness, such as personifying the spirits that "symbolize the psychological tensions and social patterns that [his] patrons experience but have no conscious control over."[41] The goal, of course, is health and wholeness, whose meanings in other-than-literate societies are somewhat different from those found in our own. Shamanic researcher Jeanne Achterberg writes that

> health is being in harmony with the world view. Health is an intuitive perception of the universe and all its inhabitants as being of one fabric. Health is maintaining communication with the animals and plants and minerals and stars. It is knowing death and life and seeing no difference. It is blending and melding, seeking solitude and seeking companionship to understand one's many selves. Unlike the more "modern" notions, in shamanic society health is not the absence of feeling; no more so is it the absence of pain. Health is seeking out all of the experiences of Creation and turning them over and over, feeling their texture and multiple meanings. Health is expanding beyond one's singular state of consciousness to experience the ripples and waves of the universe.[42]

A better description of the effect of the contents of the Yahweh-speeches could not be written. Job's much-discussed "repentance" is neither false nor an ironic expression of the futility of expecting answers about human justice from cosmic sources. Job has been tutored by the pedagogy of pain. At the end of the struggle with God in 38–42—and it should be clear that this *is* struggle, one of Propp's functions, both from the military idiom that orders Job to gird himself up as if for battle (38:3) and from the sharp tone of the rhetorical questions that follow—Job is firmly reintegrated into the web of creation that no longer needs to put human experience and the questions raised by that experience at the center of interest. The struggle here has been a real one, but it is the kind of struggle that heals. A sort of spiritual Copernican Revolution has taken place for Job, and this is why he can say in 42:6, "Therefore I recant and change my mind concerning dust and ashes."[43] The wild, marvelous creatures who act as animal helpers in the tale world have taken on the role of the shaman's power animals who teach the lessons of life and death and mark the path of ecstatic return to the human community.

Who, then, acts the part of the shaman in the book of Job, and is there any foundation for the importation of yet another "foreign" model to aid us in our reading? Survivals of shamanic thinking and practice *do* exist in societies that are no longer organized around hunting and gathering, and belief in the guardian animal spirits who protect game and aid the hunter may linger long after the society moves into other forms of economic production.[44] The literary setting of the book of Job as it stands makes an overt attempt to situate the story's action in the distant, almost primeval, patriarchal past, a time when such ancient beliefs as those reflected in the shamanic world view might reasonably be considered to retain some of their vitality. Even if we were to consider a real, factual survival of shamanic practice unlikely during the time period to which we might assign the action or composition of the book of Job, the possibility of the survival of associated traditional and literary motifs relating to shamanism could still not be ruled out. Arvid Kapelrud has examined certain evidence in the Hebrew Bible for the existence of shamanic practice and finds support for thinking that some survivals of ecstatic shamanism do exist, primarily derived from Canaanite influence.[45] While he pays no specific attention to healing practices, no doubt because so little is known about the actual practice of medicine in ancient Israel, if survivals exist in one area it is not unreasonable to think other traces of this tradition of folk healing might have lingered in the house of Israel. More

comparative work that analyzes the better-known medical practices
of surrounding cultures for shamanic survivals needs to be
undertaken before anything more than speculation can take place,
but the use of sympathetic magical procedures in healing among the
Hittites, for example, offers intriguing possibilities for reconstruction.

To return to the first question, posed earlier—who plays the role
of shaman in the book of Job?—the answer, at least at this stage of
consideration, is so big as to be no answer at all. Everyone acts out
shamanic roles; Job is the afflicted one whose illness becomes his
ecstatic cure. He has taken the grief generated by the human
outcome of the divine wager directly into his body to create an
illness whose significance goes well beyond the merely personal. By
the end of the story he has received the mandate to pray for the
reintegration of his friends into the divine blessedness to which he
has been restored. The dialogues between Job and the friends
dramatize the images by which each attempts to understand and
respond to the experience of illness at hand, so that in effect each
acts the role of shaman for the other. Even Elihu serves his purpose,
as he gestures toward the theophany to come. Yahweh, whose role
as divine healer in the Yahweh-speeches is often overlooked (see
Gammie, however[46]), spins out the parade of animal helpers who act
as the shaman's teachers, guardians, and helpers. In the healing of
Job and his (and/or the author's) society, everyone plays a part.

Perhaps the real shaman, then, is the author, whose brilliant
appropriation of the prose tale allows him to attach his audience's
conflicts and needs to mythic structures that can then be used to
reorganize the community's experience of suffering and illness.
When the story switches from the syntagamatic axis of narrative to
the paradigmatic axis of poetic speech, the audience is captured and
moved into the timeless world of pain, whose content, texture, and
taste can only be known through the metaphorical allusiveness of
poetry. The return to prose after Job's meeting and appropriation of
the divine comfort and knowledge made available through the power
of animals signals the return to health and a more ordinary state of
consciousness. The shaman has journeyed far and wide, up and
down, through and beyond. He has considered the stars and the
stones, the birds of prey and the dead tree that scents the waters

of life, the ways of humanity and the way of wisdom, and he is content. In the knowledge derived from his travels, the human community is built up and broken down and built up yet again. We, the audience, have come to know ourselves, the world, and God better by means of the journey onto which the author of Job has catapulted us, so that in the end we too can affirm with Job, the wounded healer, "We had heard by the hearing of the ear, but now our eyes have seen."[47]

CHAPTER 5

THE BOOK OF JOB AND INNER-BIBLICAL DISCOURSE

Michael Fishbane

The book of Job has a rhetorical character all its own—one that never fails to astonish and compel readers of every degree of literary sophistication. From the initial outburst of Job to his friends (in ch. 3), to the climactic speech of God to Job (in ch. 41), the argumentation often proceeds less by logic than by stylistic figure. Metaphors mix with metaphors to create a rhetorical *bricolage* of imaginative density, and one question follows another to displace apparent sureties with ever-deepening disorientation. Indeed, despite the moot trial structure overall—galvanized by an insidious test and dramatized by theological desperation—the reader (as jury) is repeatedly swayed by the magical play of images. More often than not a point is solved more by simile than by syllogism, and more by the analogical relations between images than by the patient process of reason.

Centuries of commentaries have not failed to admire the bold literary imagery in this book, but far more attention has been given to the legal and theological content of the arguments. In fact, to the extent that inner-biblical allusions in the speakers' words are considered, they largely serve to invoke the general wisdom or deuteronomic ideology that is challenged by Job and variously defended by his friends. Very little emphasis is placed on reading the stylistic figures of the book in terms of the gathering argumentation.[1] This task, I believe, will provide unexpected pointedness to many literary turns, in two respects: A comparison of a given Joban figure with others in the Hebrew Bible can sharpen the wit of the Joban usage, while comparison of comparable figures *within* the book of Job itself can enable one to appreciate the interactive relations of

86

various speeches to one another. The first procedure relates Job to stylistic conventions found in Scripture as a whole, and the second correlates figures within the book of Job alone.

Job and the Bible—Rhetorical Links and Differences

I

The powerful blast of Job against God in Job 7:17-18 is a good point to begin our inquiry into the inner-biblical dynamics of Joban discourse. As we shall see, a full exploration of this text and its cognates will open up many issues. The passage reads:

> What [*mâ*] is Man [*'ĕnôš*] that You raise him up,
>   and set [*tāšît*] Your mind upon him;
> that you take note of him [*tipqĕdennû*] each morning,
>   and check him by the minute?[2]

As often noted, this part of Job's complaint evokes the ostensibly related hymnic formulation found in Psalm 8:4-6. There the psalmist rhapsodically wonders:

> Who [*mâ*] is Man [*'ĕnôš*] that You are mindful of him,
>   the son of Man that You take note of him [*tipqĕdennû*]?
> For, Lo! You have made him little less than divine . . .
>   . . . and have set [*šāttâ*] everything for his dominion.

At the most formal level, several stylistic and verbal features connect the two passages. First, each unit begins with the interrogative pronoun *mâ* and the noun *'ĕnôš*; second, the queries are structured by the particles *kî* ("that"), *wĕ-kî* ("and that"), and *wĕ-* ("that"); third, the verb *tipqĕdennû* and the verbal stem *šît* ("to set") recur in both units; and finally, the exalted status of the human species is variously marked by the verb *tĕgaddĕlennû* ("raise him up") and *tĕḥassĕrēhû* ("made him less"). But if syntactic, verbal, and rhetorical similarities bring these texts into relation, the interpreter is still obliged to ask, in what way (or ways) is Psalm 8:4-6 a subtext or pretext for the formulation in Job 7:17-18? That is, how should we consider the relation or tension between them? Does the Joban trope build on a traditional liturgical model known to contemporary readers, so that the differences between it and the psalm would be felt as deliberate irony? Or are the texts merely similar in forms, so that the most we may do is draw attention to their stylistic relations?

There is certainly no easy answer to those questions, but the very process of engaging them takes a step toward assessing the piquancy of Job's style. Let us therefore begin by observing the condensed and balanced form of the Psalms passage, in which the opening query (*mâ*) evokes the exalted status of the human species, nearly divine and majestically dominant over all earthly life. Indeed, the word *mâ* expresses astonished joy, and the verbs that follow further heighten the point. Now this crescendo of praise contrasts sharply with the Joban unit, which is part of a larger accusation addressed to God. In this instance the interrogative *mâ* evokes a cry of despair; for Job uses the particle to increase the difference between God and persons (not to celebrate their proximity), and to hurl a confused query to heaven (not to evoke divine praise). What, asks Job, is man's account before the overwhelming power of God? The strangeness of divine providence is emphasized as well, as the speaker wonders why God can't even let mortal man swallow his spittle in peace (v. 19). "If I have sinned," Job asks, "what effect has it on You, Creator of Man?" (v. 20). Clearly the image of God here is not that of a majestic providence who delegates authority to a human overlord (as in Ps. 8). It is rather that of a dark divinity that hounds and horrifies the dreams of mortals (v. 14). Indeed, the inverted perspective of our Joban passage assumes added irony when specific topics are compared. For example, in the hierarchical structure of Psalm 8 (which mirrors Gen. 1) even the creatures of the watery deep are under human dominion. This orderly perspective clashes with Job 7:12, where rhetorical questions exaggerate God's misplaced attention. "Am I the Sea or the Dragon, that You muzzle me so?" (v. 12).[3] Job jousts with a sarcastic wit that wins at least a rhetorical victory, for his allusion to old mythic battles with sea monsters sardonically sharpens the misplaced energy of divine providence. The royal God of Psalm 8, who sets (*šāttâ*) all creatures under human dominion, is presented here as a divinity inappropriately obsessed (*tāšît*) with human sin. Our comparison of the two texts thus sharpens this ironic discordance.

II

There are other ways in which the positive ambiguity of the words in Psalm 8:5-7 is negatively employed in Job 7:17-18. Let us note, for example, the psalmist's crescendo of praise for the human species: "Who is man that You *tizkĕrennû*; the son of Man that You *tipqĕdennû?*" Two points may be made. First, the phrases are poetically balanced, so that the doubled reference to the human being ("Man," "son of Man") accentuates its hierarchical status. In addition, there is a second parallelism, marked by the Hebrew words *tizkĕrennû* and *tipqĕdennû*. This doubly enriches the whole, for beyond their obvious use as synonyms ("remember," "call to mind"), each verb has a secondary allusion; *tizkĕrennû* puns on the noun *zākōr* ("masculine") and so points back to the kingly "Man," while *tipqĕdennû* puns on the verb *pāqad* ("to appoint to office") and so points forward to his royal office in creation. The human person is thus exalted and called to God's mind for special significance. In this light, the related language of Job 7:17-18 spins wildly awry. Its own first verb, *tĕgaddĕlĕnnû*, which means both "raise him up" and "give him status," is negatively marked by God's strict accountancy—carried here by the verb *tipqĕdennû*. No longer a term referring to the special status of mankind in the mind of God, the verb now confers pointed theological irony. As the medieval commentator Rashi noted a millennium ago, God is judged here for "accounting" man's deeds on a daily basis. The "examining" quality of this picayune providence is further underscored by the parallel verb *bāḥan*, which now drifts toward the accountancy aspect of *tipqĕdennû*. In this way, its otherwise positive use to denote the refining or all-knowing dimension of divine attention is undercut.

Job's sarcasm thus has special bite in light of the psalmist's praise—and this intertextual irony may have been his intention from the start. Indeed, it seems far more likely than not that the fixed form of the psalmist's praise preceded and inspired Job's rhetoric. A final perspective on this irony emerges through a comparison of the word *mâ* in both sources. For the psalmist, the initial query "who is Man" is encased in the laudatory *inclusio,* "O Lord, our God, how [*mâ*] great is Your name in all the earth," that begins and ends the Psalm (vv. 2, 10). God's providential greatness here is that he allows for the exaltation of humans within the created order ("You have set everything beneath them," v. 7). The psalmist's rhetorical wonder is posed as an unanswerable question (*mâ*) evoking astonished praise (*mâ*). By contrast, Job's speech shifts from cosmological to moral providence—from praise to biting provocation. In fact, his sarcastic question "What [*mâ*] is Man?" (v. 17) is even more pointedly formulated in the ensuing diatribe. For in verse 20 he asks God, "If I have sinned, how [*mâ*] does it affect You?" And then, immediately following (v. 21), he goes on to wonder, "For what [*meh*] reason do You not forgive my transgression?" These variations on *mâ* highlight variations of the theological mind in Scripture, pointing to its pathos, its passion, and its pain.[4]

III

Another example further demonstrates the reuse of fixed forms in Job's rhetoric. Once again he characteristically twists his source toward a different concern. The text occurs as part of Job's final submission in 42:2. It reads:

I know that You can do everything [*kōl*]
   and that nothing [*mĕzimmâh*] is impossible [*lō'-yibbāṣēr*] for
You.

At first glance, the coda makes fine grammatical sense—a fitting finale to Job's avalanche of torment and a humble acceptance of God's wondrous ways. But how, then, may we account for the masculine verb *yibbāṣēr* in conjunction with the feminine noun *mĕzimmâh*? Surely the form *tibbāṣēr* would be more proper. And further, how might we explain the choice of this verb at all, since the noun *mĕzimmâh* has a negative connotation in wisdom literature?

An entirely different perspective emerges when we recall Genesis 11:6,[5] in which God looks down from heaven to the tower-building erected by mortals and says:

> If, as one people and one language, this is how
>   they have begun to act—
> then nothing they propose [*kōl . . . yāzĕmû*] will be
>   out of their reach [*lō'-yibbāṣēr mē*—]!

In this text, the verb *yibbāṣēr* seems to be an ironic allusion to the noun *mibṣār* ("fortress"), and thus a play on the tower theme, while the verb *yāzĕmû* is used to indicate a deliberate plan. Such a sharp formulation puts the Joban figure into relief. For we now realize that the word *mĕzimmâh* need not always have negative implications,[6] and that the masculine form of the verb is carried over to Job 42:2 *as a frozen form.* Indeed, just this frozen, ungrammatical usage suggests that Genesis 11:6 is both the ironic target and the source of Job's rhetoric.

Whereas Genesis 11:6 reflects divine fear of human power, Job now praises God for his utter omnipotence. Indeed, a comparison of the two passages strikingly highlights the hubris of the "tower generation" and Job's own vaunted challenges, and it also underscores the reclaimed hierarchy of divine privilege found in both texts. In the mouth of Job, the echo of God's ancient judgment of cultural pride is transformed into a humble confession. To be sure, there is no guarantee that the author of the book of Job deliberately alluded to the tower episode, but for the suggestive grammatical reasons just adduced I would claim this to be the likelihood. The whole matter has text-critical implications. For if rhetorical play is involved—that is, if Job's discourse turns on an allusive irony—the better part of valor would be to heighten the philological problem in Job 42:2, not emend it away!

IV

Having just focused on a textual cue latent in the personal prefix of a verb, let us turn to a related example in which a textual oddity suggests that the source of some Joban rhetoric lies in other biblical formulations. In the following case we also glean a deeper perspective on Job's personal suffering. The text is Job 5:17:

Happy is the man whom God tests [*yôkiḥennû*],
  and the reproofs [*mûsar*] of Shaddai do not despise [*'al-tim'ās*].

For comprehension, two grammatical points need to be noted: First, the overall context and consecution of the Joban passage is unclear, and second, the oblique (third-person) form of the first verb (*yôkiḥennû*) shifts—unexpectedly and oddly—to the direct (second-person) discourse of the second verb (*tim'ās*). As a further matter we may also wonder why the reproved person is deemed fortunate.

Some help comes from Proverbs 3:11-12, another wisdom source in which sapiential counsel is formulated.

The reproof [*mûsar*] of the Lord, my son, do not despise [*'al-tim'ās*],
  and do not hate his testing [*tôkaḥtô*];
For whomsoever the Lord loves, he tests [*yôkîaḥ*].

In this passage (as against the Joban one), the overall context is clear: It is a wisdom instruction formulated in the style of direct discourse common in the advice of a master to his disciple. Indeed in the master's charge suffering is deemed a sign (or proof) of God's providential care. This point comes as the explanatory climax of the instruction.

While there is no reason to assume a direct borrowing of Proverbs 3:11-13 in Job 5:17, a comparison of the two passages clarifies the latter within the overall topical and syntactic conventions of ancient biblical wisdom. Job's rhetoric emerges as a frozen fragment of ancient theological instruction—a window into an ancient Israelite—a theology of suffering (cf. Ps. 119:71). As in the preceding case, any hasty recourse to textual emendation on the basis of apparent philological oddities must be restrained by patient attention to the full canon of biblical discourse. To be sure, the ancient reader of Job would hardly think of Proverbs 3:11-12 per se. It is only we textual latecomers who need to invoke that specific proverb in order to appreciate the sapiential reverberations that echo in Job 5:17. Our eye must wander to that source because the wisdom traditions of divine testing are no longer in our cultural ear.

Inner-Joban Discourse—Other Rhetorical Links and Differences

I

In the first part of this essay several speeches in the book of Job were examined from the wider angle of inner-biblical discourse. Our present concern is now to view Joban discourse within the compass of its *own* sequence of speeches. This will illumine some striking developments in the Joban cycle. Since Job 7:17-18 was invoked earlier, I shall revert to it again here. As will be recalled, that piece was an ironic denunciation of divine providence that turned on the status of God's earthling—the *'ĕnôš*. What, Job asks, is the human privilege of being so raised up among creatures as to be the subject of God's special scrutiny?

Eliphaz, the first of Job's interlocutors, picks up the thread of Job 7:17-18 in 15:14-16 and remarks:

Who is Man [*mâ 'ĕnôš*] that he might be cleared of guilt,
    or the creature of Woman [*'iššâ*] that he be justified?
For indeed, He [*hēn*, God] puts no trust in His holy ones;
    and [even] the heavens are not guiltless in His sight.
What then of one so loathsome and foul,
    Man [*'îš*], who drinks perversity like water?!

What a caustic rejoinder! The point is now shifted away from Job's anthropomorphic theology (and his accusation of a picayune providence in heaven) to the rottenness of the very human claim to innocence. No matter that Eliphaz does not directly answer Job's charge. The fact of human sin is invoked here to undermine any thought by the plaintiff (Job) that the judge (God) has meddled beyond justification. Even the claim to innocence is deemed perverse. In this cosmic scheme of things, this creature (now, note, born of *woman!*) is even worse off than the heavenly host of the heavens themselves. To make this point, the opening question of "*mâ . . . kî*" ("what . . . that") has both rhetorical and syllogistic force—followed as it is by the *hēn* clause ("for indeed") and the seconding *'ap kî* ("what then"). Indeed, the opening question is cunningly answered by shifting the scale of perspective: The query of the opening *kî* is resumed and slammed shut by the closing *'ap kî*; and the pun on purity through the verb *yizkeh* ("*cleared* of guilt") is first mocked by saying that even the mute heavens are not pure or guiltless (*zakkû*), and then traduced by portraying mortal man as a sewer of sin ("who drinks perversity like water"). In the end, the mock logic serves to clear God himself, a God so utterly transcendent and pure that any human accusation is but the foul vapor of hubris. "What" and "who" indeed is a Man? The answer is given *a minore ad maius*.[7] Eliphaz's legal logic thus pierces Job's theology. At the same time, with a subtle turn, Eliphaz adverts to his own first speech in 4:12-18—especially verses 17-18:

> Will mortal Man [*'ĕnôš*] be acquitted by God,
>   or a Man [*gāber*] be pure by his Maker?
> Truly [*hēn*] He [God] cannot trust His own servants,
>   and reproaches His angels—
> How much [*'ap*] less those who live in clay huts,
>   formed of the dust and crushed like the moth?!

Such a speech is presented as a revelation of sorts, "a word . . . in stealth" that fills Eliphaz's dreams with hair-raising horror (vv. 12-15). As a heavenly voice, it is reported by the sage as a transcendent truth far more compelling and certain than the voice of those who are "shattered between daybreak and evening," who "die, and not with wisdom" (vv. 20-21).

These theological sentiments are doubly marked: first, by a classical twofold rhetorical question (*hă-. . . 'im*, "will . . . or"), followed by a concluding particle (*hēn*, "truly" or "indeed"), and then by the particle *'ap* ("how much"), which is normally coordinated with the *hēn*-clause. That is to say, in this passage the *hēn*-clause serves a swing function. It is at once a latch that closes the first rhetorical series and a hinge that opens the ensuing argument by analogy (from minor to major; "what" with respect to *x*, "so much so" with respect to *y*). The effect is an intensification and prolongation of the logic, such that the conclusion of one logical series becomes the initial premise for the other. But when Eliphaz reverts to this point words later (in 15:17-18), he introduces a striking change, owing to his response to Job's intervening query (in 7:17-18). To be sure, the older rhetorical pattern is ostensibly maintained, along with the double analogy (relating mortals to the pantheon and the pantheon to God). But when Eliphaz now reuses the *hēn 'ap* sequence, he subordinates it to the *mâ 'ĕnôš* ("Who is Man?") query that derives from Job's earlier point. By so splicing Job's speech with the language of divine revelation transmitted to him, Eliphaz turns the protest into a powerful syllogism. The interrogative *mâ* thus becomes the first element of a logical pattern: "what" (*mâ*) with respect to *x*, "so" (*'ap*) much the more with respect to *y*. Job's rhetorical pathos is thus pricked, and his anxious question is transformed into cool logic.

II

The thick irony of Eliphaz can be further appreciated when we note that his use of the verb *yiṣdaq* ("be justified") in 15:14 does not simply resume 4:17-18 but 9:2 as well, wherein Job himself responds to Eliphaz's point:

Truly I know that it is so;
   indeed, how can a Man be justified [*ûmâh yiṣdaq 'ĕnôš*] with God?!

He wearily goes on to say that even if he were in the right (*'eṣdaq*), his mouth would condemn him (v. 20); for (9:32):

He [God] is not a man, like me, that I can answer him [*'e'ĕnennû*],
   that we can go to the law together.

The wheel of this argument takes an unexpected turn in 33:12, when the final interlocutor, Elihu, takes up these terms and says:

Truly [*hēn*] you are not right [*lo'-ṣādaqtā*],
   on this I will answer you [*'e'ĕnekkā*]:—
God is greater than any Man [*'ĕnôš*]
Why then do you complain against Him—
   that He does not reply [*ya'ăneh*] to any one's charges?!

He goes on to emphasize that God does indeed answer mortals, in both dreams and visions of the night (vv. 13-14). Note that the conclusion is given first (v. 12) and is only secondarily followed by an explanation and the key question (vv. 13-14). This final question closes the first rhetorical move and introduces the speaker's second justification. God is not only greater (*yirbeh*) than Man but surely responds to all complaints (*rîbôtā*). It is thus Job who is inattentive; for God answered him long before!

The attentive reader—and surely Job himself!—will catch a double echo here. The first of these is the allusion to the terrifying night vision of Eliphaz in 4:12-16, *just before* the message that an *ʾĕnôš* cannot be justified (*yiṣdaq*) before God (v. 17). The second echo is Job's own wish in 7:13-14 that he not be disturbed by violent visions, *just before* his own protest *mâ* ʾĕnôš ("What is man?") in verse 17. By weaving together these two strands, Elihu poignantly reminds Job that he *already* has had visions—and though he regards them as honorific and contentless, he is wrong. Dreams and night-visions are in fact the recurrent means of divine communication to the attentive ear (33:15-16). For in dreams God "opens human understanding" to a larger reality, even as visions provide a subtle "chastening" that leaves a divine "signature" on the human heart "to suppress pride in man" (v. 17). Elihu thus charges Job with being trapped by his own arguments—high on rhetoric and pride but low on humility and inner-reflection. If he would but attend, his nightly dreams could be read as God's daily message of reproof (v. 14).

Having linked his discourse of Job's words in 7:13-14, Elihu goes on in 35:6-8 to rebut an old claim of Job. He says:

> If you [Job] have sinned, what do you do to Him? [*mah-tipʿāl-bô*]
> If your transgressions are many, how do you affect Him?
> If you are righteous, what do you give Him;
> What does he receive from your hand?
> Your wickedness affects men like yourself;
> Your righteousness, [other] mortals.

These powerful words seek to undermine Job's sense of strange providence by revealing an impartial judge, unimpeded and unimpaired by human action. On the one hand, the point serves as a supplement to the friends' argument of divine transcendence, and to Job's own misprision. But in the present context these words also complement Job's early query in 7:20-21, *after* the reference to dreams and the question *mâ 'ĕnôš:*

> If I have sinned, what have I done to You [*mâ 'ep'al lāk*], watcher
>   of men?
> Why do You not pardon my transgression
>   or forgive my iniquity?
> For soon I shall lie in the dust;
>   When you seek me, I shall be gone.

As noted earlier, these words hurl barbs at an all-too-attentive God. If he is truly transcendent and unaffected by sin, why does he so stringently hold mortals to account? Job does not deny his sin; he rather denies and objects to any sense that the punishment fits the crime; indeed, he cannot fathom why a transcendent God will not forgive. But this is not the point, and it is rightly disregarded. Just as odd is Job's attempt to affect God by an appeal to his mercy. For if God is utterly beyond the effects of sin, why should he rend justice by special favor? But in this selfish hope Job merely proves himself all too human. Elihu rightly reverts to God's transcendence at the end and strikingly reframes Job's point. God, says the interlocutor, is truly beyond the effects of sin or righteousness; but he nobly replaces Job's anthropocentric whine with a brief instruction on the anthropocentricity of ethics. Job should leave off misguided grousing and focus on how his sin affects his own soul—and the lives of others. This would lead to repentance and inner change, and leave transcendence to God.

Job catches the drift of this rhetoric, and though his ear needs the full volume of God's final speeches, something of Elihu's point has changed him. For in response to God's transcendental majesty—beyond all earthly ethics—Job comes back to a word that he used earlier along with his caviling cry of "What have I done to you?" In theological despair he wails *mā'astî* ("I am sick of it!" 7:16). Now,

after Elihu has asked him "What do you do" to God? and after
God's own awesome speeches, Job repents and says (42:6):

> *'em'as,* I recant and regret—
> being but dust and ashes.

The haunting abuse of God is finally abated, and Job's sarcastic
point that God will one day seek him out for persecution but he will
be dead in the dust is transformed. In the closing words by Job, the
mortality of dust has become a matter of self-awareness. The hero
now confronts his mutability and earthiness. He realizes that if he
cannot change God, he can at least change himself.

In conclusion, let us recollect the path of allusion and echo that
has guided this inquiry. Starting with some verbal and rhetorical
relations between Joban and related biblical discourse, and
continuing with inner-Joban correlations, it was possible to give
new edge to several speech units in the book of Job. On the one
hand, ironies and oddities were put in a new light; on the other,
chains of argumentation among the speakers were revealed. If the
first series of examples shows the value of setting Joban rhetoric
within the full spectrum of biblical language, the second shows
unexpected give-and-take among the speakers in the gathering
arguments. Perceiving this, the latter-day reader of the book may
increase pleasure and comprehension by coming to know its
speeches not just by the seeing of the eye, but by the hearing of the
ear as well.

PART II

History of the Interpretation of Job

CHAPTER 6

RABBINIC INTERPRETATIONS OF JOB

Judith R. Baskin

Comments about Job are found throughout rabbinic literature, and one could say that there are almost as many Jobs as rabbis who speak about him.[1] This wealth of interpretation results first from the composite nature of the biblical book itself, which portrays a pious and uncomplaining Job in its beginning and concluding chapters, and a raging and defiant Job everywhere else, a contradiction difficult to resolve.[2] Some rabbis chose only to emphasize Job's piety, while others sought to discover in his words and actions the reasons for his severe punishments. There are those exegetes who draw upon the dialogues of Job and his companions in discussions of larger philosophical and ethical issues, but only a very few statements about Job attempt to analyze the meaning of his behavior and experience, and most of these barely touch the profound questions at the book's core.[3]

A preeminent source of Job's great interest for rabbinic commentary stems from rabbinic Judaism's view of Job as a Gentile. Those interpreters who held high the ideal of the righteous Gentile championed Job as its concrete example; in one source he is described as the most pious Gentile who ever lived.[4] More sedulous sages attempted to undercut Job's virtues and his reward. Still others, who acknowledged his positive qualities yet were hesitant to assign them to a non-Jew, sought to prove that Job was not a Gentile at all, but one of the children of Israel.[5]

The basic elements of rabbinic discussion concerning Job are already well established in remarks attributed to tannaitic sages (first century to mid–third century c.e.), although most of these

101

remarks appear in post-tannaitic sources. Thus the second century R. Ishmael is quoted as having declared Job a Gentile,[6] while R. Eleazar of the next generation is said to have championed his Israelite origin.[7] The Talmud also describes a "difference among the Tannaim" on the question of Job's ultimate end, the first-century R. Eliezer holding that Job has no place in the world to come, and his perpetual opponent, R. Joshua, maintaining the opposite.[8] Although there are few novelties in Amoraic (mid–third to mid–fifth century C.E.) expansion of these tannaitic concerns, insistence by some amoraim on Job's Israelite origin appears to be directed against Christian glorification of Job as a Gentile witness to Christ, a topic discussed below.

The Question of Job's Ethnic Origin

In virtually all rabbinic study of Job, the primary concern is his ethnic origin, for on this all other considerations rest. Much of the discussion on this point is related to when Job lived. The talmudic tractate *b. Baba Batra* (14b-16b), in its examination of the authors and proper order of the biblical books, offers suggestions ranging from the time of Abraham to the days of Ahasuerus.[9] The midrashic compilation *Genesis Rabbah* 54:7 contends that Job lived in the days of Abraham, comparing the similarity of "Uz [עוץ] his first born" (Abraham's nephew) (Gen. 22:21) and "There was a man in the land of Uz [עוץ]" (Job 1:1). With similar reasoning, one tradition, recorded in *b. Baba Batra* 15b, declares that Job lived in the time of Jacob and married Jacob's daughter, Dinah. The proof, again based on linguistic analogy, is that in connection with his wife Job says, "You speak as one of the foolish women [ובלנת] speak," (Job 2:10), and in connection with Dinah the text declares, "Because he wrought folly [ובלנת] in Israel."[10]

The most popular estimation for when Job flourished, suffered, and flourished again was during the lifetime of Moses and was based on the belief that Job was a Gentile. *B. Baba Batra* 14b relates that Moses was the author of "his own book," and the "portion of Balaam and Job," and this statement is then used to support the opinion of R. Levi b. Laḥma (fl. 290–320 C.E.) that Job was a contemporary of Moses (16b).[11] Moreover, Job's inclusion among the seven Gentile prophets who preached to the nations assumes that this was the case. These seven were Balaam and his father Beor, Job, Eliphaz the Temanite, Bildad the Shuhite, Zophar the Naamathite, and Elihu son of Barachel the Buzite. According to a rabbinic tradition, the Holy Spirit was removed from the nations at the moment when the Torah was given to Israel.[12] Since Job was a Gentile and a prophet, he could, therefore, have lived no later than the period before Israel received the Law.

Further corroboration of this chronology comes from the midrashic assertion that Job lived in the court of Pharaoh at the time of Israel's captivity in Egypt. In fact, some rabbinic traditions explain Job's suffering as just punishment for his role as one of Pharaoh's counselors. According to these accounts, Job served the ruler of Egypt along with Balaam and Jethro. When Balaam persuaded Pharaoh to decree that all male Israelites must be drowned, Jethro fled, but Job remained silent and did not voice his disapproval. It was for this that he was afflicted.[13] That there was a reason for his suffering was axiomatic for the rabbis, whose view of divine justice precluded the possibility of undeserved misfortune.[14]

Indeed, a further midrashic tradition describes the apt moment of Job's torment:

> When Israel departed from Egypt, the angel Samael [Satan] arose to accuse them. . . . It can be compared to a shepherd who was leading his sheep across a river when a wolf came to attack the sheep. What did the shepherd, who knew well how to deal with such emergencies, do? He took a large he-goat and threw it to the wolf, saying to himself, "Let him struggle with this until we cross the river, and then I will return and bring him back." So when Israel departed from Egypt, the angel Samael rose to accuse them, pleading before God, "Lord of the universe! Until now they have been worshipping idols, and now You divide the sea for them?" What did God do? He delivered into his hands Job, one of the counsellors of Pharaoh, of whom it is written, "And that man was whole-hearted and upright" (Job 1:1), and said, " 'Behold, he is in your hands' (Job 2:6). While Samael is busily occupied with Job, Israel will go through the sea! Afterwards, I will deliver Job." This is why Job said, "I was at ease, and he broke me asunder." (Job 16:12)[15]

Through this fitting turn of events, Job received his deserved punishment, while at the same time he helped preserve the children of Israel.

Other rabbis believed that acting as Pharaoh's counselor was not Job's only misdeed. He was also accused of blasphemy and speaking against God in his heart. Raba, one of Job's most severe critics, maintains that "In all this Job did not sin with his lips" (Job 2:10), which implies that Job did sin within his heart, saying, "The earth is given over into the hand of the wicked, He covers the faces of the judges thereof: If it be so, where and who is He?" (Job 9:24).[16] Raba's point is that even though Job did not utter any blasphemies until after his suffering began, God knew that he was harboring such impious thoughts in his heart and was therefore compelled to punish him. Job's sin, in this instance, was that he doubted God's justice. Several of Job's other remarks, such as "If a man died, may he live again?" (Job 14:14), were also seen as heretical by various sages because they seemed to deny the resurrection of the dead. Likewise, in *b. Baba Batra* 16a, Raba is quoted as saying of the verse, "As the cloud is consumed and vanishes away, so he that goes down to Sheol shall come up no more" (Job 7:9), "This shows that Job denied the resurrection of the dead."[17]

In such hostile remarks about Job, rabbis such as Raba may also be responding to pietistic treatments of Job that emerged from non-Pharisaic Jewish circles. Such texts as the *Testament of Job* and a *Life of Job,* the latter written by a certain Aristeas,[18] had glorified the pious sufferer of Job 1 and 42 as an innocent and paradigmatic model of patience under duress. The outraged and outspoken Job of the rest of the book is completely ignored in these works, which had an immense impact on Christian views of Job. The rabbinic respect for Scripture could not sanction so cavalier an approach to the divine word and instead demanded descriptions of Job's obvious wrongdoings, justifications of his undoubtedly deserved punishment, and condemnations of his intemperate and occasionally blasphemous complaints. The flawed figure who emerged explains the hesitation some rabbis felt in granting Job full forgiveness and access to the world to come. At the same time the rather one-dimensional Job, championed by the authors of those pietistic texts and their adherents, was also disavowed.

Yet it seems clear that rabbinic ambivalence about Job stems not only from his questioning of God but also from misgivings based on his apparent Gentile origin. The rabbis present Job as evidence of the righteousness a Gentile may attain, but they also wish to define the limits of his distinction. Thus Job is often compared unfavorably with various Israelites. It is said, for example, that had Job borne his suffering without complaint, he would have risen to a renown equivalent to that of the patriarchs. Time and again, the rabbis ask a complaining Job to compare his suffering with the greater tests the patriarchs endured with faithful silence. A comment from *Pesiqta Rabbati* 47 is typical:

> The Holy One, blessed be He, said to Job: Why do you raise a cry? Because suffering befell you? Do you perhaps consider yourself greater than Adam, the creation of my own hands? Because of a single command to which he did not pay attention, I decreed death for him and for his progeny. Yet he did not raise a cry. Or perhaps you consider yourself greater than Abraham? Because he ventured to say "How shall I know that I shall inherit it?" (Genesis 15:13), I put him to trial after trial, saying to him, "Know for certain that your seed will be a stranger" (Genesis 15:13). Yet he did not raise a cry. . . . Or perhaps you consider yourself greater than Moses. Because he spoke in anger to Israel, saying, "Hear now, you rebels" (Numbers 20:10), I decreed as his punishment that he could not enter the land. Yet, he did not raise a cry.

As in the preceding passage, Job is often compared, always to his disadvantage, with Abraham. Thus in the '*Abot de Rabbi Nathan* 2, Job is praised for his modesty. Yet the text hastens to point out that Job's modesty could not compare with Abraham's, commenting, "Job refrained from looking at other men's wives. Abraham did not even look at his own, as it is written [in reference to Sarah], 'Behold, now I know that you are a beautiful woman' (Genesis 12:11), which shows that up to then he did not know."

Similarly, '*Abot de Rabbi Nathan* comments on the greatness of Job's hospitality. "Nevertheless," the midrash continues, "the Holy One, blessed be He, said to Job, 'Job, you have not yet reached half the measure of Abraham. . . . That is why he was granted delight of spirit.' " R. Levi, in *b. Baba Batra* 16a, is even

recorded as having taught that Satan acted from pious motives in
tormenting Job, "for when he saw that the Holy One, blessed be He,
was inclined to favor Job, he said, 'Heaven forbid that He should
forget Abraham's love.' "[19]

According to such interpretations, even Job's supposed connection with the household of Israel is not to his credit. In describing
Job's marriage to Jacob's daughter, Dinah, *Genesis Rabbah* 80:4
offers the following exposition of "And Dinah the daughter of Leah
went out" (Gen. 34:1):

> R. Huna [fl. 220–250 c.e.] commenced in the name of R. Abba
> Bardela the Priest [a late Tanna], "To him that is ready to faint,
> kindness is due from his friend" (Job 6:14). The Holy One, blessed
> be He, reproved [Jacob]: You have withheld kindness from your
> brother; when she married Job you did not convert him. You would
> not give her in marriage to one who is circumcised [Esau]. Lo! she is
> married to one who is uncircumcised [Job]. You would not give her
> in legitimate wedlock. Lo! she is taken in illegitimate wedlock;
> accordingly it is written, "And Dinah the daughter of Leah went
> out."

This comment is based on the tradition that on his return to Canaan,
when he was preparing to meet Esau, Jacob concealed his daughter
Dinah in a chest, lest his brother wish to marry her and he be obliged
to give her to him. God spoke to him, saying, "Because you have
acted unkindly towards your brother, Dinah will have to marry Job
who is neither circumcised nor a proselyte."[20] While this midrash
does not deny Job's merits, it is clear that righteous Gentile though
Job may be, he is deemed inferior both to descendants of Abraham,
such as Esau, and to proselytes.

From these comments it is evident that while some rabbinic
exegetes would not deny the possibility of a righteous Gentile, few
could accept the notion that a Gentile might be more righteous than a
father of Israel. In the same way, the midrash contrasts the prophetic
gifts of Moses and Balaam in a fashion unfavorable to Balaam. The
Gentiles are not denied their prophet, but his inferiority to the
visionaries of Israel is made manifest.[21]

Job in Jewish-Christian Disputation

The multiplicity of opinion concerning Job's national origin, the time in which he lived, and his character traits and ultimate righteousness is prompted in part by the lack of consistency and specific information in the book of Job itself. Some views, however, seem to have been prompted by particularistic or polemical considerations as well. The effort to represent Job as an Israelite, or conversely, to compare him unfavorably with Israelite exemplars because he was a Gentile, is certainly evidence of contradictory Jewish attitudes toward Gentiles in the rabbinic period. *B. Baba Batra* 15b records a dispute between R. Eliezer and R. Joshua on Job's merits. Since these sages are quoted in rabbinic literature as disagreeing over whether or not a Gentile could attain a place in the world to come, it is clear that the issue in dispute is the possibility of Gentile righteousness:

> There was a certain pious man among the heathen named Job, but he [thought that he had] come into this world only to receive his reward [here], and when the Holy One, blessed be He, brought chastisements upon him, he began to curse and blaspheme, so the Holy One, blessed be He, doubled his reward in this world so as to expel him from the world to come.[22]

In a similar vein, *j. Sota* 20d and *Genesis Rabbah* 57:4 attribute to R. Ḥiyya the following teaching: "God said: One righteous man arose among the nations of the world, and I gave him his reward and let him go. Who was that? [It was] Job." This negative comment seems anxious to establish the Gentile's essential inferiority. Job's rich reward is a thing of this world only, while the suffering of Israel will be far more amply recompensed in the world to come.

A likely explanation for the denigration of Job, or conversely, for the assertions that he was actually an Israelite, has to do with Christian claims. Texts *adversus Judaeos* are common in patristic literature, but less obviously polemical exegetical writings also show evidence of such controversies.[23] Polemics as such are more difficult to discover in rabbinic literature, given its comprehensive nature, but here too traces of such disputes can be discerned, especially where discussions of similar import, based around the same biblical verse or biblical figure, can be found in both literatures. Such a controversy appears to have centered around Job.[24]

One of the major areas of Jewish-Christian contention was the place of the Jewish people in God's dispensation following the advent of what Christianity believed to be the messianic era. A popular and effective Christian argument proclaimed that with the incarnation, biblical Israel had been displaced by the new Israel, the community of Christian believers drawn from the Gentile nations. The destruction of the Temple in 70 c.e. and Israel's further debasement after the failed rebellion of 132–136 c.e. seemed to support this position. Christian claims of a preexistent community of believers outside the nation of Israel, one that took precedence over the Levitical priesthood, only lent fuel to the fire. Prominent among the saintly pagans who were said to have been a part of this primeval Christian community, existent even before the birth of Jesus, is Job.

The rabbis responded to these claims of succession by reiterating proofs of continuing divine love for Israel. Rabbinic insistence that prophecy ceased among the Gentiles after the giving of the Law at Mount Sinai constituted one line of response. Further modes of attack would insist that such "saintly pagans" as Job and Melchizedek were actually Israelites. As Louis Ginzberg has written, Job is claimed as an Israelite because some commentators "could not allow that a man of the kindness and piety of Job should be a non-Jew and therefore make him a Jew."[25] This is the conclusion of the third-century Palestinian Amora, R. Johanan, the head of a studyhouse in Tiberias, who taught that Job was among those who returned from the Babylonian exile and founded a house of study in Tiberias.[26] Tiberias was also a Christian center, and it seems likely that R. Johanan had contact with Christian scholars or was at least aware of some Christian teachings. A Christian of the same locale who was a contemporary of R. Johanan and whose exegeses show knowledge of Jewish traditions was Origen (d. ca. 253). The two scholars appear to have been aware of and to have responded to each other's "exegetical tendencies," certainly in the case of the Song of Songs.[27] In light of R. Johanan's determined advocacy of Job as an Israelite who lived at the time of the return from Babylonian exile, it is interesting to find that Origen, who glorifies a Gentile Job as a model of Christian patience,[28] maintains the view, cited by various Tannaim, that Job's lifetime spanned the period between Jacob and Moses. In his championing of Job as a Jew, it seems likely that Johanan is responding to such Christian appropriation and adaptation of Jewish tradition.

Further indications that Job was a subject of discussion between Jews and Christians are found in the writings of Jerome (d. 420). Again the disputed question is Job's origin. Jerome was one with Christian tradition in placing Job in the tradition of pagan priests, outside of the Levitical priesthood. In a letter, he describes the traditions of his predecessors concerning Melchizedek and his spiritual descendants, concluding, "They say too that Job himself was not of the race of Levi, but of the descendants of Esau; although the Hebrews declare the contrary."[29] Jerome probably learned of Jewish views about Job from the Jewish teacher he hired to instruct him on the difficulties in the Hebrew text of Job,[30] rather than from Jewish-Christian disputation, but it is significant that the issue remained alive in fifth-century Palestine, and that the Jewish point of view made known to Jerome was that Job was an Israelite.

The rabbis saw the happy sequel to Job's suffering as a symbol of hope to sufferers in all times. Job's death, when he was "old and full of days" (Job 42:17), was seen as enviable. R. Johanan, who glorified Job as an Israelite, believed that Job would serve as a model for all. According to *b. Berakot* 17a:

> When R. Johanan finished the book of Job, he used to say the following: The end of man is to die, and the end of a beast is to be slaughtered, and all are doomed to die. Happy is he who was brought up in the Torah and who has given pleasure to His Creator, and who grew up with a good name; and of him Solomon said, "A good name is better than precious oil, and the day of death than the day of one's birth." (Eccl. 7:1)

Similarly, Job's return to prosperity is explicitly linked in consolation texts to the rewards that will eventually come to the children of Israel in the days to come. *Pesiqta Rabbati* 26:7, for example, contrasts the chastisement of Zion with the chastisement of Job: Both lost sons and daughters, both were robbed of gold and silver, and both were cast upon a dungheap. The intention of these parallels, of course, is to reassure Israel that just as Job was comforted for his suffering, even more will Israel be consoled for the miseries she has endured. For, as R. Joshua, the son of R. Neḥemiah, teaches in *Pesiqta Rabbati* 20/30, "If Job, who sinned, eventually had given to him a double recompense, so Jerusalem will eventually be given a double recompense of comfort, as Scripture says at Isaiah 40:1, "Comfort ye, comfort ye my people." The repetition of "comfort" is understood as proof that Jerusalem's recompense, as Job's, will be twofold. Jerusalem's destiny, as the midrash has shown, has been presaged in every particular by Job's; surely the final boon will not be lacking.

In conclusion, there is no rabbinic consensus on Job. Even those sages who grant his good qualities cannot deem him, a Gentile and arrant blasphemer, quite the equal in righteousness of an Israelite. Some rabbis, out of a general sense of hostility toward perceived sectarians as well as the Gentile nations, do their best to emphasize his iniquities and denigrate his rewards. Even the glorification of Job as a model Israelite by such rabbis as Johanan has as much to do with scoring points against Christian arguments as with genuine esteem for the character himself. For the rabbis, who could neither deny divine justice nor explain innocent suffering, the quandary of the Gentile's place in God's creation remained the central exegetical issue of the book of Job.

CHAPTER 7

PROVIDENCE IN MEDIEVAL ARISTOTELIANISM

MOSES MAIMONIDES AND THOMAS AQUINAS ON THE BOOK OF JOB

Martin D. Yaffe

Despite current uncertainty and wide-ranging disagreement over the meaning of the biblical book of Job, little scholarly attention has been paid to the philosophical interpretations of it by the medieval Aristotelians. Yet the greatest of the Jewish Aristotelians, Moses Maimonides, devoted two full chapters of his *Guide of the Perplexed* to God's answer to the suffering Job, in the belief that it constitutes the authoritative answer to the philosophical question of divine providence.[1] Following Maimonides in this belief, his Christian counterpart Thomas Aquinas composed a line-by-line commentary on the biblical book—virtually unread, however, by modern scholars.[2] Reasons for the current neglect of these works, both philosophical and theological, are not hard to find. First, philosophically, there is the suspicion that the Aristotelianism common to Maimonides and Aquinas may be either obscurantist or outmoded. Second, theologically, similar suspicions may arise about the dogmatism of Maimonides' or Aquinas's pre-philosophical (sc. Jewish or Catholic) commitments. These suspicions must be addressed by anyone seeking to restore the respectability of Maimonides' and Aquinas's interpretations for purposes of the modern discussion.

The present essay maintains that Maimonides' and Aquinas's interpretations deserve a restored respectability; support for this assertion is obtained by examining the connection between their theological analyses and the Aristotelianism on which those analyses are, at least in part, based. Both Maimonides and

Revised from *Hebrew Studies* 20-21 (1979–80) 62-74, with the editor's kind permission.

Aquinas may be said to write on two distinct levels; their surface meaning, easily accessible to members of their respective religious communities, contains a deeper meaning, accessible only to philosophers. The surface and the deeper meanings are connected in that Maimonides' and Aquinas's intentions are *protreptic*[3] that is, meant to introduce (or reintroduce) their coreligionists to philosophy. Thus (1) the charges of philosophical obscurantism and obsolescence may be answered by pointing out that Maimonides and Aquinas use Aristotelian terminology not so much as an end in itself but primarily as a means for facing philosophical questions hitherto unresolved by the received theology. Likewise, (2) the presumption of theological dogmatism may be answered insofar as Maimonides and Aquinas themselves are concerned to show their immediate addressees the need to question their prior theological assumptions.

The evidence for our claim lies in the symmetry of Maimonides' and Aquinas's differences of interpretation. Whereas Maimonides argues that God's answer to Job's question about divine providence implies that Job himself though perfectly just remains unwise, Aquinas argues on the contrary that Job though perfectly wise is nevertheless blameworthy. Job's fault in either case corresponds to a shortcoming in the religious community to whom the interpretation is addressed. The shortcoming of Maimonides' coreligionists is their religiously authorized intolerance of philosophical wisdom; the shortcoming of Aquinas's coreligionists is their religiously authorized underestimation of the need for practical moderation in theological arguments informed by that wisdom. Thus both men wish to alert thoughtful coreligionists to their common shortcomings and to suggest a philosophical or quasi-philosophical corrective.

We proceed by simply comparing Maimonides' and Aquinas's approaches to the most obvious features of the Job story. We begin with some preliminary remarks on what both men share philosophically and theologically, namely, their common Aristotelianism and biblical heritage. Afterward we will examine their divergences with respect to the following points: the addressee or reader for whom their respective comments are intended; the figure of Job himself; the role of the three friends whom Job first confronts in dialogue about his suffering; the role of the fourth friend, Elihu; and the speech of God that resolves Job's drama.

Aristotelian and Biblical Heritage

Let us begin considering what Maimonides and Aquinas share philosophically and theologically. First, philosophically, both men are Aristotelians. What does this description mean? To state it in a way that highlights their difference from modern thought, it means that they accept the premodern or at any rate Aristotelian identification of philosophy with "science."[4] "Science" here is not, or not yet, the results of the experimental work of Galileo, Newton, or Einstein and their followers. Aristotelian "science" has a much more speculative meaning, which connects closely with the original, unsophisticated meaning of the term. The original meaning of "science" (ἐπιστήμη, *scientia*) is "knowledge" in the strict sense, or knowledge of causes, as Aristotle says. In Aristotle's Greek, *epistēmē* suggests *technē*, meaning "art," or the knowledge of the causes of artifacts as understood by artisans. These Aristotle reduces to the well-known doctrine of the four causes: (1) the material of the artifact (e.g., the wood of a table); (2) the "beginning of the change," or efficient cause, whereby that material begins to be shaped into the form proper to that artifact (e.g., to a table); (3) the form itself (called in Greek the "look" [εἶδος or θεά] and similarly in Latin [*species*]), which we might also call the artisan's pattern or blueprint; and finally, (4) the purpose or good of that artifact, namely, the job or work (ἔργον or *operatio*), the activity it is to perform (e.g., to hold a vase, or to write on). To know these four causes of an artifact is then to be "scientific" about the artifact.

Yet Aristotelian philosophy is scarcely coextensive with *technē*. Philosophy originates for Aristotle here with the attempt to become as "scientific" about *non*-man-made things as artisans are about their own products. Aristotle's "scientific" terminology, we would argue, is consciously designed for this task. So, at any rate, Maimonides and Aquinas seem to have understood Aristotle.[5] A difficulty, however, remains with Aristotle's "scientific" project—and this Maimonides and Aquinas also seem to have understood—namely, that there is no human guarantee that we can be as *successful* in understanding the causes of non-man-made things as artisans appear to be with regard to their own products. The reason is clear enough. Artisans have much closer access to the artifacts that are the special objects of their attention, because these artifacts are products of their own making. But obviously philosophers do not *make* the things they know, which include what they call "natural" things. They have access to them only by their continuing observation and inference (called in Greek θεωρία and in Latin *speculatio*). Philosophy as understood by Aristotle and his followers thus remains an inherently speculative—that is, a tentative, provisional, ongoing, unfinished—project. It is therefore better understood in terms of the active quest on the part of the philosophers, that is, the continual activity of questioning, than in terms of any putatively settled results. It is for this reason that Maimonides and Aquinas, who recognize and share Aristotle's protreptic aim, cannot be considered simply dogmatic. They are well aware that they may not possess complete certainty, free from all doubt, about what they would understand. On the contrary, they are concerned, as vehicles of philosophy, to introduce their readers as well to their doubts.[6]

Besides Aristotelian philosophy, Maimonides and Aquinas share a common heritage of biblical theology, which includes the book of Job. The book of Job presents itself to them as the story of a perfectly pious man who is allowed to suffer in order to test his piety. Yet Maimonides and Aquinas do not read the book of Job exactly as modern biblical critics do today.[7] For example, whereas modern critics tend to cast doubt on the unity or coherence of the book as we have it, both Maimonides and Aquinas accept the book's unity and coherence as a matter of course. In this they defer to rabbinic and Catholic tradition, respectively. We may however say that both men pay a hermeneutical price for their deference. For neither rabbinic nor Catholic tradition reads the book as a single work to be understood altogether in its own terms, but each considers it instead in the broader context of rabbinic or Catholic doctrines, which it is said to confirm.

Chief among these doctrines for Aquinas appears to be that of the immortality of the soul, which, however, is nowhere set forth explicitly in the book of Job itself.[8] Similarly, Maimonides appeals to an authoritative rabbinic opinion that the book of Job is entirely parabolical and in no way historical, even though other rabbinical authorities disagree here, and even though Maimonides himself nowhere sufficiently demonstrates the grounds for his own opinion.[9] Let us speak, then, of Maimonides' and Aquinas's own "pious" readings of the book, understanding by this term their willingness to attribute such doctrines to it as may agree with some version of rabbinic opinion or Catholic faith, yet that may not be derived from the original text itself. The chief question arising here, for our purpose, concerns whether Maimonides and Aquinas here *recognize* the difference between a pious and a literal reading. It is our contention that they do—at least to the extent that each deliberately employs that very ingredient which we have just cited (viz., in Maimonides' case, the doctrine of the immortality of the soul) and which serves to set off his pious reading from a strictly literal one, in order to accomplish an ulterior purpose that cannot be called simply pious but that we have called protreptic. For both men wish not simply to confirm the established theology in question but rather to introduce (or reintroduce) their intended addressee to philosophy. Yet in so doing, as we shall see, they function admirably within their respective sacred traditions, of which the book of Job remains a part.

Maimonides, Aquinas, and Their Intended Readers

Maimonides writes characteristically as a rabbinic authority.[10] He presupposes his reader's competence in talmudic casuistry. What his reader wishes to learn from him instead concerns homiletical speculation and apologetics. He is particularly aware of the apologetical doctrines that are influenced by philosophical more than religious sources and which are called by Muslim theologians *kalam*. The question therefore arises: Does the *kalam* succeed in proving logically what it claims about the nature of divine providence, or not? Maimonides' reader is admittedly not in a

position to judge competently here, since his training is in legal-
istic casuistry at the expense of philosophical speculation. In
particular, as Maimonides indicates, he does not know natural
science but merely what Scripture and traditional homily say about
this subject, more or less naively. Indeed, natural science would
tend to upset scriptural authority here and so is prima facie excluded
from the rabbinic curriculum of study. Yet from Maimonides'
Aristotelian viewpoint, at any rate, natural science is a prerequisite
to knowing what may or may not be demonstrated about divine
providence. The training of Maimonides' reader is therefore at odds
with what that reader ultimately needs to know. Nor does
Maimonides wish to upset the reader directly by confronting him
with the possible inadequacy of his rabbinic preconceptions as such.
Instead he proceeds cautiously. By fortunate coincidence, the book
of Job is admirably suited to his task. Maimonides can identify the
views of the three friends Eliphaz, Bildad, and Zophar,
respectively, with three of the apologetical views with which his
reader is most familiar: Eliphaz is said to represent the authoritative
viewpoint of the Torah or Jewish tradition, which believes that all
things are ultimately governed by divine justice;[11] Bildad, the
viewpoint of the so-called Mutazilite *kalam,* which argues from the
premise that all things are governed by divine wisdom; and Zophar,
the Ash'arite *kalam,* which argues instead from the premise that all
things are governed by divine will. Job himself assumes the
philosophical viewpoint of Aristotle, which admits divine providence concerning species or universals but not individuals. Job thus
confronts these three apologetical views and examines their
limitations with special reference to his own particular case. Yet Job
does not know those limitations from the outset because, as
Maimonides tells us, Job at the outset is perfectly just but not
necessarily wise. He must acquire wisdom in the course of his
questioning; wisdom itself thus becomes the object of his quest. Job,
as Maimonides views him, therefore becomes the example of a
perfectly just man, the ideal follower of rabbinic law, who
nevertheless stands in need of a quest for wisdom—that is, who must
become a philosopher. The story of Job is thus a parable that
Maimonides' addressee may apply to his own comparable
circumstance.

Aquinas, on the other hand, writes characteristically as a

professor of theology.[12] He instructs students of theology in Catholic doctrine. Philosophy, far from being excluded from the curriculum of such students, is generally accepted as necessary in order to defend the faith. Aquinas's students, typically, must undergo oral examinations or cross-examinations in order to become masters of theology; in particular they must know how to argue in defense of correct church doctrine on any matter against rival claimants. But Aquinas discovers a practical difficulty here. As he explains in the prologue to his own *Summa Theologiae,* the teaching of theology remains somewhat ineffective—disorderly and confusing to students—because of the idiosyncratic demands of professorial examiners and because of the tiresome repetitiveness of current teaching methods. Differently stated, Aquinas's students may find themselves in a situation of having to give their professors what the professors want to hear, rather than acquiring a clear and orderly grasp of Christian doctrine in all its ramifications. Aquinas wishes to correct this shortcoming. He therefore writes his *Summa* "as befits the erudition of beginners"[13] by rethinking and reorganizing the entire curriculum from the beginning, in the interests of improved pedagogy. In this way, Aquinas himself is no simple authority, but a philosophical one. Yet he addresses a practical rather than a strictly theoretical shortcoming of Christian theology as it affects his students: Their grasp and defense of the correct conclusions as required for their final examinations do not guarantee that they have understood the full practical implications of those conclusions.

Such is the situation also of Aquinas's Job; he is the ideal student, or perhaps professor—perfectly wise, yet somewhat naive in practical matters. He is therefore able to refute Eliphaz, Bildad, and Zophar, and even Elihu, for their faulty intellectual grasp of church teaching. But he does not do so without revealing a practical fault of his own, which must be corrected. In Aquinas's interpretation, Job, though perfectly wise, is imprudent in his manner of communicating his wisdom.[14] As we shall see, he gives his friends the impression that he is blaspheming. Job must therefore reassess his relationship to his friends whom he would instruct. The story of Job—a historical fact, according to Aquinas—is thus the story of a man who is wise in the divine truth as taught by the church, yet who must reconsider the possible ill effects involved in his professing that truth to others in society. His Christian wisdom must therefore become the object of his own practical reassessment, or his own quest for forgiveness from sin. In the course of his sufferings, the need is revealed for a renewal of his study of the meaning of the wisdom that he has hitherto taken for granted. In this way, Aquinas's Job induces the student or professor of Christian wisdom, who is seen to be perfectly wise, to re-examine the practical limitations of the wisdom he professes—and so to communicate that wisdom in a more moderate or considerate way than his training may have suggested to him hitherto.

Interpretation of Job's Speeches

Consider, in this light, Maimonides' and Aquinas's conflicting interpretations of Job's own speeches. Maimonides tells us that Job, given the full onset of his sufferings, comes to doubt whether God cares for human beings at all. Maimonides quotes Job as follows: "It is all one—therefore I say: He destroyeth the innocent and the wicked. If the flood slay suddenly, He will mock at the calamity of the guiltless" (9:22-23). And further: "One dieth in his full strength, being wholly at ease and quiet. His pails are full of milk. . . . And another dieth in bitterness of soul, and hath never tasted of good. They lie down alike in the dust, and the worm covereth them" (21:23-26). Again: "Even when I remember I am affrighted, and horror taketh hold on my flesh. Wherefore do the wicked live, become old, yea, wax mighty in power? Their seed is established in their sight" (21:6-8).

These verses tell us, Maimonides says, that Job believes that the righteous and the wicked are alike regarded as evil by God. God has only contempt for humanity. He casually ignores human beings. For example, when a torrent suddenly kills and sweeps away all in its path, God merely laughs. He is unaffected by human suffering. Worse, he even allows the wicked to prosper—a prosperity that is in no way diminished even if the children of the wicked man perish after his own death. As Job says, "For what pleasure hath he in his house after him, when the number of his months is determined?"

(21:21). In short, Maimonides' Job is said to deny all hope of resurrection after death; God is merely indifferent to the human individual. And yet this opinion is seen to remain perplexing and problematical to Job himself, for it appears to contradict the accepted belief in the divine origin or creation of the human individual. "Hast Thou not poured me out as milk, [Job wonders,] and curdled me like cheese?" (10:10). Maimonides indicates that Job's opinion about divine providence—namely, that individual suffering is a matter of chance—is also Aristotle's opinion. Maimonides' addressee, insofar as he may vicariously identify himself with the opinion of Job, thus begins to become aware that his opinion on the subject in question may have philosophical implications that he has not yet been able to articulate adequately.

In Aquinas's exposition, on the other hand, the words of Job that Maimonides cites do not appear to carry the same meaning. Whereas Maimonides interprets Job's complaint that God "destroys both the innocent and the wicked" (9:22-23) to mean that God is indifferent to undeserved suffering, Aquinas on the contrary interprets these words to mean only that death is the common punishment for all, since no one is without sin. Similarly, Job's remark—that "one dieth in his full strength, being wholly at ease and quiet. . . . And another dieth in bitterness of soul, and hath never tasted of good" (21:23-25)—for Aquinas means neither that God lacks adequate knowledge of the merits of humans nor that God lacks the will to reward or punish them on their merits, but only that no one can tell what a person's true merits are merely from the person's bodily condition at the moment of death. Further, Job's query, "Wherefore do the wicked live, become old, yea, wax mighty in power?" (21:7), Aquinas understands rhetorically, as Job's way of rebutting the presumption of his three friends that virtue has an earthly reward and that earthly suffering is a punishment for sin. Unlike Maimonides' Job, who views his suffering as undeserved in light of his own perfect justice, Aquinas's Job views his suffering rather as a practical challenge in the light of his own perfect wisdom. Aquinas's Job wishes to convert his three friends to his superior wisdom. Nor does that wisdom, according to Aquinas, exclude the doctrine of life after death (here Aquinas's Job opposes the materialism of the three friends, who deny, as we shall see, the immortality of the soul). Rather, Job's statement about the wicked, which Maimonides uses to prove that Job denied immortality and resurrection—"For what pleasure hath he in his house after him, when the number of his months is determined?" (21:21)—for Aquinas carries no such connotation; it proves merely that whatever punishment the wicked person will suffer does not include the future misfortunes of his descendants, "especially since a sinner after death would not know this."[15] Finally, Aquinas's Job does agree with Maimonides' Job in attributing his own origin to the divine: "Hast Thou not poured me out as milk, and curdled me like cheese?" (10:10). But whereas for Maimonides Job's having been created by God may well be compatible with God's subsequently neglecting to care for him as an individual, for Aquinas this verse shows only that Job attributed all works and operations of nature to God, including the very release of sperm and synthesis of bodily mass in the womb that generated him as an individual, which he compares figuratively to the pouring out of milk and curdling of cheese. Evidently the wisdom of Aquinas's Job is not called into question by the mere occasion of his suffering, any more than is the justice of Maimonides' Job. The progress of the story depends, in either case, rather on Job's confrontation with his friends.

Interpretation of the Friends

Maimonides' Job confronts three friends who share the common conviction that Job's suffering is somehow caused by Job's own sin. Yet Maimonides emphasizes the intellectual differences among those three, whereby they purport to explain to Job the connection between suffering and sin. The position of the first friend, Eliphaz, Maimonides tells us, is the position of the Torah, according to which the world is created by a God whose ultimate concern is justice. Accordingly, humans have freedom to act for good or evil, and bodily pleasure is God's reward for good acts while pain is the punishment for evil ones. Eliphaz therefore says to Job, "Is not thy wickedness great? And are not thine iniquities without end?" (22:5). According to Eliphaz, everything that has befallen Job is deserved; Job's past sins have led to his present misfortune. In order to rebut Job's implicit rejoinder that no

one could demonstrate his sinfulness from the obvious facts of his
life (since Job is for all practical purposes a perfectly just
individual), Eliphaz replies as follows: "Behold [God] putteth no
trust in His servants, and His angels He chargeth with folly; how
much less in them that dwell in houses of clay, whose foundation is
in the dust?" (4:18-19). That is, for Eliphaz, although everything
befalling Job is deserved, yet Job's sins may remain hidden from our
merely limited human perspective.

The position of the second friend, Bildad, is the position of the
Mutazilite *kalam,* according to which the world is created by a God
whose primary attribute is wisdom. Accordingly, as humans are
endowed with freedom to act as they see fit, evil is the practically
inevitable consequence of that freedom. It follows that the human
suffering that results from evil must be seen in terms of the wisdom
of the divine plan. As Bildad says to Job, "If thou art pure and
upright, surely now He will awake for thee, and make the habitation
of thy righteousness prosperous. And though thy beginning was
small, yet thy end should greatly increase" (8:6-7). That is, Bildad
believes that if Job is truly innocent, then he will receive wise
compensation for his present suffering, so that Job's own good will
ultimately be increased in the future.

Finally, the position of the third friend, Zophar, is the position of
the so-called Ash'arite *kalam,* according to which the world is
created by a God whose primary attribute is will. Accordingly,
divine providence is said to control everything that happens in the
world, including what happens to every individual, so that
everything that happens is ordained (or preordained) by God
directly. Otherwise, Zophar implies, whatever happens would be
impossible. An unfortunate consequence of this view is that God
wills apparent evils, so that injustices in the world seem not only
permitted but also positively endorsed by God. To account for this
consequence, Zophar replies as follows: "O that God would speak,
and open His lips against thee; and that He would tell thee the secret
of wisdom, that they may teach thee doubly. . . . Canst thou by
searching find out God? Canst thou find out the Almighty to
perfection?" (11:5-7). As Maimonides explains, Zophar here
argues that since everything follows from God's will alone,
therefore no reason should be sought for God's actions; Zophar
insists that the question should not even be raised.

From the viewpoint of Maimonides' reader, who naturally sympathizes with Job's wish to defend his own justice, two things are noteworthy. First, the three friends disagree not only with Job but also among themselves. One emphasizes God's justice, another God's wisdom, and the third God's will. Given only these available options, how can the fair-minded person know which to choose? Second, therefore, any intelligent choice requires investigating the basis of those apologetical opinions further. This, of course, is what apologetics claims to be, namely, a reasoned defense of one's prior theological commitments. Yet that is exactly the difficulty at the moment, namely, which prior commitment, if any, is correct? This difficulty points to the very difference that Maimonides' addressee, like Job, must learn, namely, the difference between a mere defense of a preconceived commitment and a full understanding of the entire situation, including those very causes that would lead persons merely to defend preconceived commitments. For Maimonides, following Aristotle, that difference accords with the difference between imagination and reason, or between a merely apologetical theology and a truly philosophical one.[16]

Similarly, Aquinas's Job also confronts three friends who share the common conviction that Job's suffering is somehow caused by Job's own sin. Yet whereas Maimonides emphasizes the *intellectual* differences among the three friends as theologians, Aquinas emphasizes their *practical* differences as accusers of Job. Eliphaz is said to accuse Job of mistakenly believing that he is innocent of all sin; Bildad, to say that Job wrongly believes that God does not reward virtue or punish sin; Zophar, to say that Job erroneously thinks that his friends are mocking him in his suffering by calling themselves "witnesses of God." We learn from Job's replies that each friend has some grounds for his accusation, but that those grounds are ultimately inadequate and their accusations misinterpretations. Thus in reply to Eliphaz's claim that Job believes himself innocent of all sin, Job states only that he is innocent of that quantity of sin which would justify his present quantity of suffering. To Bildad's claim that Job does not believe that God rewards virtue or punishes sin, Job replies that he does *not* believe that God does so in *this* life, but only in another life. Finally, to Zophar's claim that Job thinks that his friends style themselves God's witnesses in order to mock his sufferings, Job answers that he *does* believe (along with

1 Cor. 15:15)[17] that a true witness of God must speak the truth, but that none of the three friends has truly or adequately accounted for Job's sufferings. Of course the three friends' false accusations of Job, Aquinas tells us, are not simply a practical or ad hoc convenience to support their adversarial position vis-à-vis Job but are connected to an intellectual shortcoming: Their false impressions of Job would be corrected if they simply took into account the doctrine of the immortality of the soul, in which Job himself is said to believe and that is the reason despite all for his equanimity. But Aquinas also tells us that the doctrine of the immortality of the soul in its explicit form is unknown in the Old Testament; it is revealed only in the New. It follows that although Job is said to be motivated above all by a wish to convert his three friends completely to his own viewpoint, he nowhere completely divulges to those friends the grounds for his viewpoint but limits himself to arguing *ad hominem*. Accordingly, if Job is to succeed with his three friends, then the friends must arrive at that viewpoint on their own, presumably as Job himself did. We interpret this last to mean that Job arrived at his viewpoint by his own reasoning, that is, as a philosopher. This is why Aquinas himself quotes 1 Corinthians 15:15 in the context we have mentioned; in the Vulgate it reads as follows: ''Now we are found to be even false witnesses of God, since we have given testimony against God that He raised Christ, Whom He did not raise if the dead do not rise.'' In the original context, Paul would appear to be referring to the resurrection of the body of Christ, which resurrection should be believed in, Paul tells us, only if it is true that God resurrects the bodies of the dead generally. But in endorsing life after death, neither Aquinas nor Job dwells on the resurrection of the body; on the contrary, Aquinas emphasizes that the next life is the life of the soul separate from and unacquainted with the particular bodily details of earthly life, and that this truth is at least akin to if not identical with the speculations of Aristotle.[18] Perhaps, then, Job's wisdom is humanly accessible only by means of Aristotelian philosophy, and his friends would be converted only if they somehow discovered this fact on their own in passing. Aquinas's Job indeed tries to make that discovery possible for them by debating with them in effect as an Aristotelian philosopher, who however uses the parabolic language of the biblical tradition. Even so, his

prospects for success are not favorable, since even if the three
friends were to become open to the possibility of another life after
death, they might still wish to interpret that life as corporeal or
bodily, according to the surface meaning of the New Testament;
thus the three friends' corporealism or materialism would obstruct
their full understanding of the nature of divine providence as it
operates in human affairs—an understanding that requires a more
philosophical mind in order to be grasped. Yet this understanding
(Aquinas tells us in his own prologue to his *Exposition*) it is the
"whole intention" of the book of Job to provide.[19]

Interpretation of Elihu

The attitude of Elihu toward Job, for both Maimonides and
Aquinas, lies somewhere between that of the three friends, who
have been reproaching Job all along, and that of God, who will end
the discussion by vindicating Job. In either case, Elihu deviates from
the three friends in such a way that, had the three friends chosen to
follow Elihu, they would be brought closer, though not completely,
to the viewpoint ultimately endorsed by God. Both Maimonides and
Aquinas thus view Elihu as a kind of corrective for the three friends
(albeit an incomplete one), and for Job too, insofar as he must
confront his three friends' viewpoints *ad hominem.* For both
Maimonides and Aquinas, Elihu mediates between Job and his three
friends on the one hand and God on the other. How he does so in
either case corresponds to the symmetrical difference we have been
describing all along.

According to Maimonides, Elihu adds little to the three previous
reproaches of Job, except for the following. First, Elihu agrees with
the three friends in trying to refute Job's denial of particular
providence, but he does so by speaking of the practical
intervention of angels to relieve human sufferings (cf. 33:23-24).
For example, an angel may intervene when an individual is
desperately ill to the point of death, so that the individual is saved
and restored to perfect health. At most, however, this practical
intervention may happen only two or three times in an individual's
lifetime (33:29)—that is, Elihu (unlike, say, Zophar) does not speak

of continuous miraculous intervention. Second (again like the three friends—Eliphaz, for example), Elihu speaks of dreams or night visions whereby God communicates with individuals. But again (unlike what the friends imply) these visions also happen infrequently in an individual's lifetime and moreover are generally ignored or misinterpreted: "For God speaketh once, yea twice, yet [man] perceiveth it not. In a dream, in a vision of the night, when deep sleep falleth upon men"(33:14-15). Such visions are tantamount to parables and may admit of instructive interpretations in entirely natural terms, that is, reasonable or philosophical interpretations. In this way, we may say, God is said to intervene in an individual's life not only practically (*sc.*, by relieving bodily suffering unexpectedly) but also intellectually (*sc.*, by provoking philosophical wonderment imaginatively). Finally, Elihu alone among the five is said to speak consciously in the form of a parable. Elihu thus speaks both in parables and about parables. In this, Elihu's manner of communication resembles that of the book of Job as a whole, as Maimonides read it, and it is this parabolical manner of communication that Job (as well as Maimonides' own reader) must learn to recognize in order to begin to acquire philosophical wisdom.

According to Aquinas, however, Elihu does not need to teach Job about parables in order for Job to become more philosophical, for Job himself already speaks philosophically and in parables. Unlike Maimonides' Elihu, Aquinas's Elihu and his Job are already intellectually close; both men, according to Aquinas, believe implicitly in the doctrine of the immortality of the soul. Indeed, only because of this belief is Elihu said to be able to differ from the three friends in his reproach of Job. Because, like Job, he already believes in another life, Elihu, unlike the three friends, need not limit himself to misinterpreting the individual's suffering in this life as caused simply by that individual's own sin—yet in Job's case Elihu does exactly that! According to Elihu, Job *is* being punished for the sin of blasphemy—for attributing injustice to God as the cause of Job's suffering in this life. Elihu arrived at this mistaken notion, Aquinas tells us, by misconstruing Job's previous words to his three friends. For example, when Job had said (to Bildad), "Behold, I shall clamor when suffering force [*vim*], and no one will hear; I shall raise my voice, and there is not anyone who will judge" (19:7 Vulgate).

Elihu interpreted these words as Job's contentious denial of particular providence. But in fact, as Aquinas reminds us, Job was not speaking contentiously but only philosophically (albeit parabolically). In these and like speeches, Aquinas says, Job "was desiring to know the reasons for divine wisdom";[20] that is, as we might say, he wished to know the causes of the forces of bodies surrounding him and understood that he would not acquire that knowledge merely because he had phrased his request aloud. By misinterpreting Job's words, Aquinas's Elihu becomes the example of a man in possession of intellectual wisdom who through practical naiveté overestimates that wisdom—in this Aquinas's Job (unlike Maimonides') stands to learn only from Elihu's bad example. Elihu and Job for Aquinas stand related, we may say, like the professor and student of the prologue of Aquinas's *Summa Theologiae*. It is the *practical* defect of presuming the adequacy of his intellectual wisdom that Aquinas's Christian intellectual must overcome, even as Maimonides' rabbinic Job (who has no such practical defect) must overcome the *intellectual* defect of not having recognized a parable for what it is.

The Speech of God

God's speech, in either case, is intended to remedy the defect in question. Neither Maimonides nor Aquinas allows that speech anything but a protreptic meaning. The main speech, which begins "Where were you when I laid the foundations of the earth?"(38:4), is in either case said to be designed entirely to reveal to Job (and his like) his own ignorance.

For Maimonides, Job's ignorance is primarily of an intellectual sort. God's speech therefore reveals to him the things of which he is ignorant. Yet it reveals these in the form of a parable, so that Job may know that he still needs to investigate further in order to acquire the knowledge he lacks. God's speech is said to concern natural things only; it mentions the firmaments and the heavens, Orion and the Pleiades (for Aristotle divine things), only insofar as these influence sublunary nature (cf. 38:4-5, 31-32). God's questions to Job therefore indicate for Maimonides that our merely human intelligence is incapable of grasping fully how natural things are connected with the divine—that is, how they are created or produced in time—since, as Maimonides tells us, those things do not quite resemble what we make. "How then [Maimonides asks] can we wish that His governance of, and providence for, them, may He be exalted, should resemble our governance of, and providence for, the things we do govern and provide for?"[21] As natural activities differ from the activities of artisans, Maimonides' reader is told, so divine governance and providence must be said to differ from that of the human—which is to say, of course, that they do not *entirely* differ, as we have already pointed out for Aristotle, but that their problematic similarities-*cum*-differences are not a matter of settled knowledge but must become the subject of further, continuing investigation. To show this, for Maimonides, is the (philosophical) purpose of the book of Job as a whole. "If a man knows this," Maimonides concludes, "every misfortune will be borne lightly by him."

For Aquinas, on the other hand, Job's ignorance is of a more practical sort. God's speech is therefore said to reveal not merely sublunary nature (as for Maimonides) but what Aquinas calls "[God']s effects."[22] By this expression may be understood God's effectiveness in providing for each creature's practical needs, just as a proper artisan—a builder, for example—knowingly provides for what he has built. Nor does God overlook human beings, even though humans fail to grasp the full extent of the divine wisdom and virtue, which are the cause of those effects—presumably because, in the first place, they are insufficiently attentive to those effects themselves—that is, they are not sufficiently philosophical. Aquinas therefore intersperses God's speech describing his effects with observations drawn from Aristotelian books on the subject, with which the speech is said to coincide parabolically. God's awesome speech itself stuns Job into silence and repentance— although or because Job is a philosopher. Job recognizes that he has indeed sinned, not from pride or impurity of motive but only from "levity" or superficiality of thought[23]—presumably in thinking that he could accomplish the practical conversion of his friends to Christian wisdom merely by debating with them. God's speech then concludes with a parabolic description of Satan, or what Aquinas calls "the malice of the rational creature,"[24] under the figures of

Behemoth and Leviathan. About this much more could be said. Suffice it to say here only that Aquinas's reader, like Job, is reminded of the need to be more attentive to the full meaning, practical as well as intellectual, of divine parables, as God's way of providing both practical and intellectual guidance to rational creatures, nonphilosophers as well as philosophers.

CHAPTER 8

"WHY DO THE WICKED LIVE?"

JOB AND DAVID IN CALVIN'S SERMONS ON JOB

Susan E. Schreiner

In the sixteenth century, both Catholic and Protestant exegetes found in the book of Job an opportunity to analyze the difficult issues of suffering and providence. These commentators inherited two exegetical traditions that bequeathed to them penetrating insights on these subjects. In the allegorical tradition, influenced primarily by Gregory the Great, the book of Job became the occasion for discussing, among other topics, the beneficial nature of affliction. In the literal tradition, formulated by Thomas Aquinas, the story of Job was interpreted as a debate about the nature of divine providence. In all of these commentaries, one issue continually emerges as a critical interpretive element, namely, the problem of human perception or, rather, the clash of varying perceptions. The reader of these commentaries gradually discerns that the following questions structure precritical interpretations of Job: Does suffering elevate or alter one's perception of reality? Is there any discernible order in human events? What can one perceive about providence in times when the wicked prosper and the good suffer? What does suffering, particularly inexplicable suffering, mean for one's understanding of history?

This essay analyzes the way in which Calvin's sermons on Job probe these perceptual issues by combining the themes of suffering and providence. We shall see that Calvin thereby fully exploits the perceptual tension inherent in the book of Job. Insofar as he sees the book of Job as a debate about the nature of providence, Calvin's sermons are a continuation of the Thomistic tradition.[1] Moreover, Calvin follows Thomas by developing the perceptual implications inherent in the arguments about the character of human history that constitute the Job text. Unlike Thomas, however, but like the allegorical tradition, Calvin is intensely interested in understanding the nature and purpose of the inexplicable suffering endured by Job. He unites these two themes, then, by placing Job's suffering within the wider context of the providential issues that permeate the book.

Calvin undertook his sermons on Job during the year 1554–1555. During the last decade of his life, he was intensely preoccupied with the exposition of several biblical books that discuss the often inscrutable nature of divine providence: Job, the Psalms, and 1 and 2 Samuel. In these texts Calvin found two figures, Job and David, both of whom were loved and afflicted by God. This concern with perception and suffering becomes so intertwined that Calvin frequently discusses David's afflictions while commenting on the book of Job. Therefore, as Calvin charts the tragedies of Job, he does so hand in hand with those of David. We will best detect Calvin's concern with the perceptual issues in the book by following his use of Job and David as paradigmatic figures for the type of suffering he saw as lying at the heart of Job's tragedy, a suffering caused by the inscrutability of divine providence. By defining Job's suffering in terms of providence, the reader is able to discern how Calvin employs the Thomistic interpretive framework in a way that makes the book of Job a story about suffering, perception, and history.

Job and David in the History of Interpretation

The exegetical decision to link Job and David occurs at least as early as Ambrose's series of four sermons entitled *On the Prayer of Job and David*.[2] These sermons serve as a particularly suitable point of comparison with Calvin because both Ambrose and Calvin take this exegetical turn of interpreting Job through the person of David. Furthermore, it is fruitful to compare Ambrose with Calvin because he typifies a spirituality of suffering that would find fuller expression in the Gregorian tradition. Our discussion will show that Calvin understands the suffering exemplified by Job and David in a way significantly different from that of his predecessor.

According to Ambrose, Job and the Psalms address the same problem, namely, doubt about divine providence caused by the prosperity of the wicked and the seemingly unjust suffering of the good. Interpreting Psalms 41 (42) and 72 (73) in conjunction with the book of Job, Ambrose cites David's confession as typical of the temptation that haunts all believers: "My feet were almost moved, my steps had nearly slipped, for I was envious when I saw the peace of sinners."[3] In the afflictions of Job and David, Ambrose depicts the often inexplicable spiritual and physical suffering of the faithful, suffering that Job and David shared with Abraham, Moses, Peter, and Paul. As models for future generations, Job and David were, to Ambrose's mind, teachers for the faithful on how to suffer well.

Ambrose uses two themes to explain the suffering endured by Job and David. One theme, reminiscent of Paul, is that of strength and athleticism. Since "strength is made perfect in weakness[es]," suffering enables one to gain spiritual fortitude.[4] To describe this muscular benefit of suffering, Ambrose says of Job that "even though he felt the arrows of the Lord were in his body and that he was pierced by them, yet like the good athlete who does not give way to pain or refuse the hardships of the contest, Job said, 'Let the Lord, having begun, wound me but not destroy me in the end.' "[5] In Ambrose's view, Job was like an "athlete of Christ" in order that "he might be fashioned by temptations and attain to the crown of a greater glory."[6] Comparing Job's judgments to those of his friends, Ambrose observes that "he was stronger than those who appeared healthy and sound. . . . For Job was stronger when sick than he had been when healthy, according to that which is said, 'Strength is made perfect in weakness.' And so when Job was suffering weakness, then he had the greater strength."[7] This athletic interpretation of suffering recurs in Ambrose's descriptions of David. Commenting on Psalm 73, he says that "the man who has not struggled or been exercised in the combat of various contests will not be able to hope for future rewards."[8] "Because [Job and David] were scoured here," Ambrose explains, "they had strength in their afflictions."[9]

The second theme used by Ambrose to describe the salutary

nature of adversity is that of freedom leading to wisdom. His descriptions of the purpose for the afflictions endured by Job and David are governed by references to insight, knowledge, and judgments. Job's friends are said to have suffered from "feeble insight," while Job was able to speak "in mysteries," to make "distinctions in the spirit," and to utter truths according to a knowledge of spiritual things.[10] The knowledge gained by Job and David led to a wisdom that granted them a deeper insight into the illusory nature of earthly happiness. When Ambrose's Job cried, "Why do the wicked live, reach old age, and grow mighty in power?" he saw that the life of the wicked is "at first glance clearly a good but in a deeper and more mysterious sense, you will discover that what is considered good is not good and what is considered evil just men reckon preferable."[11] So, too, David overcame his temptation by seeing that "[God's goodness] is not to be weighed by the appearance of things present but by the advantages of things to come."[12] Repeatedly Ambrose uses Paul to interpret the experiences of Job and David, as, for example, in his allusion to 1 Corinthians 2:15, "Distinguish these matters and because you are spiritual, judge between them."[13]

If we recognize that suffering produces a deeper strength, freedom, and perception of the world, we can see why Ambrose argues that believers such as Job and David *desire* adversity because "the Father scourges the son whom he receives."[14] Suffering strengthened and freed Job and David by turning them away from the "waves" or "sea" of the ever-fluctuating temporal realm.[15] In his descriptions of detached transcendence attained by Job and David, Ambrose gave expression to that ancient identification between suffering and freedom. Only suffering leads to a truer perception of reality, a perception that liberates one from enslavement to that which is illusory and fleeting. Suffering, then, did not pose to Ambrose the problem of theodicy, as it often does for the modern reader, because affliction was not seen as an evil. The greatest evil was not adversity but rather the acquiescence in the goods of temporality, or what Gregory the Great calls "fatal tranquillity."[16] This spirituality of suffering becomes so predominant in the medieval moral interpretations of Job that both Gregory and Denis the Carthusian completely invert Job's question: Rather than asking why the righteous suffer and the wicked prosper, they argue that providence is most *indiscernible* when the good are happy and the wicked suffer.[17] To leave someone in a state of "fatal tranquillity" is to condemn that person to a life without the curative power of suffering.

The Order of Providence

Calvin places his comparisons of Job and David not in the context of detachment, freedom, and transcendence but rather in terms of the incomprehensibility of divine providence. He explores the theme of God's hiddenness within history by accentuating certain elements of the Thomistic exegetical tradition. Both Calvin and Thomas interpreted the book of Job through the question of immortality. According to Thomas, Job alone believed in personal immortality while Eliphaz, Bildad, and Zophar denied belief in the afterlife.[18] Although he makes the issue of immortality the point of debate between Job and his friends, the problem that really lies at the heart of the controversy is the perception of order. Thomas explains that both Job and his friends believed in providence and saw in the orderly course of nature evidence for the existence of God's governance. Following Maimonides, however, Thomas explains that doubts about providence arise regarding human events because "no certain order" appears in them.[19]

Thomas sees that this latter point is the source of disagreement: Do human events exhibit order? He argues that because Job's friends denied immortality, they restricted providence to the earthly life. In order to defend the justice of this earthly providence, they were forced to conclude that adversities were punishments for past sins and that happiness was the reward for virtue.[20] In the speeches of the friends, Thomas sees what modern scholars call the deuteronomic view of history, a view that portrays history as justly ordered, intelligible, and predictable. This theory is not one that Thomas wants to discard completely. He also believes that human events are justly governed and that at times adversities are indeed punishments for sins.

Nonetheless, Thomas believes that Job's friends were funda-

mentally wrong and that their error was a perceptual one. Their
mistake was the claim to perceive within history an order that was
not discernible to the human eye; the justice they professed to see
was often a justice reserved to the afterlife. Job "spoke rightly"
about God because his belief in immortality provided him with a
perceptual superiority over that of his friends, a truer perception into
the nature of history and providence. To explain how Thomas
understands Job's perceptual advantage, we must appreciate the
connection in his mind between immortality and a justly ordered
view of history. The existence of the afterlife functions as an
extension of history so that God can exercise justice after death.
Without the doctrine of immortality, the burden of proof for God's
justice lies within history.

Exegetically Thomas presents Job's arguments by giving to his
laments a thoroughly literal reading. A hard look at human events
finds not the order claimed by the friends but the injustices
described by Job. Job's complaints were not expressions of
detachment from the earthly realm but rather his honest and
experiential observations about the nature of history *if* that history
is judged without a doctrine of immortality. If one is limited to
"that which appears from experience," it is indisputable that the
wicked prosper and the good suffer.[21] Thomas's Job was asserting
that if his friends insisted on restricting providence to history, then
this disorder was the true character of that history over which they
claimed God ruled; to restrict providence to the earthly life is to
accuse God of *injustice.*[22] A realistic view of history leaves Job's
opponents with the dilemma that an unjust God determines human
events.

This dilemma disappears, however, if there is an afterlife.
According to Thomas, Job's purpose was to show that it was *not*
incompatible with divine providence to show that the wicked
prosper in this life;[23] because of the afterlife, God "had time" to
remedy the injustices of history. By appealing to immortality,
Thomas construes Job's bitter complaints as both an honest view of
history and a *defense* of God's justice.

Calvin, too, sees the story of Job as a book about the nature of
providence and history. He also portrays Job as the one who insists
on defending the doctrine of the resurrection and, thereby,

extending divine justice to the "last day."[24] More importantly,
Calvin uses the doctrine of the afterlife to set up the same perceptual
opposition between Job and his friends as did Thomas. According to
Calvin, the friends spoke many true things in their defense of God's
justice but were rebuked by God because of their insistence on
restricting providence to history. This restriction made them
misperceive the nature of earthly events. Judging only by what they
could "see with their eyes," the friends claimed that God punishes
and rewards in this life, a doctrine that made them conclude that
Job's afflictions were due to past sins. Their determination to
"enclose all of God's grace" within the present life made them
argue that history must always be justly ordered.[25] Like Thomas,
Calvin portrays Job as arguing that history appears to be confused
and abandoned by God.

Calvin, however, differs from Thomas in that he more deeply
explores the incomprehensibility of providence and defines Job's
suffering in terms of the hiddenness of God. For Thomas,
suffering plays no instrumental role in Job's perceptual superiority; in fact, Thomas interprets suffering as an "impediment" to the
free use of reason or the contemplation of truth.[26] Calvin's interest
in the nature of Job's suffering leads him to use the exegetical
device of linking Job and David as paradigmatic figures for that
type of spiritual torment caused by the hiddenness of God. Since
Calvin does not cite his sources in these sermons, it is not possible
to determine whether he appropriated this device from Ambrose.
Nevertheless, regardless of the question of influence, Calvin too
made the same exegetical discovery. The context, now, is not
fourth-century Milan but sixteenth-century Geneva. In this latter
age, characterized by religious turmoil, dissent, and persecution,
the question of suffering led Calvin to discussions about the
incomprehensibility of providence and the hiddenness of God.[27]
We shall show that in his attempt to understand Job's anguish,
Calvin struggles with a recurring tension between God's visibility
and hiddenness, revelation and silence, knowability and incomprehensibility. Continually he tries to hold these antithetical
strains together so that the God of history does not recede into utter
inscrutability.

Job and David in Calvin's Sermons

As Calvin explains, Job and David led parallel lives; God both elevated and afflicted them. Just as Job was upright and withdrew from evil, so too David was a faithful servant and a prosperous king who was elevated by God.[28] Yet the lives of both men were filled with tragedy. Just as Job lost all of his possessions, his children, and his health, so too David was pursued by Saul, his son died, his women were raped, his enemies surrounded him, and his son Absalom conspired against him. In Job and David Calvin sees the preeminent proof that God afflicts those whom he loves.[29]

When confronting the problem of suffering, Calvin is keenly aware that different explanations for affliction coexist in the Bible. He tenaciously defends the retributive and pedagogical theology of suffering espoused by Job's friends and often recognized by David in the Psalms.[30] According to this theory, the reason for adversity is knowable because it functions pedagogically as correction and discipline. As justification for this theory, Calvin cites Eliphaz: "Behold the man whom God corrects is happy; refuse not the chastening of the Almighty" (Job 5:17). Calvin is delighted that David expresses the same insight in Psalm 119:67: "Lord it has been to my profit that thou hast humbled me." This statement explains Calvin's preference for David over Job and the reason why he continually appeals to David at Job's expense.[31]

Calvin's favoritism for David stems from his own theological anthropology. Ironically, David is, for Calvin, the bigger hero because he is the greater sinner. It was David's frequent confessions of sin that so endeared him to the Reformer. Continually, Calvin uses the Psalms throughout his sermons in order to hold up David's confessions as a corrective to Job's self-justification.[32] The difference between the attitudes of Job and David are best expressed by Calvin's sermon on Job 14:4 where Job cries, "Who can bring a clean thing out of impurity?" As did earlier exegetes, Calvin interpreted this verse as describing original sin. In Calvin's view, however, Job did not so readily confess his guilt; instead he sought "some subterfuge in order to lessen the condemnation that is upon all men." In contrast to Job, Calvin continues, David willingly confessed the guilt of original sin in Psalm 51 "not in order to seek some pretext with which to justify himself before God but to pass condemnation on what he was."[33] By using David to correct Job, Calvin continually wants to insist that the proper attitude toward suffering, regardless of the cause, is humility. Although Calvin reiterates the traditional view that Job was intended to be a model for imitation by future generations, the reader soon realizes that this title more rightly belongs to David.

Calvin uses David to support his retributive theology of suffering not only to support his view of human sinfulness but also to confirm the essential rationality of history. Like Thomas, Calvin affirms this interpretation of suffering because it portrays a rational, intelligible, and predictable universe where God rewards and punishes according to the Law. In such a world God's justice is knowable, visible, and comprehensible to the human mind. In his effort to retain this theory, Calvin reminds his audience that there are times in history when God does act as Job's friends argued, by restoring order and punishing the wicked. Because God's justice is sometimes knowable, Calvin can recommend the works of God in history as well as the study of history as a means for perceiving divine providence.[34]

Nonetheless, Calvin is also aware that there are times when divine providence is not visible. He knows, for example, that the adversities of Job and David cannot be explained only as punishments. In Job's story, Calvin confronts the reality of truly *inexplicable* suffering inflicted by God "without cause," that is, without a cause knowable to human reason.[35] Calvin seeks to interpret this more problematic type of affliction by again appealing to David, and he cites Psalm 41:1 ("Blessed is he who judges wisely of the poor . . .") as a warning that one must judge cautiously with regard to another person's suffering so that "what happened to Job's friends does not happen to us."[36] Here Calvin aligns David with Job in *opposition* to the retributive theology of suffering preached by the friends. By reading the laments of Job and David as realistic descriptions of history, Calvin comes to consider the darker side of divine providence. In the tragedies of these men, Calvin recognizes the torment endured by the faithful not because of sins but because they are caught in a world where God remains hidden.

When moving within the realm of inexplicable suffering, Calvin

bases his comparisons of Job and David on the fact that both men
underwent the same "spiritual combat" or "temptation" caused by
the disordered appearance of human events. Gazing upon the
"confusion" of history, Job and David fell prey to the same
"temptation" as described by Ambrose, namely, doubt about the
reality and justice of God's providence. Throughout the Job
sermons, Calvin intersperses Job's complaints with verses from the
Psalms in order to define the spiritual conflict experienced by Job
and David as the fear that God had abandoned their cause or
forsaken the realm of human events.[37] The happiness of the wicked,
described in Psalm 73, caused Calvin's David to fall prey to the
same temptation experienced by Job when his wife told him to
"curse God and die." In these moments, Calvin explains, both men
feared that God had "become their enemy" and no longer heard
their prayers.[38] Calvin repeatedly explains that Job's greatest
temptation was a spiritual one—that is, the fear that God had
"become his enemy," that God had "taken the side of the wicked,"
or that God had turned away, as if asleep in heaven, and no longer
cared for human events.[39] According to Calvin, Satan bombarded
Job with "evil fantasies" by asking, "Do you believe that God
thinks about you? Do you not know that he has abandoned you? Do
you believe that God even deigns to have regard for human
creatures?"[40] Finally, Job's cry that "God has turned against me and
become cruel" reminds Calvin of similar statements made by David
in Psalms 22:15-16, 69:2-4, and 31:10-11.[41]

In these texts, Calvin sees an existential connection between Job
and David that he turns into an exegetical device with which to
interpret suffering. Emphasizing the incomprehensibility of God's
governance, Calvin invests the stories of Job and David with an
urgency about the "inner spiritual combat" or "despair" caused by
their realistic confrontation with the nature of history. And yet he
insists that in the depth of this despair, believers such as Job and
David must "rise above the clouds" and trust in God's providence.

The composition of the Psalms allows Calvin to believe that
David arrived at this trust more quickly than did Job. If we
compare Calvin's comments on the Psalms with his reading of
Job's laments, we discover that in the Psalms Calvin finds, or
inserts, more visual imagery about the perception of faith or the

"watchtower" upon which David stood to survey divine providence.[42] Even in the times of darkest silence, Calvin's David more
quickly concluded his lament with praise for a providence he could
not discern. In the search for a way to trust in providence during
times of divine hiddenness, the book of Job is simply more
convoluted than the Psalter. In contrast to David, Job took longer to
trust in God; he traveled more detours, complained more bitterly,
fell into blasphemy, argued his own self-justification, accused God
of wielding an "absolute power," and questioned divine justice
more deeply than did David.[43]

Nonetheless, Calvin is intent on finding grounds for Job to trust in
providence in spite of the "disorder" he perceives in history. The
most important argument Calvin employs is the invocation of God's
essential nature. Repeatedly he insists that God's will is the rule of
justice and that therefore his decisions cannot be judged or
questioned. God does not rule by a "naked will" or by a tyrannical
and capricious power. Calvin protects God's transcendence from the
charge of arbitrariness by appealing to the inseparability of the
divine attributes. When Job was confronted by a history he could not
understand, he was recalled to the unity of the divine essence, an
essence in which the power, goodness, and justice of God cannot be
separated.[44] Thus when Calvin's Job was tempted to doubt divine
justice, he could trust in God because God could not exercise a
power separate from his justice and goodness. This appeal to the
essential and inseparable nature of the divine attributes rests on the
assumption that God is immutable and will act in harmony with his
unchangeability. In these passages, Calvin tries to find a God whose
reliability is rooted in his essence so that his hiddenness cannot
throw his faithfulness into question.

Because of the vast transcendence of God, however, this appeal to
the inseparability of the divine attributes does not leave the realm of
hiddenness. Believers such as Job and David are simply told to trust
in God's essence even when they cannot understand it. But Calvin
does not stop here. Continually he directs Job and David not merely
to God's incomprehensibility but to his knowability, which stands,
Calvin promises, in continuity with his hiddenness. It is the
juxtaposition of the *opera Dei* that finally serves as a source of
confidence in the midst of the present "disorder" of history.

Throughout the sermons on Job, Calvin commends the appeals made to God's revelation in nature, whether those appeals are made by Job, the friends, or David. Nonetheless, Calvin makes it clear that the revelation provided by creation must be understood properly; one cannot claim that the same order present in nature is discernible in human history. The order visible in nature demonstrates the power and wisdom of God in his creation and control over the cosmos. In contrast to the beauty and order of creation, however, stands the inscrutability of God's actions in history. Calvin sees that the Job text combines descriptions of nature with statements about the character of history. As he works his way through the book, Calvin articulates the principle that would properly account for both types of passages, namely, that one can rightly contemplate God's providence in creation but that history does not exhibit the same order. In Calvin's exegesis, only Job rightly perceived the difference between God's revelation in nature and in history and, thereby, squarely faced the ambiguity that pervades the realm of human events.[45] In these sermons, therefore, the perceptual concerns are intensified by the fact that Calvin juxtaposes the two realms of nature and history as an opposition between revelation and hiddenness.

In the whirlwind speech, however, we have *God* arguing on the basis of nature. And, not surprisingly, we see Calvin appealing to David as he cites the Psalms throughout chapters 38–41 in order to describe the wonders of creation and to commend the contemplation of the cosmos.[46] In the end, therefore, Calvin's Job hears not only God but also David. In this concluding section of his sermons Calvin uses creation imagery to combine visibility and invisibility by placing in the heart of nature itself a dialectic between hiddenness and clarity. On the one hand, the mirror of nature reflects the wisdom of God's providence. Nature, however, also transcends human comprehension and leaves us with only a ''glimpse'' or ''taste'' of divine governance. As Calvin repeatedly argues, we can never *fully* understand the wonders of the earth, stars, and animals.[47] Job learns, therefore, that the very majesty of nature infuses it with a kind of hiddenness.

For Calvin, the descriptions of nature in the book of Job, especially in the divine speeches, show that the governing of history requires a wisdom and power *beyond* that revealed in the cosmos. Nonetheless, despite the ultimate incomprehensibility of both nature and history, Calvin leaves Job with a promise, namely, that the same God who brought the order of creation into existence is powerful and wise enough to govern human events and, on the last day, to bring order out of the present confusion. On the basis of the revelation present in nature, Job is to trust that despite appearances, God is still ordering human events with justice and wisdom. Throughout his sermons on the dialogues, Calvin argues repeatedly that God's will is the rule of justice, that there is no continuity between God and Job, the infinite and the finite, God's justice and human justice.[48] In his sermons on the whirlwind speech, however, Calvin holds out the promise of continuity between God's revelation in nature and his governance of history. In the midst of inexplicable suffering, Calvin's Job must hold on to the "outskirts of God's ways" and grasp the promise offered by creation—the promise that the goodness of God reflected in creation is an inherent and inseparable part of God's now-hidden providence.[49]

Conclusion

Calvin stood in a long line of exegetes who used the story of Job to confront the issues of suffering and providence. The retributive nature of suffering, espoused by Job's friends and expressed in the Psalms, allowed Calvin to conclude that God sends afflictions as pedagogical chastisements for sins. The problem with the retributive theory was not that it misinterpreted suffering; like most precritical exegetes, Calvin was irresistibly drawn to the arguments of the friends, which extolled the justice of God. Like Thomas, Calvin saw that the problem with the retributive theory was a perceptual one; that is, it granted to history an order and intelligibility that was simply not discernible to the human eye.

Calvin's sermons continued the Thomistic interpretation by portraying Job as the personification of the ambiguous nature of history. In contrast to Thomas, however, Calvin explored the nature of Job's suffering. For Calvin, Job's correct doctrine of immortality was not enough to explain the full meaning of his laments; the text demanded an understanding of the nature and purpose of the suffering expressed by those laments. Both Calvin and Thomas read Job's complaints not as expressions of detachment but as realistic observations about human history. Calvin proceeded further by trying to grasp the perceptual implications of the suffering caused by the disordered nature of that history. Calvin agreed with the exegetes of the moral and allegorical tradition of Joban commentary that suffering changes perception; the sufferer perceives truths that the nonsufferer cannot understand. However, if we compare Calvin with this tradition, represented here by Ambrose, we see a significant difference in the object of that perception.

According to Ambrose, suffering was intrinsically linked to strength, wisdom, and freedom. Through affliction the soul gains fortitude and is released from earthly entanglements. Loss produces freedom. Suffering effects detachment, and the soul, extricated from the temporal world, ascends to the eternal realm. Suffering teaches the soul to recognize its true home above the realm of time and change. In this Neoplatonic view of suffering, affliction aims at an anthropological wisdom, a knowledge of the self and the true home of the soul in the hierarchy of reality.

For Calvin, the inexplicable suffering endured by Job and David is not defined as loss leading to detachment. It is not described in terms of freedom, transcendence, and ascent. With Calvin we have a suffering intrinsically linked to, and caused by, the inscrutability of providence. Calvin views the suffering of Job and David in terms of the perceptual limitations and doubts caused by the disordered appearance of human history. The afflictions of Job and David caused them to seek out a God who was silent and hidden. In comparison to Ambrose, then, we see in Calvin a suffering that aims not at *anthropology* but at *theology*. To be sure, Calvin's Job and David suffered real pain, a pain defined as spiritual wrestling against despair. Their agony, however, led them not so much to the brink of self-realization as to the edge of the abyss. What they feared most, according to Calvin, was a world abandoned by God. Their greatness was their triumph over despair. Although their afflictions did not effect in them a detachment from history, nonetheless they did find a deeper faith in God. Through suffering, Job and David pierced through the swirl of personal and political chaos to trust, despite the evidence of history, that God is in providential control of the earthly realm.

That providential God, they learned, is both hidden and revealed. For Calvin, people like Job and David cannot abide the total silence of God. As he states in his sermon on Job 14:13-15, "There is nothing that a person ought to fear more than to be forgotten by God."[50] The whirlwind speech promised that even the apparent disorder of history was not completely engulfed by darkness. The dialectical tension between hiddenness and revelation that cuts through all the sermons on Job is maintained by the witness of nature. Even the transcendent God of chapters 38–41 does not recede, finally, into utter inscrutability. Job was promised (by both God and David) that the "glimpse" of God's nature offered by creation is sufficient reason for trusting that God will always act in continuity with the power, goodness, and wisdom revealed in the cosmos. Through suffering, Job was directed to a God whose essential character he could trust, even in times of the darkest silence.

This was a message that would have been welcomed by Calvin's congregation. Calvin's task as a preacher and exegete was to create, in the terms of Robert Bellah, a "community of memory,"[51] and to re-present the figures of Job and David as "models" in the minds of his hearers.[52] Calvin clearly saw the role of memory involved in his own exegesis and preaching as an aid to trust in providence. Therefore, Calvin evoked the past by seeing the book of Job as a historical work intended for present use or profit, by identifying Job and David as models for instruction and imitation. He summoned past sufferers to tell their tales. That past was not only historical but also paradigmatic. Just as Job and David looked to the *opera Dei* as a basis for their trust, so too Calvin directed his people to Job and David as grounds for hope in the present.

CHAPTER 9

JOB AND HIS FRIENDS IN
THE MODERN WORLD

KAFKA'S *THE TRIAL*

Stuart Lasine

If the testimony of theologians and literary critics is any indication, the most important modern interpretation of Job may have been written by an author who never refers to this biblical book. Assertions of a strong relationship between the book of Job and the work of Franz Kafka have been made and reiterated since the decade of Kafka's death, when Margarete Susman declared that none of the achievements of Western Jews bears the traits of Job's primeval dispute with God more purely and profoundly than does Kafka's work.[1] Northrop Frye states that from one point of view the writings of Kafka "form a series of commentaries of the Book of Job."[2] Buber considered Kafka's work to be the most important Job commentary of our generation.[3] Other theologians agree. Scholem counseled Walter Benjamin to begin any inquiry into Kafka with the book of Job.[4] Rosenzweig goes so far as to suggest that "the people who wrote the Bible seem to have thought of God much the way Kafka did."[5] Similar claims have been made concerning a specific relationship between Job and Kafka's *The Trial,* a novel that Frye calls "a kind of 'midrash' on the Book of Job."[6]

Several factors have prevented these and other comparisons from providing a satisfactory analysis of the perceived relationship between the book of Job and *The Trial.* First, comparisons of the trials of Job and of Kafka's protagonist Joseph K. have not adequately considered the function of technical legal terminology in the two works, or the way the trial metaphor prompts readers to take on the role of juror in order to make ethical judgments about characters and events. Most important, scholars making this comparison generally accept Joseph K.'s distorted perception of the Court as corrupt and nefarious, if not his perception of himself as an innocent victim.

In this essay I will argue that the Court in Kafka's novel actually affirms the same set of moral values as the book of Job and biblical law. Biblical legal collections include many exhortations designed to prevent individuals from acting in unethical ways, or even feeling negative emotions toward others.[7] These laws carry no penalties, for individuals could not be prosecuted by the state for failing to live up to such moral dictates. In his "oath of clearance" (ch. 31), Job demonstrates that he has not been guilty of failing to live up to these ideas.[8] In *The Trial*, the Court system is activated by K.'s failure to put these values into practice. In effect, the novel answers questions like these: What would a Court be like that *did* prosecute an individual for failing to live up to such moral standards, even in his most private emotions and attitudes? What would happen if such a person had none of the self-knowledge that Job possesses to such an extraordinary degree—if, in fact, he displayed the same tendency to twist the facts to fit his theories that characterizes Job's *friends,* rather than Job himself?

Job and Josef K. are both tried according to "justice" in its most fundamental sense, as the virtue that puts another's good ahead of one's own. At every point, Job and K. mark opposite poles of moral behavior and attitude in relation to others. This opposition extends to their status as scapegoats. While Job may well be the community's failed scapegoat, as Girard contends, K. merely adopts the pose of victim in order to evade his personal responsibility toward others. For this, K. is held accountable by the Court and tried in very much the way that God tries the guilty in the Hebrew Bible. In contrast, Job's claim of innocence and his charge that God allows the poor to be victimized, are adjudged correct by God himself.

While readers of the book of Job are led to share Job's perception of social injustice and divine inaction and challenged to take a stand on Job's indictment of God, readers of *The Trial* are led to identify with a self-obsessed protagonist who refuses to accept responsibility for his predicament and then challenged to renounce that identification and pass judgment on K.[9]

The Function of the Trial Metaphor

A number of biblicists[10] have recently detailed the pervasive use of legal metaphor in the book of Job. Similarly, Kafka scholars[11] have given increasing attention to the role of legal vocabulary in *The Trial*. One must still ask whether the basic trial metaphor and its attendant legal terminology serves a comparable *function* in the two works. Biblical scholars like Habel[12] explain legal metaphor in Job as a means of organizing narrative and theological components of the book in a creative and dramatic way, or, like Dick, suggest that it is a forceful way of communicating "the bankruptcy of conceiving the man-God relationship along the lines of legal justice."[13] In studies of *The Trial,* the function of legal metaphor is usually discussed only in very general terms, and in ways that support the commentator's prior interpretation of the novel's meaning.

Such explanations do not consider the possibility that one function of the legal metaphor may be to determine the reader's relationship to the text. This possibility *is* entertained by Cox, who asserts that the legal metaphor in Job serves as "a vehicle for involving the reader in the affair" as "the 'judge.' "[14] Because the prologue has established the reader in the position of being the only one who stands outside the action, it is the reader who is "called on to decide: who is 'in the right.' "[15] And when W. H. Sokel asserts that the court functions as K.'s observer and audience and that "we the readers are an extension of K.'s court,"[16] he is placing readers of Kafka's novel in the same position in which Cox places readers of the book of Job.

General comparisons between jurors and readers have been made by a number of writers and critics.[17] Recently, critics like Mailloux have analyzed the ways in which authors create an implied ethical reader by conducting a "trial of the reader's judgment," which makes possible "the *experience* of an ethical position."[18] Mailloux notes that for reader-response critics, judging characters often leads to "having the reader judge himself . . . in everyday life" as an authorial means for educating the reader.[19] In this scenario, the reader is put in the position of K. and biblical figures who listen to parables aimed at increasing their self-awareness and ability to accept responsibility (see below).

The way in which the trial metaphor leads readers to make judgments similar to those made in daily life can be illustrated by contrasting the structure of the trial with that of the drama, a genre to which both Job and *The Trial* have been assigned.[20] Scarry contends that "the trial audience, the jury, is there to 'make-real' what the audience of a play can ordinarily only 'make-up.' "[21] Nevertheless, because at one level readers pretend to believe what narrators tell them,[22] readers who are invited to play the part of jurors will tend to make the same kind of judgments that they would want to "make-real" if they were members of an actual jury. While Spinoza[23] envisioned the author of Job as something of an armchair writer who never suffered like his protagonist, the book itself may prompt readers to "rise from *their* chairs" to pass judgment on perceived injustice, as did Job, before and during his trial by God. Conversely, readers may convict Josef K. for his *failure* to abandon the pose of detached spectator in order to help others.

The Proceedings

Having discussed the basic function of the trial metaphor, we are in a position to compare and contrast the two trials at each stage of the proceedings. The trials begin when Job and K. are visited by higher powers because of the way they had conducted their lives up to that point. Both are "fallen upon" (Job 1:17; *The Trial* [hereafter "P" for *Der Prozess*] 12, 18)[24] without being told why, an experience neither expected. Both then go through a process of testing that shows whether they have reacted to the initial reversal of their life patterns by altering their attitudes and character.

Once their lives have been turned upside down, both Job and K. feel "hunted."[25] Both demand to know the charges against them (Job 10:2; P 11, 58). Both are "impatient" (Job 21:4; P 223), as they repeatedly proclaim their innocence, and insist that they are victims of injustice. However, while readers are told that Job is innocent in the first verse of the book, the first sentence of Kafka's novel merely reflects *K.'s* assumption that he has done nothing wrong. K.'s guilt is assumed by the Court. For Job, who is being tried precisely because his innocence is assumed by God, the only remaining possibility of guilt is if he becomes guilty by the way he reacts to being made to suffer unjustly (which is precisely what the Satan predicts will occur [1:11; 2:5]).

Job demonstrates his innocence of any social injustice by going over the details of his past ethical conduct in his oath of clearance (Job 31). While Job even offers to announce "the count of his steps" (31:37),[26] K. merely speculates on the need to examine his past in detail (P 137, 154-55), without submitting even a *Beweisantrag,* that is, a motion to receive evidence, as do other accused persons (P 82).[27] Admittedly, it is difficult to envision K. making an oath like Job's when one considers that in contrast to Job, K. *was* attracted to a married woman (Job 31:9; P 72), *was* willing to raise his hand against poor children (Job 31:21; P 49), and *did* rejoice at the idea of his enemy's ruin (Job 31:29; P 75).

While both Job and K. perceive judicial authorities as corrupt, their basis for this opinion differs considerably. Job describes corruption among authorities primarily to indict God for elevating and sustaining such immoral and incompetent leaders (Job 9:24; 12:17-25). While these descriptions are often taken to be hyperbolic, nothing in the book implies that they have no basis in fact. In contrast, at the time when K. levels his charges at his first interrogation (P 57-61), he knows practically nothing about the workings of this Court or the status of the other accused persons he purports to represent. Although he has witnessed the behavior of the warders at his arrest, he nevertheless accuses them of misdeeds they have not committed (cf. P 57-58 with P 9-18). When K. visits the corridors of the Court soon thereafter, he acknowledges that his visit is motivated by his desire to affirm his prior assumption that the inside of this legal system is just as repellent as its outside (P 85).

During their ordeals, both Job and K. receive some sort of advice and comfort from "friends." If K. begins with the theory that he cannot be guilty and accuses the court of guilt and injustice, Job's friends begin with the theory that God cannot be guilty of injustice and then accuse Job of guilt. Eliphaz's specific trumped-up charges against Job (22:5-11), to which Job responds in his oath of clearance, are just as groundless as the accusations made by K. at his interrogation.

While Job can only long for an impartial umpire or referee (9:33; 16:19; 19:25), K. fails to seek help from those agents of the Court who do not share the partiality and ignorance of the defense lawyers and their minions, none of whom works with the full approval of the Court. Thus K. misses the opportunity to seek direction from the examining magistrate, the information officer, and the Court chaplain. K.'s *false* helpers are not only those who tell him to accept guilt, in the manner of Job's friends, but also those who support his desire to evade responsibility by accepting as a working premise his claim to innocence.

Because both Job and K. argue against injustice both on a personal basis and as human beings *per se,* both have the opportunity, based on this double perspective, to act on behalf of other humans as their advocate or intercessor. However, only Job acts in good faith on behalf of others, both on principle (the human condition is the same for master and slave [3:19; 31:15; cf. 7:1; 14:1]) and in response to the sufferings of victims, which he now perceives with his new worm's-eye view of the human world (24:1-12; 29:12-17; 31:13-22).[28] K., on the other hand, appeals to humanity in general ("we are all simply human beings here" [P 253]) only to exculpate himself as an individual;[29] he is unconcerned about the suffering of others. This is true even when K. is told that he may be able to help to alleviate that suffering (e.g., P 79; cf. 66), and even when he *says* that he is acting on others' behalf (P 57). In fact, K.'s pretended advocacy of other victims may actually cause new victimizations.[30]

The Court may well be interested in granting K. a close-up, worm's-eye view of the poor, so that he might identify with and feel concern for these fellow-citizens. The Court directs K. to its offices, which are located in a neighborhood composed of tenements, a neighborhood familiar to K. only through impersonal business dealings. In *The Trial* the Court is (literally!) on the side of the poor, as was the regal Job before his trial, and as is the ideal just king of Israel (e.g., Solomon in 1 Kings 3:16-28).

Finally, toward the end of their trials both Job and K. are given the opportunity to understand their delusion about the workings of the higher powers, by being granted visions that they must interpret themselves. In Job's case the opportunity takes the form of God's speeches, while in K.'s it is given by means of the prison chaplain's doorkeeper legend. While the chaplain's words are intended to enlighten K. about his delusion concerning the Court, God's attempt to correct Job's perception of cosmic governance is also his legal response to Job's countersuit (*rîb* [31:35; 40:2]).[31] Job has succeeded in having his legal charges taken seriously by the higher powers and has even seen God (42:5). In contrast, K.'s last thoughts before his execution still question the whereabouts of the judge he has never seen and the high court to which he has never come (P 272).

The Character of the Accused

Comparing the trials in this way highlights the fact that the Court in Kafka's novel investigates and punishes K. according to one biblical concept of divine administration of justice. Like the judicial procedures practiced by the Court, a divine trial can be aimed at establishing the true character of the accused. While God can determine a person's true nature "without investigation," as Elihu puts it (Job 34:24; cf. 1 Kings 8:39), a divine trial can take time for a different reason. God may sentence people by allowing "suspects" freely to act out their character, in effect giving them what they ask for. As the rabbis say in reference to God's treatment of Balaam, God leads a man down the path he chooses to tread.[32] In so doing, he may show himself to the wicked as perverse, as the psalmist puts it (Ps. 18:26). Because such trespassers are corrected by God "little by little" (Wisd. of Sol. 12:2), their trials give them the opportunity to gain more knowledge of themselves and God, so that they might change themselves and thereby annul their sentence.

K. is arrested precisely because the Court knows his true character without investigation. The Court is attracted by guilt and must send out warders (P 15). The Court tests K. "little by little" by consistently taking him at his word, following his lead, over a yearlong period, always showing him where the resolution lay, but never telling him. The Court shows itself to K. as shoddy and corrupt in order to hold up a mirror in which K. could recognize, and then rectify, his perverse behavior. For example, while K. assumes that the "dirty books" he discovers in the empty courtroom are evidence of the examining magistrate's corrupt character, they clearly portray his own character and even his situation at the very moment he is perusing them (P 67).[33] It is because K.'s continuing insistence on his innocence prevents him from acknowledging his moral failings that he is executed on the eve of his next birthday.

Victimization and Responsibility

René Girard has recently made a bold and provocative interpretation of the book of Job in terms of his scapegoat theory.[34] Girard believes that there is a "universal tendency of human beings to transfer their anxieties and conflicts on to arbitrary victims."[35] He highlights passages in the book of Job that show the friends and other representatives of the community to be unanimous in their perception of Job as worthy of being hunted down and violently punished. The God who persecutes Job is the God of the friends, comparable to the Greek Erinyes, who signify collective, social vengeance.[36] Noting the presence of a "cluster of metaphors centered on the hunt," Girard identifies this deity as "the god of the manhunt."[37] Job is a failed scapegoat, however, because he refuses to accept the community's image of him as guilty and culpable, thereby preventing the complete unanimity required for the maximal efficiency of the scapegoat mechanism.

Girard's reading of the book of Job invites comparison with *The Trial,* precisely because many readers of the novel view Josef K. as the victim of a brutal transcendent power that hunts down and persecutes its arbitrarily chosen prey.[38] According to Girard,[39] commentators on Job have ignored the fact that it is the community that is responsible for the misfortune of this scapegoat. In contrast, Josef K.'s perception of himself as a victim of hostile groups is merely another attempt on his part to ignore personal responsibility for his deeds. Once more the stories of Job and Josef K. prove to be diametrically opposed. If biblical scholars have failed to recognize Job as the community's intended victim, Kafka scholars have failed to recognize that K. is *not* such a victim, when they identify with K. and accept his self-presentation.

Critics who interpret K. as a victim typically point to the court artist Titorelli's portrait of "Justice" (P 176). As K. observes Titorelli's work on this figure, which also represents "the goddess of Victory," it no longer looks like either deity; rather, it looks completely like "the goddess of the Hunt" (P 177). Spann[40] suggests that this goddess might lead readers to recall the Erinyes, "the unrelenting huntresses of the guilty," that is, the same figures Girard had compared with Job's divine persecutor, the god of Job's friends. However, the many commentators[41] who take "the goddess of the Hunt" as an emblem of the Court's conception of Justice do not take account of the fact that it is only to K. that the figure appears as such. The novel itself does not identify Justice and Victory with "the Hunt." Like other books and pictures viewed by K., this depiction of Justice and Victory is more reflective of his own nature than it is of the Court's.

K.'s perception of the goddess figure is often linked with a later remark made to K. by the lawyer's nurse (and K.'s mistress) Leni, to the effect that K. is being "goaded" *(gehetzt)* by the Court (P 244). Leni's view is accepted not only by K. but by a number of scholars,[42] in spite of the fact that from the Court's point of view, she is the parade example of the wrong kind of help K. has been getting, particularly from women (P 253). Adopting Leni's perspective allows K. to continue projecting responsibility for his plight onto others, the nebulous "they"[43] who are allegedly after him. From the Court's perspective, an accused person who views himself as "goaded" may be attempting to obscure the fact that it is his own actions that have brought the Court down on him. According to one Kafka aphorism, evading responsibility by claiming the status of victim *is itself* "the original sin, the old injustice." This sin consists in the reproach that humanity makes, and does not cease making, that an injustice has been done to it, that the original sin was committed against it.[44]

The Practice of Justice

Human nature is an open question at the beginning of the book of Job. Can human beings—even those who possess total integrity—display disinterested piety when their world is turned upside-down by the God who created and sustained that world? Is it conceivable that persons reduced to such a pitiful condition could forget themselves and their own cases against God in order to become advocates for the masses of suffering victims they now see from their worm's-eye vantage point in dust and ashes?

While many issues are left unresolved at the end of the book of Job, these questions *are* answered, with a definitive yes. In addition, the audience learns that Job was correct (42:7-8) in his perception that God does not intervene swiftly to rescue victims of injustice by crushing their oppressors. It is only humans who react to perceived injustices with immediate action, as Moses acted to stop the Egyptian overseer from beating the Hebrew (Exod. 2:11-14). God does not see as humans see (Job 10:4). If God sees the cosmos under the aspect of eternity, human moral agents view the human social world under the aspect of urgency. Moses' reaction to the victimization of the Hebrew illustrates the rabbinic maxim "If there is no man, try to be one" (*m. 'Abot* 2:6; cf. Isa. 59:15-16).[45]

Kafka himself was as personally troubled by social injustice as is the character Job.[46] The fact that as a writer "Kafka is incapable of the god's-eye view of human suffering," as Robertson puts it,[47] also aligns Kafka with the biblical Job. Kafka also assumes that suffering viewed from the human worm's-eye view urgently calls for moral action by the viewer, while the godlike posture of the detached spectator, a posture adopted by K. whenever possible, removes moral urgency from what is seen, allowing the viewer to withdraw from "the scene of the crime."[48] One cannot act heroically to rectify injustices when these are perceived from "up in the gallery."[49]

The detached beholder observes events as though he or she were in an audience watching a play. When K. beholds the whipping of the warders, the most urgent of the Court's presentations on his behalf, he is unable to disengage himself completely. To be sure, he quickly rationalizes away the thought of going on stage to offer himself as a substitute victim (P 109). Instead, he himself uses violence to silence the victim Franz (P 106-7), after offering a bribe to the whipper.[50] Both modes of intervention are typical of K. Throughout the novel he "identifies with the aggressor" against accused persons[51] and attempts to control others by obligating them to him financially.[52]

According to Robertson, K.'s failure may merely testify to the moral weakness of *all* human beings. He contends that while the Court can begin to arouse K. "from his previous moral indifference into the beginnings of self-awareness," it would still be "superhumanly difficult" for K. to escape his guilt.[53] As evidence, Robertson cites an aphorism written several years after the novel, in which Kafka is said to imply that since the Fall "no human being is strong enough" to "lead a good life."[54]

At first glance, this interpretation might seem to increase the similarity between the novel and the book of Job. The weakness of humanity is repeatedly emphasized by all speakers in Job, as well as in other parts of the Hebrew Bible.[55] Moreover, humans are said to be incapable of knowing whether they are truly innocent, while quite capable of self-deception.[56] At the same time, however, many biblical texts depict human beings as morally strong and vigorous, and, in the case of Job, having complete moral self-knowledge. Indeed, the Fall story should not be used to gauge the high moral potential of human beings in either the Hebrew Bible or *The Trial*.[57] In both cases it is clearly possible to choose "a good life."[58] In fact, both Kafka and biblical speakers imply that what prevents people like Josef K. from "choosing life and good" is their tendency to obscure the fact that they already possess the knowledge necessary to make this choice, by positing such knowledge as a goal still to be reached.[59]

Finally, Robertson's interpretation does not consider how little is required to "do justice," either in Kafka's view or from the biblical perspective. Admittedly, it takes a superlative human being like Job to forget his selfish interest and even his pain, in order to intervene on behalf of many others (see, e.g., 29:17), even though, as a human being, he is unable to answer God's challenge (40:9-14) and abase *all* the proud. Ancient Jewish tradition is no less sober in its assessment of human selfishness than modern theorists, as is evident from the proverb "Man is close to his own bones."[60] Indeed, the social virtue of justice is most remarkable precisely because it goes directly against the grain of human nature. At the same time, the fact that justice means putting another's good ahead of one's own implies that one can practice justice if, in the words of Camus's guilty character Clamence, one can "forget oneself for someone else, one time, at least."[61] Nothing in Kafka's writings implies that humans cannot achieve this goal, even if Josef K. chooses to die "like a dog" (P 272) rather than to fully live as a human being.

PART III

Themes from Job in Contemporary Theological Reflection

CHAPTER 10

POWER, ORDER, JUSTICE, AND REDEMPTION

THEOLOGICAL COMMENTS ON JOB

Langdon Gilkey

These remarks are theological ruminations inspired by a rereading of Job and a glance at one or two major commentaries. They represent, therefore, neither an informed commentary on Job nor a developed theological resolution of the immense problems raised in the book of Job—though admittedly these reactions do reflect a particular sort of theological direction and so they point the way to a more inclusive understanding of the issues swirling around the poem's treatment of God, history, justice, and evil.

On reading Job twice, my attention was caught by the juxtaposition throughout its course of four important religious categories or themes: power, especially the power of God, order, moral justice, and redemption. In this document—and throughout theological literature—these themes seem to conduct a strange dance together, sometimes uniting, sometimes separating, sometimes opposing or defying one another, and then coming back to some sort of unity.

In Job one is struck at once by two interesting points. First, it is the *moral justice* of God, not God's relation to the order of things, that is radically—and justifiably—questioned. To our surprise, because we tend to associate them, order—the order of nature, for example—is here distinguished from, in fact separated from, justice, the rule of natural law in the cosmos *from* the rule of moral justice in history.

Second, throughout the poem the power of God, the creative power that brings all that is into existence, is regarded as the

ground or basis of the order evident in nature, the "bounds" or
"limits" that keep natural forces from chaos (38:10-12, 20ff.), and
the forms, often the bizarre forms, that each kind of thing represents
(33ff.). It is through God's power to bring things into being that the
order characterizing each thing and its relations to other things is
established and preserved; the evidence of God's power is,
surprisingly, the evidence that such order has been given to
everything that is. Thus here power and order are both associated
with the Almighty, even the Omnipotent, God, while the moral
justice which that God purportedly also represents and defends is
found by Job, and apparently by the poet, to be utterly wanting.
Since this point is not always made about Job's protest, it is worth
recording.

Power, Order, and Justice

This point raises some interesting questions about perhaps the
most important contemporary theological interpretation of the
problem of evil, namely, that of process theology. As is well known,
in order to disentangle the good God from responsibility for evil, the
almightiness of God rather than the virtue of God is here qualified.
God and the power of things are no longer identified, the latter being
the effect of the principle of creativity; correspondingly, in God's
primordial nature God is associated metaphysically with order and
particularly with novel order, with increasing value, and in that role
with the fulfillment and so the "virtue" of each type of entity. In
God's consequent nature, God rescues all that has achieved value in
creation and so performs a redemptive role, preserving value and the
experience of value despite the transitory nature of things. Power on
the one side and order and value on the other are metaphysically thus
sharply distinguished. God as representing both order and value
is therefore good, and the temporality, the variety, and the
self-formation of process itself are responsible for evil—in our
poem, for the lack of moral justice in the world. God is, therefore,
"justified," the problem of evil in its relation to God being resolved
by denying God's power in favor of God's role as the principle

of order and value. Generally it is assumed—as it is also in *J.B.*—that this sort of resolution through the radical disjunction of the principles of power and of value finds its first and most powerful expression in the book of Job.

It seems to me (as apparently it did to the ancient Hebrew tradition, at least as represented by Job) that the unequivocal identification of order and moral value on the one hand and the disjunction of power and order/value on the other constitutes a mistake, possibly a Greek and not a Hebrew error. First of all, order seems to be no closer to moral justice, or in fact to the principle of redemption, than is power—though a liberal (as a Hellenic) culture seems to feel that it is. All evil in existence represents a form, some mode of identity and some minimal principle of order, else it does not exist at all and is no threat; and order in the hands of ideological will is doubly menacing (cf. the familiar phrase "law and order"). If God presents possibilities of order or of principles of order, therefore, God seems to be as responsible for evil, for the forms of evil entities or events incarnate, as God would be if God provided the power to be for these same entities or events. If God is a metaphysical principle of any sort, in fact, God is responsible in some significant measure for all beings that are; hence God is *ipso facto* involved in the evil that beings represent—unless one makes the further Greek error and blames matter unequivocally for the evil that "good" forms incarnate, against their will, so to speak.

Second, as this poem reiterates, order depends on power—the two principles are united in the coming to be of things. The power to be expresses itself as much in the order, form, or logos represented by creatures as it does in their material, physical substratum. In fact, there is no material substratum without its own intrinsic order, as modern physics shows. Hence the principle of being, the "force" or "power" of existence, is in some way identical with the principle of order. The power of being is also the source of the forms of being, its bounds or limits, as this poem reiterates. Ancient religious tradition, and certainly the Hebrews, took for granted this identity of the power of being and the form of being, of being and logos, and used it against Job's protest. It is not merely the God of power who silences Job but the God who establishes an ordered, defined, and limited set of powers on earth. Modern tradition, seduced, one may say,

by the Hellenic error, on the one hand distinguishes power and order
and on the other unites order and moral justice and hence argues not
against Job but against God.

The real issue clearly is the relation of God, the principle of being
and of order, to moral justice: Does the source of the power of being
and of the natural order of existence support, guarantee, or further
the moral justice of life generally and of history? Posed in this way,
we see that this question is not only "biblical"—as the poem shows
it is—but represents also the more penetrating form of the modern
question of God, the question whether the impersonal or universal
order of things, certainly assumed by scientific naturalism, has any
relation to or relevance for the pursuit of the good in history (cf.
Haeckel, Russell, Dewey, Monod, etc.). In this sense the poem
entitled "Job" is both Hebrew and naturalistic modern in its
sensibilities and not, so it seems to me, either Greek or "liberal."

Clearly, Hebrew tradition, represented by the major speeches of
Job's friends, asserted that the God of power and of order also
established and upholds moral justice in history: The good are
rewarded and the evil punished. Thus when Job suffers, this means
ipso facto that Job is not as innocent as he claims to be but is in fact,
in some hidden way, a sinner, and a fairly hefty one at that. We note
two important presuppositions of this traditional argument. First,
God plans, wills, and effects all that happens in history, down to the
least detail. Hence evil events in a person's life do not merely
happen but are divine acts and thus a divine punishment for that
person's sins. Second, it is assumed, as a correlate, that history, the
sequence of human events in time, is morally intelligible. The good
are rewarded and the wicked punished, and this spectacle of moral
justice is plainly visible to any unbiased eye that surveys history's
course. Since each speech critical of Job makes these two
assumptions, each one in its own way concludes that the Job who
suffers is therefore a Job who is guilty of wrongdoing. Job of course
objects to this argument and insists that he is innocent; whether or
not he may also question one of these other two presuppositions,
namely, the effective or active omnipotence of God or the moral
intelligibility of history, *besides* his insistence on his own
innocence, is hard to determine from the text. In any case, he

never abandons his claim to innocence. On this basis, granted his suffering, he insists that historical events, especially those relevant to him, are not morally intelligible, and therefore that God is not, as is claimed, just in relation to him. Hence his protest.

One may question the reality of his innocence. Is anyone, even the most obviously righteous, that good? Since most (though not all) who are considered good also consider themselves good, they are therefore in that at least self-righteous and at worst hypocritical, hiding the reality of their spiritual pride from others and even from themselves. Much of the orthodox Christian tradition would say as much of Job. Granted the possible validity of this traditional argument, it is, I think, irrelevant to the main issue raised in the poem, and hence to its three subpoints: (1) Does God do all that happens in history? (2) Does all that happens therefore illustrate the moral law of reward and punishment? and (3) Is history therefore morally intelligible? Do the events in history manifest justice and hence manifest God's justice?

Autonomy and Virtue

In tackling this set of issues it is, I think, important to recall that even believers in original sin—if they have any sense at all—do discriminate morally between different shades or levels of evil in history (what Reinhold Niebuhr called "the equality of sin and the inequality of guilt"). If that is so, it can also be concluded—though Niebuhr does not draw this conclusion to my knowledge—that a just God also makes roughly the same sort of discrimination—whatever she may decide to do with this variety of offenders. God does distinguish levels of responsibility and so levels of guilt, to use Niebuhr's phrase. The question still stands of whether the divine moral discrimination between the relative evil and the relative good has direct effect on the course of events in history, that is, whether the relatively good are in fact rewarded and the relatively unjust are in fact punished during the course of history's sequences. In other words, the symbol of original sin does *not* relieve the theologian of the question of the moral justice of history and so the question of theodicy, the justification of God's providence in the face of historical evil and personal suffering.

For the moment, setting aside the question of Job's innocence and the divine responsibility for personal suffering, let us note two aspects of Job as a person that seem to me to be remarkable. First, there is his *courage* in challenging God, as well as traditional religious piety, in accusing God—as God is usually understood and defined—of moral ambiguity at best and of radical indifference to morals at worst, and in asserting against both God and tradition the moral incoherence of history under God. This act of religious rebellion horrifies his friends and finally evokes the grudging admiration of God, as it has of countless lesser readers since. Second, Job's *integrity,* or perhaps more accurately—in the light of the modern Enlightenment—his insistence, on his own *autonomy* or defense of that *autonomy* is remarkable. Job will not under any circumstances admit to any phony or contrived sin, certainly not to mollify his friends, and not even in order to mollify God and relieve his own sufferings. He will assent only to that judgment on himself which his own conscience and own consciousness of himself can allow or affirm, to which his own autonomous self assents. This is an interesting point. Job's insistence here on an autonomous self-judgment makes great sense to us; it makes no sense at all either to Paul or to Luther: "I know nothing against myself, and yet the Law reveals my guilt." In any case, it is this courage and autonomy, not his innocence (which to many is hardly credible), that gives to Job his immense human stature. It is also this that inaugurates, or helps inaugurate, the *dialogic* relation to God supremely character-istic of Judaism and, in vastly reduced form, of Christianity. There are here, as in the figure of Socrates, the seeds of the much later Enlightenment in which this principle becomes explicit and central, and so of the modern veneration of autonomy—though note how reductionistic science, also a consequence of the Enlightenment, if taken as a philosophy progressively endangers this same inherit-ance.

As it is important to distinguish the principle of order from that of moral justice if one is to understand Job—and life!—so it is important to distinguish courage and autonomy from innocence or virtue, freedom from the virtuous exercise thereof. Modern culture is inclined to collapse virtue and autonomy into one identical principle, to understand freedom as *good* if only it is able to exercise itself, as it tends to assume the identity of order and justice. Unfortunately not all those who are autonomous, nor all those with the courage to assert their autonomy, are virtuous. And for this reason the value or worth of a human being, centered on her or his autonomy, responsibility, or personhood, is distinguishable—and must be distinguished—from the "virtue" of that human being. Most liberals are rightly against oppression and exploitation, affronts to the value of those oppressed because they represent a denial of their autonomy and so of an important aspect of their personhood. Liberals are apt to mistakenly assume that since these exploited persons are of course of value, they are by the same token *virtuous* or *good*—that is to say, that autonomy and personhood are equivalent to virtue. Sadly, the facts do not bear out this assumption; the downtrodden of one era—for example the bourgeoisie prior to the seventeenth century—may well become the oppressors of the next era. Their value as autonomous persons is relatively constant; their virtue—that is, what they do with their autonomy—is another matter entirely. Only if, in other words, one identifies the exercise of autonomy or freedom with virtue and so assigns evil to some extrapersonal source (genetic inheritance, social tradition, class, etc.) can one so assume the identity of autonomy with virtue and so the goodness as well as the value of autonomous persons. But again, if evil arises outside the self in forces that determine the self from beyond itself, then respect for autonomy, which respect encourages that view of evil, finds the very autonomy it represents itself becoming precarious, even vanishing; for then the whole self as well as the evil self becomes merely a function of extrapersonal genetic, historical, social, or psychological forces, and autonomy, virtue, and value disappear together.

Three Constructive Theological Suggestions

Let me in conclusion make three constructive theological suggestions on the basis of this discussion to date. By constructive theological suggestions, I do not mean proposed doctrines. Rather I

mean that these suggestions look to me fruitful; I intend therefore to
follow them out a bit further and hope that at some time they may
with care and feeding become a developed theological proposal, a
set of doctrinal statements of some sort. At present I am not at all at
that stage. Specifically, these three suggestions seem to me to
promise, if thought through with some care, a reinterpretation that
will in part answer Job's protest against the tradition he inherited,
and yet one that will in its way "justify" both God's "godness" as
the source of power and order and God's goodness.

First Suggestion

Prominent in the theology of the last two hundred years is the
rejection of the notion that God—however else she may be
described—is the direct author and effector of all events, outward
and inward, large and small, significant and insignificant. What the
divine rule may entail is the subject of endless debate; but that it does
not entail a divine "causation" or "determination" of all events is
almost universally agreed upon. There are many ways this
"limitation" on God may be effected: by metaphysically reducing
the divine power and status; by theologizing only about revelation
and faith, sin and grace; by dodging ontological issues; by a torrent
of rhetoric; and so on. Few, however, explicitly challenge the claims
of creaturely autonomy, of the necessity for the self-constitution of
the person (as Kierkegaard put it), and thus for the self-constitution
and autonomy even of the response of faith (Brunner, Barth,
Bultmann), understood as implications of the presence of
spontaneity, autonomy, and freedom present in creaturely existence
generally as well as in the human experience of human inwardness
(Whitehead, Tillich, Reinhold Niebuhr). As we have noted, this
tradition of autonomy, enlarged into a central credo of the
Enlightenment, traces itself at least back to Job—though there its
ontological implications vis-à-vis the relation of God to human
autonomy were not drawn out.

Generally—at least for this ideology—God is the power in all, the
order in all, and the redemptive end of all. But the autonomy and
integrity of creaturely life intervene; and since that autonomy
is the divine intention at creation, God "steps back" in creating, as

Kierkegaard put it, in order to establish an autonomous creature dependent yet also free to direct itself—a creaturely co-creator. God constitutes all and preserves all; but all that is, natural and historical life alike, also constitutes itself according to the structure and order given to it by its creator. Thus the world does not illustrate directly the justice either of God or of human creatures but a puzzling combination of both; it is therefore an order within disorder, a justice within injustice, an ambiguous mystery nevertheless laced with meaning (Reinhold Niebuhr). The strict identification of what happens in nature or in history with the will of God and so with the moral will of God is now largely denied. As a consequence, despite its temporary return via the theory of progress, the complete or evident moral intelligibility of history is no longer an article of faith for most Christians or Jews. Needless to say, the question of *what* sort of relation might obtain between the will of God and the course of history remains an unanswered query in modern Christian and Jewish thought. But at least one of the presuppositions of the Joban dialogue, namely, that God directly causes to happen all that happens, is no longer with us.

Second Suggestion

There is another challenge to the tradition Job disputed. That tradition identified God's intention with earthly rewards and hence regarded earthly suffering as a sign of divine punishment. Here suffering is taken as solely *negative* and thus as having no positive relation of any sort to the divine will. Suffering indicates divine displeasure as clearly as it does divine punishment. Now despite the prominence of this view in the so-called deuteronomic understanding of history and the common Christian understanding of providence in history, one can see this view challenged at significant points throughout the greater tradition. For example, in the symbols both of the Suffering Servant and of the atoning Son of God, it is through participation in suffering that redemption takes place. Here suffering, and even more surprisingly and mysteriously, *innocent* suffering, almost becomes an instrument or medium of the divine rather than the antithesis of the divine, sure signs of the divine judgment and displeasure as in Job.

This same theme, once it is recognized, appears also in many unexpected places. The life of nature, even as viewed through the eyes of modern biology, represents a strange union of new life with suffering and death, the arising of new generations and of new forms of life only through the suffering, elimination, and death of old generations and old forms. This was seen with great clarity by our earliest ancestors and is expressed vividly in primal religion; the sun sets before reappearing, the moon dies before becoming whole again, seeds die before reappearing as new life, and so on. Hence the conditions of new life, new birth—the power and the value of life—are linked inexorably with suffering and even with death. Something must be given, even sacrificed, if these divine gifts are to be received. Hence arise countless rites of sacrifice and myths of dying saviors; hence each major symbol of the divine fertility is also, at one and the same time, a symbol of death, and in the end of life after death: tree, blood, earth, water, womb, snake, moon, sun.

This strange dialectical unity of power and order, of death and life, illustrated in nature, in the primordial religious response to nature, and in these two central biblical symbols of Suffering Servant and of atoning, dying Son of God, has reappeared in much contemporary theology in the theme of the suffering of God as a central mode or instrument of divine redemption. God reconciles our existence to ourselves and to God's self through participation with us in the sufferings that we bear. This notion has of course hovered uneasily since the beginning over all concepts of the Atonement; never before, however, have theologians had the nerve to associate this suffering directly with God, with God the Father. Now they do; one finds the theme of the participation of God in suffering explicitly in some of the neo-orthodox, in Tillich, and of course now especially in Moltmann. One finds it also in the interesting notion of God as a polarity of being and of non-being now being worked out by some under the influence of Buddhism as well as that of the other sources already mentioned: nature, other religions, and atonement. I mention this because the dialectical relation of suffering to the divine redemptive presence represents the possibility of a quite different interpretation of the classical problem of evil, not least of that problem as seen in the suffering of the innocent Job.

Third Suggestion

This second point—the strange unity of suffering, death, life, and redemption—leads into my final comment or suggestion. For the tradition that Job challenged, and for much traditional Judaism and Christianity, God represents above all a principle of moral justice, what is later termed the Law, the moral law, blessing the good and punishing (or at least chastising) the evil. Certainly no interpretation of either Judaism or Christianity can deny aspects of this representation, or question long the justice of God and the divine concern for the morally and socially good. The question is whether there are other principles alongside this one, or even superior to it. In both traditions God is also redeemer from evil as well as chastiser of evil, a slightly different character and role. That is, here God does not so much judge, repudiate, condemn, and destroy evil—God as moral law—as God transforms it, embraces it, participates in it, and overcomes it. This is the theme we have in part just rehearsed; let us push its implications a bit further.

This theme of redemption is hinted at in Job (39:19ff.). I do not agree with those neo-orthodox interpretations that see the triumph of divine grace over the distinctions of the law, over the divine judgments on evil and sin, as representing the main point of Job (cf. Samuel Terrien's commentary in *The Interpreter's Bible*). Nevertheless, hints of grace as transcendent to law, to the distinction between good and evil, righteousness and unrighteousness, are surely present in Job. The important point in our discussion is that the principle of grace, and back of that the reality of the divine rescue from evil as opposed to the divine judgment on evil, represents a different relation to the fact of evil on the part of God and a different posing of the problem of evil than does the question as posed in Job, the question of the divine justice in relation to the innocent suffering of history.

How is this difference manifest? The redemptive activity or "work" of God, via suffering, via atonement, the acceptance and justification of the sinner, resulting in a new reconciliation and out of that a new life, represents or points to an aspect of God that *transcends* the distinction between good and evil and thus overcomes that distinction. To say with surprise that God loves (*agapē*) the sinner is to counter the more expected phrase: God judges and condemns the sinner. Clearly in both Judaism and Christianity God does both; and as noted, Job hints at both. But the point is the centrality of this principle of transcendence and its paradoxical relation to the divine justice; for in neither tradition does the moral distinction of good and evil, resulting in the moral distinction of righteous and unrighteous, innocent and guilty, represent the final word about God or God's will toward us. There is for both a grace in the divine that accepts the unworthy, even the sinner, and even in his or her sin (again, *agapē*); what is needed therefore for redemption is initially not righteousness, not good works, but trust and commitment in response to grace; and out of this transcendence of the law (of order and of moral order) a new mode of moral life may be possible. Once again, grace represents a different resolution to evil than does moral judgment—and so the interpretation of Job is itself set on a different course.

One final word: The transcendence of grace over law, over the moral distinction of good and evil, righteousness and unrighteousness, morality and immorality, that is to say, the divine *agapē*, is importantly if dialectically related to the other transcendence over the principle of justice already mentioned, namely, the transcendence of the principles of power and order over moral law, the transcendence of the divine being itself. This latter transcendence is crystal clear in Job: When Job challenges God for lacking moral justice, Job is answered by a *hierophany* of the divine power and order, a hierophany of sheer transcendence, of divinity, of the holy in Otto's sense, that overwhelms Job—quite illegitimately to most moderns. While the problem of the divine justice remains, to be sure, this manifestation of transcendence is nevertheless important. As divine power and order together transcend in the poem the divine principle of strict justice, rewards to the good and punishment for the bad, so in the divine redemptive purpose the divine being also transcends the divine justice. In the experience of atonement and justification evil is rewarded not by punishment but by grace—and the capacity for moral justice follows thereupon. In both cases the divine transcendence is clear. This transcendence appears in the poem in the dialectical relation of divine power and order to the divine justice, and it appears (here in hint, later explicitly) in the subordination of the issue of moral justice, of the law of righteousness, to redemption by the grace of the divine *agapē*. Alike the divine being, the order of creaturely being, and the hope of divine redemption seem to require that transcendence. Thus as a final suggestion, the overwhelming appeal to the transcendence of the divine source of being and order in this poem—which has outraged so many moralists—represents perhaps the necessary presupposition, if not the full articulation, of the same divine love and grace that in all probability these same moralists do not wish at all to relinquish.

CHAPTER 11

A RESPONSE TO THE BOOK OF JOB

James M. Gustafson

Rabbi Robert Gordis wrote that just as every actor harbors a secret ambition to play Hamlet, "so every biblical student nurtures the hope of some day writing about Job."[1] Whether the observation is accurate or not is an empirical question to which I do not have an answer. I would aver, however, that any theologian who is moved to use human experience as one criterion for testing traditional religious affirmations of radical trust in the benevolence and beneficence of God cannot help but be occupied with the book of Job. Further, if she or he takes seriously contemporary accounts of the determinants of nature, from the vastness of the cosmos to the minuteness of genes, aspects of the struggle of Job have a particular poignancy.

To be occupied with the book of Job, however, does not certify competence to write about it; this must be acknowledged. The historical and literary technical credentials of Marvin Pope and others evoke no small measure of admiration and anxiety.[2] A technically informed theological and religious interpretation that reorders the sequence of the text and sheds insight in the light of other literature can take one through an unfolding drama in a way that a single chapter cannot.[3] A book of sermons governed by a systematically coherent theological vision may lead one to "bow in humble reverence before the face of our God" and provoke both affirmation and dissent, but to respond would take as many sermons from a different vision.[4] Any reduction of the issues to a two- or three-sentence conundrum captioned "the problem of theodicy" will bleed the vitality out of the poetic, dialogic, and dramatic passions that pervade much of the book. The philosophical theological reduction removes the rich texture of the language, which enables the reader to empathize effectively as well as intellectually not only with Job but also with all who speak. But even if one had sufficient talent, poetic or homiletic discourse is not appropriate to the occasion of this chapter.

I have selected three themes from the book of Job that are, in my judgment, of particular pertinence to our contemporary moral and religious circumstances.

Conventional Religious Trivialities

First, the book of Job powerfully portrays the triviality, indeed the fatuousness, of a great deal of conventional and traditional religious discourse. Job's resistance to the assurances and indictments of his friends reflects religious and moral honesty and integrity that, if felt to ring with some truth, is not always forthrightly articulated by ministers of religion and even theologians.

Everyone remembers Job's impatient, indeed despairing question, "Why did I not die at birth, come forth from the womb and expire?" (3:11 RSV). That such a question is not unreasonable under utterly repressive and bitter circumstances can be seen in numerous modern reflections by various persons. It recurs in various forms, for example, over and over in Solzhenitsyn's *Gulag Archipelago*. Even if the life-destroying powers do not lead to such a radical question, many conventional religious utterances must ring hollow to countless persons living in the half-ruined ghettos of American cities, the barrios of Lima, the disease-ridden villages, camps, and cities of South Asia and sub-Saharan Africa, and elsewhere. I need not, I think, attempt to visualize or verbalize many such conditions to communicate my intention. One need only imagine oneself as unemployed and living in the Woodlawn area of Chicago, or suffering from AIDS, to ask how meaningful it would be to hear, for example, the words of Eliphaz to Job in his first speech. How smug and complacent they sound! If under such circumstances we would find the words that follow to be trivial or fatuous, what words can be said in similar circumstances? And what alterations in conventional religion and traditional Western theology are required to say them? Listen to Eliphaz:

> As for me, I would seek God,
>> and to God would I commit my cause.
>
> Behold, happy is the man whom God reproves;
>> therefore despise not the chastening of the Almighty.
> For he wounds, but he binds up;
>> he smites, but his hands heal.
> He will deliver you from six troubles;
>> in seven there shall no evil touch you.
> In famine he will redeem you from death,
>> and in war from the power of the sword.
>
>>>>> (5:8, 17-20 RSV)

One cannot but honor Job's moral and spiritual integrity, as one would honor that of our contemporaries subjected to pious banalities in similar circumstances, when he responds,

> Therefore I will not restrain my mouth;
>> I will speak in the anguish of my spirit;
>> I will complain in the bitterness of my soul.
>
>>>>> (7:11 NRSV)

No doubt such banalities are spoken by some contemporary clergy, but perhaps not often even by the heirs of theological traditions that would support them. The Protestant Reformers counseled those who suffered, apparently innocently, to ask in effect, "What sins have I committed to bring this on?" While they could be realistic about the miseries of life, they remained assured that such suffering was a part of the providential purpose and activity of God. Calvin, for example, marvels at the fact that infants "immediately on coming forth from the womb . . . find food prepared for them by [God's] heavenly care" in their mothers' breasts. Then he continues to observe that "some mothers have full and abundant breasts, and others' are almost dry," and concludes that "God wills to feed one more liberally, but another more meagerly.'"[5] Certainly the Reformers would have us commit our causes to God.

An enlightened contemporary religious and theological response would be something like this: For some of Job's afflictions we would turn to medical science, for others to ecology, and so forth. To the unemployed in Woodlawn we would respond with economic, political, and social programs, to those ridden by disease we would respond with programs to provide pure water, adequate nutrition, and whatever else is needed. We would not charge those who suffer innocently with being culpable for events beyond their, or any, human control. Even for persons whose suffering can be traced in some part to behavior for which they have some accountability, we invoke mitigating circumstances, if not excusing conditions; we certainly never tell them they ought to be happy because of a divine reproof. Our personal and professional utterances would avoid the triviality of Eliphaz's words.

Have modern religious pastors and even some theologians thought through the background theological affirmations that would support these ways of coping with conventional religious trivialities? Surely many have. God is not an immediately active agent with intentions for the sufferer in every human event. Secondary causes have a significant degree of independence from any divine causality, and the purposes of God are not so readily discerned. This is a significant shift from much that is important in the biblical experience of life, and much of the Western theological traditions. Job, like many after him, would have affirmed some words of Calvin about a Christian: "It is with God he has to deal throughout his life."[6] Dealing with God, it seems to me, is not primarily a matter of finding theological justifications for distinguishing between secondary causes and some divine purposes. It is a matter of rich and complicated human experience as individuals, communities, and participants in the order of nature as we confront powers beyond our control that, to a considerable extent, determine human life. Conventional religious trivialities, such as those I cited from Eliphaz, can be avoided; indeed, the powerful experience of having to deal with God can be interpreted as misguided and even pathological. So what are the implications of this for the use of traditional religious language in both ministry and theology?

Sometimes it leads to cognitive dissonance. I once heard a sermon that relied heavily on the book *Why Bad Things Happen to Good People,* followed by a pastoral prayer by the same minister in which intercessions were made that utterly contradicted the tenor of the sermon. Sometimes it leads, very appropriately, to a communicative silence before the mystery of human suffering and the mystery of the divine. Often it leads to an eschatological ''out'' which is convinced that in the *telos* of the divine benevolence there will be a redemptive fulfillment, a re-creation, so that the true human good will be realized individually, collectively, or even cosmically.

Job, in honesty and anguish, protests against Eliphaz's conventional, smug, religious assurances. This is one powerful theme in the book. If there is some untruth in the trivial interpretation (indeed, if it is false), contemporary religious leadership and theology is left with questions: First, is the *un*-truth integral to cherished ''truths'' of the Western theological tradition? If so, what honest alterations of that tradition are required to eliminate or correct them? Second, what do we have to say to the suffering of the innocent, particularly if we experience and know that it is God with whom we have to deal throughout life?

God and Human Well-Being

My second theme follows from, or even continues, the inquiry of the first. If, like Job, it is with God we have to deal throughout life, how we deal both with life and with God depends in large measure on what we experience as ultimate reality (its constraints and its supports) and how we articulate the object of that experience. The book of Job, because its unfolding drama and dialogue point to various human experiences of the divine power, presence, and purposes, raises very contemporary questions. How is the reality of the divine, the ultimate power, experienced in the lives of persons and in and through historic and natural events? Do various experiences confirm traditional beliefs about God? If there is dissonance between some of those beliefs and human experiences in which the human good is threatened or destroyed, are the beliefs to be affirmed in spite of contrary evidence? Or must they be altered?

An intensive detailed analysis of the book of Job along the following lines is beyond the scope of this chapter, and probably has been done somewhere. What significant shifts or changes are made in the articulations of the reality of God in Job's experience and in his interactions with other speakers? From the text, what would appear to be the decisive evidences in experience or in religious affirmations that sustain each expression? What has counted most decisively in the alterations that are made? At what points is the significance of suffering overridden not only by Job but also by the other speakers? Do other human experiences override it? Is the memory of a longer history than Job's personal history invoked, one in which other, particularly beneficent, "deeds" of God are recalled? Is it the authority of traditional religious beliefs? Is it a kind of leap of faith that makes suffering bearable? (One recalls the heading in the Battles-McNeill edition of Calvin's *Institutes* given to I, 17, 10: "Without certainty of God's providence life would be unbearable.'"[7]) This agenda of questions is evoked both by a reading of the book of Job and by contemporary human experience of the powers that bear down upon us and sustain us.

Jon D. Levenson has made a strong case against a frequent oversimplification of the theology of the Hebrew Bible in his *Creation and the Persistence of Evil: The Jewish Drama of Divine Omnipotence*.[8] I select one of many citations that support Levenson's critique. He quotes Douglas Knight's "conventional view" that "the Hebrew myths dealing with the birth of the cosmos envision no struggle between the creator and any other beings." Knight argued that the most detailed evidence for this is found in Job 40–41, which "can picture Behemoth and Leviathan as mere playthings in YHWH's Hand." This supports Knight's general conclusion that "what is primordial is the goodness of this world and of humanity; what is radically intrusive is the evil which humanity does." To this Levenson remarks, "This statement is inadequate to capture even the theology of Genesis 1.'"[9] This is not the place to fully develop Levenson's theme of the relations between covenant and creation, but only to affirm the importance of his argument against what can be interpreted as an oversimplified interpretation of the God of the Bible being unambiguously good for humans and their endeavors, and being free from accountability for all that is evil for man.

The issue in the book of Job is similar to, if not the same as, a contemporary issue. Is God experienced (not simply thought) as indifferent to the well-being of humans? As providentially caring for the good of humans through the course of events? Or as being the source, but not the guarantor, of the well-being of humans? While our contemporary accounts of the universe and of life, including human life, provide more detailed accounts of the dependence of the human on natural forces and set in different terms a cosmogony and cosmology, including a probable demise of life as we know it in some very far distant future, the religious and moral issues raised are not novel. Nor are they novel when we consider how human well-being or ill-being is the result of social, economic, and political choices and events beyond our power to influence, not to mention control. For example, Cicero poses what are both biblical and contemporary alternatives; the first is this:

> There are and always have been some philosophers who believe that the gods have no concern whatever with the affairs of men. But if this belief is true, what becomes of piety, of reverence and of religion? If the gods cannot help us, and would not if they could, but care nothing about us, and do not even notice what we do: if in short these immortal beings exert no influence whatever on human affairs, then why should we revere them, honour them or pray to them?

The second is this:

> There are however other philosophers . . . who believe that the whole universe is administered and governed by the mind and purpose of the gods and who believe also that the gods are concerned to make provision for the life of man. The fruits of the earth and all that it bears, the times and the seasons, the changing aspects of the sky, by which everything to which the earth gives birth is grown and ripened; all these they regard as the gifts of the immortal gods to man. . . . It almost goes to prove that the gods have actually created all such things for the benefit of man.[10]

Levenson's interpretation of Job, similar to others, argues that "a most disquieting book" has a "comforting conclusion" in the prose epilogue, similar to Cicero's second alternative. He contrasts that conclusion with Yahweh's speech in Job 38:

> Where were you when I laid the foundation of the earth?
>   Tell me, if you have understanding.
> Who determined its measurements—surely you know!
>   Or who stretched the line upon it?
> On what were its bases sunk,
>   or who laid its cornerstone,
> When the morning stars sang together
>   and all the sons of God shouted for joy? (38:4-7)

Levenson states the point of this "harangue" in the following terms:

> [It] is that creation is a wondrous and mysterious place that baffles human assumptions and expectations because it is not anthropocentric but theocentric. Humanity must learn to adjust to a world not designated for their benefit and to cease making claims (even *just* claims) upon its incomprehensible designer and master.

In the prose epilogue, however, Levenson notes, "We find the covenantal counterpoint to this severely heteronymous and theocentric idea of creation. . . . The God of creation grants humanity a reprieve from the cold inhumanity of the radically theocentric world."[11] The harsh experience of an indifferent God experienced through the limiting and destructive, as well as sustaining, forces of nature is altered by the memory of Yahweh's covenant with humans, a traditional religious conviction grounded in, perhaps, a different set of historical experiences, in a different "revelation" of God.

Samuel Terrien concludes from "the poem proper" (3:1–42:6) that the poem does not attempt to answer the question "Why do the righteous suffer?" While it powerfully portrays the effects of suffering, it also "through the medium of suffering . . . shows how the self is discovered in relation to society, nature and the ultimate." It contains "a sharp critique of the traditional formulations of the nature of God" that goes beyond the common understanding of "monotheism." One has defined "in poetic terms the reality by which men can live in an indifferent, hostile or, at most, meaningless world."[12] It is not the philosophical problem of theodicy that is the nub of the book; rather the poem is based in "the deeply religious anxiety that rises from doubt over God's intentions for man."[13] Terrien comments on Job's final speech (42:2-6): "Existence is fulfilled when man is aware, not of his ultimate concern but of becoming the concern of the ultimate," and thus the resolution is finally as comforting as the one proposed by Levenson.[14]

As I suggested earlier, there are three possibilities for dealing with ultimate reality as experienced in human life and in and through events both historical and natural. Many interpretations of the book of Job, and indeed many in the history of Christian theology, note two of them: (1) God is experienced as indifferent to the well-being of humans, indeed, is the enemy (Terrien notes this response particularly in 9:31 and 9:20),[15] or (2) God is experienced not as the enemy but as the friend, a comforting conclusion based on Yahweh's covenant or on the Christ event, on a belief that one has become "the concern of the ultimate." Why, in much theology and religious literature, are we given only these two possibilities? My third was stated as God being the source but not the guarantor of the well-being of humans. Of course, the issue itself is significant only if one has, like Job, Calvin, and others, a gnawing conviction that it is with God one has to deal throughout life. The third possibility licenses a deep and continuing ambivalence toward the deity based on the ambiguous (with reference to human interests) effects of power beyond human control. It is grounded in the ambiguities of individual life, historical events, and our involvement in nature itself. To support this third possibility with evidences and arguments from contemporary human experience and from contemporary interpretations of nature is beyond the scope of this chapter.[16]

The Symbol of a Redeemer

My third theme follows from the second. It is the longing for a Redeemer.

It is from Job's answer to Bildad in 19:25 that the famous and favorite line comes, etched in memory especially by Handel: "for I know that my Redeemer lives" (NRSV). The textual problems with this have to be noted. Marvin Pope translates "vindicator" for "redeemer." He points out the different usages of the Hebrew *gō'ēl* in the Bible and concludes that it "is not clear here whether Job has in mind a human agent who will act as his vindicator. The strongest point in favor of taking the vindicator and guarantor as God is the specific reference to seeing God in 26b."[17]

For the purposes of my comments, whether the Redeemer is a human agent or the divine is not as important as it would be from other standpoints. Whether grounded in legal and religious tradition or in the desires of the soul, the longing for a vindicator in the book of Job points toward an aspect present in many religious traditions. There seems to be a deep desire for certainty that restless souls will find rest; that injustices in life will have an ultimate rectification; that there is some agent somewhere who will set things right, resolve objective ambiguities and subjective ambivalences—all according to human standards; and even that God guarantees this. Even that sternest of moralists, Kant, on the basis of pure practical reason posited the existence of God and the immortality of the soul to vindicate justice; logic requires that those who suffer innocently for being righteous should find happiness, that virtue be rewarded.

Surely there are many passages in the book of Job that claim that God is just. God's justice seems to be stated in terms of human standards of deserving: if one suffers, one must deserve it; if one is innocent, that will be recognized by God and be compensated for in some way. But experience of God as loving, or belief and trust in God as loving even in the face of needless or innocent human suffering, is also invoked by interpreters. Terrien made this point in very contemporary terms: "Existence is fulfilled when man is aware . . . of becoming the concern of the ultimate." "A God who concerns himself for man is a God who loves. There is no love without sharing and a God who loves is a God who suffers."[18] Thus one longs for a God who is love, who reveals Godself fully to be God the Redeemer.

The antidote has to be proportionate to the poison if it is to heal. That is put too strongly, but only to make the point that how a theologian or any interpreter of life interprets the general salient characteristics of it prefigures to a great extent what she will propose as the resolution of its perceived problems. If the problems of persons living in the Woodlawn area of Chicago are diagnosed in economic, social, and political terms, the resolutions will also be proposed in those terms. If the problems of life in the world are the outcome of sin, one response is a vicarious atonement and a regenerating efficacious grace.

The story of Job seems to warrant the observation that God is in the details. The details in human experience are surely as often a mixture of pain and pleasure, achievement and failure, suffering and joy, anger and gratitude, as they are simply and singly one or the other. Extremes do overwhelm, sometimes in the despair that prompts suicide or utter destruction of society in rebellion or riots, sometimes in the ecstasy of a fulfilling personal experience or the promising breakthrough of peace at the end of a brutal war, or the emergence of a new regime after years of oppression and injustice. But the ardor of expectations that flourishes in the great moment of hope, of the possibility that all things can be made new, is quickly tempered by the details that rapidly intrude. And the causes of despair, individually or socially, are always more complex than the attribution to a satanic fallen angel or a single political factor can bear. Our experience of both what is beneficial to us and what is detrimental to our proper interests comes in and through the details.

Does the book of Job provide sufficient evidence for that beloved sentence ''I know that my Redeemer lives''? Even in appropriately modest terms, is there one who will vindicate Job's rightness in the face of his disasters? Obviously that depends upon what counts for evidence. One can understand the deep human longing that leads to such an affirmation; it is not dissimilar to the certainty that those suffering from a fatal disease sometimes have that there is somewhere a cure, or that if there is none now there will be in the future.

It is my judgment that human longing for a Redeemer who will rectify all injustices, who will fulfill all true human values, who will make all things new, comes close to being an illusion. A more orthodox theologian than I will agree with that with reference to individual experiences and to historical events. And so the Christian Bible and the tradition eschatologize the fulfillment of the longing, though some theologians use that presumed certainty to ground a great deal of hope in history as well.

If human suffering and human fulfillment both result from complex factors, interdependent with one another, and if it is God with whom we have to deal throughout life—God who is present in the details—then no Redeemer for whom humankind longs can radically alter the conditions of life. Conditions for relief from human suffering occur; they are dependent upon the patterns of interdependence of life in the world, and ultimately on the divine powers. But they come usually within the confines of the details of life, in the interstices of interaction that enable human intervention to alter the course of events and of individual lives—that is, in the details. At best, in my judgment, the longing for a Redeemer is a symbol; it points to the expectation that life is not altogether fated to be what it is in its occasions of misery and oppression and points to those occasions in which, through either luck or intentional activity, release from Job-like afflictions and fulfillment of Job-like successes occur. At worst, in my judgment, the longing for a Redeemer can focus the eyes of human aspiration on an end in such a way that the realities of human life and the possibilities of participating in them to the benefit of humanity and the world are badly blurred.

Conclusion

In sum, this person, who like Job, Calvin, and others has to deal with God throughout life, responds to the three themes I have isolated from the book of Job in the following ways. Ambivalence toward God, times of anger and of gratitude, is warranted in human experience, and the religious honesty that expresses it is to be prized. The fatuous banalities of much conventional religious language are either hyperbolic or false. If they are integral to traditional religious beliefs and theological affirmations, those have to be reconsidered.

Human experience warrants the recognition that the powers that bring life into being, bear down upon it, and sustain it do not focus on Job's well-being, mine, or that of any and all of humanity. They are the source of appropriate well-being for humans, but they do not guarantee it even for those who "love the Lord." But we have capacities to participate in the various conditions of life; the response to affliction is appropriately related to the events and "spaces" in experience, in the details where the powers of God are met as limits and possibilities. I cannot affirm that "my Redeemer lives," but I can affirm that the inexorable limitations of life, our dependence upon powers and events beyond human control to which we must consent, are also conditions of modest possibility for resisting what is evil to humans and enhancing what is good.

The book of Job, perhaps, is in places too despairing, and in others too assuring. But it is painfully honest. Any theologian or minister needs to be equally honest in response to it, whether that involves pain or not.

CHAPTER 12

JOB AS FAILED SCAPEGOAT

René Girard

The book of Job poses considerable problems as to its unity. It begins and ends in a fashion very different from that of its middle section. It is common to speak of this beginning and ending as a folktale serving as a kind of frame that was gradually filled in with very different material. The folktale served as a point of departure or a pretext for a theological debate that was more sophisticated than the tale but still very uneven. Modern commentators have always been more or less in agreement in preferring the discourse of Job himself over the speeches of the three friends. But they interpreted this superiority in a very different manner. Concerning the faith involved in Job's repentance *in extremis*, the pious past accentuated the final acceptance of the hero. They saw an unfortunate subjectivity in the vehement complaints of Job, an interior expression of rebellion that could be admired without danger because it is mastered in the end.

In the end this thesis remains faithful to the basic position of what has been called the folktale: Job represents patience rewarded. But it has the major drawback of minimizing the central part of the work, the part that moves us the most, and for reasons that remain enigmatic.

The modern adversaries of this traditional thesis—whether we are religious or not—have little difficulty in showing its incoherence, which is somewhat the incoherence of the text itself. Carried along by the force of his own discourse, Job finishes by complaining to God with such violence that one may ask whether Satan has not won his bet, whether he has not made the afflicted Job curse God.

This is just what the four friends think who try to persuade Job to have a more humble and submissive attitude. They reproach him for his rebellion, and they see in Job's insolence the fault that justifies his punishment, satanic pride and the will to independence.

Our centuries of revolt and unbelief see in the author of the central section of Job a precursor of their own vision. The suffering of the innocent leads us to put all religion and God himself on trial. Job would surely suspect what is absurd and even abject in a religious faith that is always led to justify God against human beings and particularly to counsel patience to the oppressed, the famous patience that appears so admirable to conventional readers. The book of Job would thus be a naive theodicy that would serve as a paradoxical pretext to its contrary, the questioning of this theodicy, and from there the shaking up of religion, which modern interpreters consider the necessary goal of all sincere reflection on the misfortune of human beings.

So concerning what is essential in the book of Job, there are two responses. The first is the patience of Job, his obedience to the will of God. The second, the modern response, is Job the rebel, Job the protester en route toward the virulent atheism of the contemporary Western world.

The second response has the advantage of placing emphasis on the central and better section of the work, the speeches of Job before his final submission. But does it correctly understand what Job says? It poses the problem in exactly the same fashion as the traditional reading, but it inverts the response. It sees in Job a man essentially maltreated by God, troubled by God, or, one should say, since those responding in this way do not believe in God, it sees in him a man who suffers for reasons totally independent both of what he is himself and of the others around him. He is a victim of evils totally exterior to the will of humans, to human action in the world.

Neither thesis succeeds in escaping the folktale. Satan cannot act except with the permission of God. When all is said and done, he is a divine agent, and the real debate of the book bears upon the suffering of the innocent. If God exists, then it is surely he who treats us as he treated Job when we lose our children and our wealth, when we are afflicted with some horrible bodily malady. The cause of Job's suffering is exterior not only to Job but also to those around him, his family and his friends. The fact that we are perpetually threatened by such ills demonstrates the nonexistence of a just and good God and the folly of religion.

The complaints of Job do not justify the second thesis any more than the first. It is true that Job suffers enormously, but he never complains of the ills that come to him from outside—the loss of his children, his disease, all the uncontrollable misfortunes that struck him like lightning and from which no one is really protected. He complains first of all and above all about the persons surrounding him, about his relatives, about whoever remains of his family, about his entire village (19:13-20).

The principal suffering comes from these others who condemn Job without exception and say he is justly punished. Job himself says that what God gave he will take back; we left our mother's womb stark naked, and we shall be buried that way. All that is still tolerable; intolerable, however, is what is added to these ills: the universal disapproval that they bring about, the mockery, the insults, the universal ostracism. The most terrible thing is to be the last of the last. Job is treated like a scapegoat even by the traditional scapegoats of the society he was dominating. He has become the pariah even of those who are treated as pariahs. He is despised and rejected by a sort of minority group, a subproletariat. Even though we cannot exactly identify the latter, it resembles the persecuted minorities in all ancient and modern societies (see 30:1-6, 9-10).

Finally, Job has the impression that the entire world turns against him. Even the objects most intimately belonging to him are dealt with in a scapegoating manner: "My very clothes recoil from me" (9:31 JB). Far from being the exception in this extraordinary concert of bad treatment, the interlocutors of Job, supposedly his friends, add to the oppression of the sufferer. They do not speak the words Job would need in order to assuage his misfortune; they are not helpful—this is the least one can say. They are the friends of happy days, like those wadis that overflow when no one needs them and do not provide even a drop of water in time of drought in order to quench the thirst of the traveler in distress. Very quickly the tone rises from one friend to the other. The more Job attempts to justify himself against the friends, the more they attempt to justify themselves against him, that is, to prove that he is not an arbitrary victim of his ills; his children, they say, or Job himself must have committed concealed crimes that have provoked the punitive action of God. There is less and less difference between the coarsely persecutory behavior of the crowd and the behavior of the so-called friends; there is simply more method in the latters' argumentation. Those that seize upon Job, following the example of the people, formerly flattered him, always after the example of people. They saw in him the chosen one of the Almighty. That is why Job can say to them, "No doubt you are the people" (12:2 RSV). *Vox populi vox Dei.* Job sees himself, therefore, confronted with an infallible coalition. It is necessary to insist upon this unanimity; it constitutes the essential structural feature of the phenomenon that is described for us, that of the scapegoat.

And this phenomenon is especially clear; it occurs here as it occurs in Greek tragedy. Job himself describes his own happiness in the period that preceded his misfortune; like Oedipus, Job passes from an excess of good fortune to an excess of misfortune. The resemblance between what is produced here and what is produced in Sophocles is striking. The quasi-royal grandeur of Job prior to his misfortune gave him the status of arbiter and judge of the community, a sort of prophet, a sacred personage. The behavior toward him was exactly the reverse of what has come about since:

> Oh, that I were as in the months of old,
>   in the days when God watched over me:
>   when I was in my prime,
> when the friendship of God was upon my tent.
>
> When I went out to the gate of the city,
>   when I took my seat in the square,
> the young men saw me and withdrew,
>   and the aged rose up and stood;
> the nobles refrained from talking,
>   and laid their hands on their mouths;
> the voices of princes were hushed,
>   and their tongues stuck to the roof of their mouths.
>
>   (29:2-4, 7-10 NRSV)

Just as the individual rejected by God is none other than the individual rejected by fellow humans, the individual favored by God is none other than the chosen one of the community. The God that Job becomes occasionally capable of repudiating is no longer completely an idol, but he maintains the fundamentally idolatrous character of the God of the crowd. The adage *vox populi vox Dei* must be understood in two senses, for if the voice of the people is the voice of God, so also the voice of God is the voice of the people. This is indeed the god of Greek tragedy, the god that is purely and simply one with the decisions of the crowd—now exalting Job because he succeeds at everything, now putting him lower than the dirt because misfortunes have struck him. But the crowd never understands itself as taking these decisions. It does not know it takes them, for they are purely mimetic; they are taken automatically by reciprocal contagion, and their accumulative effect is so rapid, spectacular, and terrifying in its consequences that it appears simply to be an act of God.

The exegetes have generally observed that what Job emphasizes recalls the penitential psalms, and this is not astonishing since the one persecuted by the group speaks as he is surrounded by the menacing circle of his persecutors. There, indeed, is the formidable novelty of the prophetic spirit. These psalms present not simply any victim, nor a victim in the style of Oedipus who quickly agrees with his persecutors, but a victim who defends the justice of his cause, who dares stand against the collective will (Ps. 31:11-13).

Certain psalms mention not only declared enemies but also friends supposedly true, who end up by joining the enemies of the victim and are thus the crowning blow of his sufferings. This is indeed what characterizes the scapegoating process: Beginning at the moment that the persecution acquires a collective character, it exercises an irresistible attraction upon those who in principle should remain faithful to the victim and support him in his distress—his relatives, his wife, his intimate friends, his domestic animals. This distress is as individualizing as possible since it separates the one who suffers from all the others, whereas there is something impersonal and mechanical about the persecutors. The proof of this is that the mechanism is described in the same fashion both in Job and in the psalms that greatly resemble Job, not

necessarily because these psalms are influenced by Job, but because
it is a universal and terribly banal mechanism that they describe.
Therefore we have here texts that, for the first time, allow the victim
to speak in the midst of his persecutors, in place of giving the usual
mythological point of view of the persecutors concerning a victim
who is perceived as guilty.

> My enemies wonder in malice
>   when I will die, and my name perish.
> And when they come to see me, they utter empty words,
>   while their hearts gather mischief;
>   when they go out, they tell it abroad.
> All who hate me whisper together about me;
>   they imagine the worst for me.
>
> They think that a deadly thing has fastened on me,
>   that I will not rise again from where I lie.
> Even my bosom friend in whom I trusted,
>   who ate of my bread, has lifted the heel against me.
>   (Ps. 41:5-9 NRSV)

In his second discourse Eliphaz the Temanite reproaches Job for
responding with reasons floating in the air, for filling himself with
the east wind, for speaking vainly and ruining piety. Eliphaz thinks
that the very arrogance of his discourse condemns Job and reveals
his culpability. The very fact that he defends himself is culpable; his
defense itself demonstrates the contrary of the innocence he asserts.
In order to lessen the gravity of his case, Job would do better to
accommodate himself and come to agreement with his accusers. Job
responds:

> I have heard many such things;
>   miserable comforters are you all.
> Have windy words no limit?
>   Or what provokes you that you keep on talking?
> I also could talk as you do,
>   if you were in my place;
> I could join words together against you,
>   and shake my head at you.
> I could encourage you with my mouth,
>   and the solace of my lips would assuage your pain.

If I speak, my pain is not assuaged,
　　and if I forbear, how much of it leaves me?
Surely now God has worn me out;
　　he has made desolate all my company.
And he has shriveled me up,
　　which is a witness against me;
my leanness has risen up against me,
　　and it testifies to my face.
He has torn me in his wrath, and hated me;
　　he has gnashed his teeth at me;
　　my adversary sharpens his eyes against me.
They have gaped at me with their mouths;
　　they have struck me insolently on the cheek;
　　they mass themselves together against me.
God gives me up to the ungodly,
　　and casts me into the hands of the wicked.

　　　　　　　　　　　　　　　　　(16:2-11 NRSV)

If I am right, Job is a scapegoat in the current sense, that is, in the sense that neither the four friends of Job nor those who persecute or ridicule him understand him, since they take him to be justly punished and responsible for his own misfortune. Job sometimes declares himself not responsible, and he protests his innocence. But the theology of the four friends is nothing but an expression, a little more refined and evolved, of the theology of violence and the sacred. Any sufferer could not suffer except for a good reason in a universe governed by divine justice. He is therefore punished by God, and pious conduct for those surrounding him consists in their conformity with the divine judgment, treating him as guilty and so multiplying further his sufferings. This is indeed the theology of the hidden scapegoat. Every sufferer must finally be guilty because every guilty person ends up by falling into misfortune, and if God delays a little too long in executing his justice, human beings will take it upon themselves to speed up the process. Everything is thus for the best in the best of worlds.

I must dwell here on archaic religious survivals that continue in the discourse of the four friends, and in particular in the three first ones. By archaic I do not mean that they are necessarily extremely ancient or that this theology has not continued intact until a recent era in numerous societies, but that they are archaic in relation to the end toward which the entire Bible directs itself. These survivals are accents that recall the great maledictions of all the primitive religions and that one finds also in Greek tragedy. We find these maledictions also in the prophets, but it is not upon the individual victim that they fall but upon the persecuting community that is unfaithful to the Law.

The evil one is cursed by God, and the worst disasters will certainly befall him. And when the friends of Job speak to him, they evoke plague, the sword, fire, flood, famine, and poison (see 20:22-29).

Here it is God alone who directs all this, but the evils that bear down on Job are all in the plural, and they range about him in a circle like a hostile mob that harasses him as the three friends are doing. God alone in principle directs this attack, but one senses the hostile crowd behind the attack.

In order to convince Job that he is wrong, the three experienced twaddlers are not able to muster up anything except to celebrate anew their litany of ritual maledictions. For example, the last discourse of Zophar the Naamathite, an extraordinary text, contains once more all the elements of the primitive game, with disasters of all sorts, terrifying visions, whirlwinds and tornadoes, hordes of nomads, and finally:

> The womb that shaped him forgets him
>   and his name is recalled no longer.
> Thus wickedness is blasted as a tree is struck.

(24:20 JB)

This recalls the striking down of mythological figures, Semele or the Titans destroyed by Zeus.

In his second speech Bildad the Shuhite describes the destruction of the wicked in terms that are consistently religious and that so closely resemble the misfortunes striking Job that one is obliged to ask whether these misfortunes are not a reprise of the fate traditionally ascribed to the one accursed of God; perhaps the entire text is a deconstruction of a very old myth that made of Job one truly guilty of offending against the mythical order. So, as Bildad finally says, to purify the places polluted by his presence, ''People scatter brimstone on his holding'' (18:15 JB).

What makes the interpretation of Job so difficult is that the theology of the three friends, in a form scarcely less primitive than the preceding citations, remains very potent in our own time. It is still very powerful in all the traditional churches; it is also strong in the modern anti-religion, which is avidly attached to this theology in order to make a weapon of it against the very existence of God. But it remains powerful also in the language of Job. In a segment of his complaints Job attributes to God himself the blows that strike him, without any longer distinguishing those that come from without and those that come from the friends. Therefore, he ends by describing himself as a scapegoat not only of the community but also of God; that is to say, he utilizes, in order to defend himself, a language that too closely resembles the language used against him by his adversaries. The effect of his use of his opponents' language is to confuse the commentators.

In the first passage cited, where Job presents himself as the victim of all his neighbors, of his friends and his relatives, he continues in speaking to his friends:

> Pity me, pity me, you, my friends,
>   for the hand of God has struck me.
> Why do you hound me down like God,
>   will you never have enough of my flesh?
>
> (19:21-22 JB)

This passage is quite revealing, as it places precisely on the same plane the punishment from God and the punishment from humans, and in order to put them on the same level Job must distinguish them. But in other passages Job no longer distinguishes them and speaks exactly like his friends. There is, then, in Job's discourses too much confusion with a purely social notion of God, that of a divinity who necessarily participates in the misfortune of the sufferer, in punishing those who suffer, in rendering the helpless helpless; this is a divinity who is the same as ''fate,'' the Nemesis of the Greeks, and who in Job is called "the first-born of death" (18:13 RSV). Sometimes Job places God at the side of the false friends, those who cause him distress. This is particularly clear in the following passage:

How long will you torment me,
and break me in pieces with words?

If indeed you magnify yourselves against me,
and make my humiliation an argument against me,
know then that God has put me in the wrong,
and closed his net around me.
Even when I cry out, "Violence!" I am not answered;
I call aloud, but there is no justice.
He has walled up my way so that I cannot pass,
and he has set darkness upon my paths.

His troops come on together;
they have thrown up siegeworks [Hebrew "their way"] against me,
and encamp around my tent.
(19:2, 5-8, 12 NRSV)

The moment that Job declares God responsible, the circle of enemies—that is, the circle of the social order—closes in around him. Job recognizes that the divine condemnation of which he has been made the object is actually a collective hate for which he is the prey, a sort of total mobilization against him. The adversary is always collective, as in the tragedy of Sophocles. But unlike Oedipus, who finished by submitting, Job plunges into the debate frantically. Just like the personage at the center of the psalms, he returns the accusation to his enemies. He conducts himself after he has been unanimously condemned as Oedipus did before; he accomplishes the unheard, he resists the violent unanimity, even if he quite often resists in the language of that violent unanimity.

Now I come to the passages that are the most interesting, when Job, all of a sudden, comes to a point of seeing himself no longer as the friends see him, as condemned by God; when he sees the punishment no longer as divine punishment, but as the punishment inflicted by human beings alone. Job almost succeeds in describing the religious system of which he is the victim. He starts to take up the case openly against his accusers. Far from speaking their language, he makes a real critique of it, and this constitutes the most original part of the text of Job, a veritable revelation of traditional religion insofar as it is based on the scapegoating process.

In chapter 17 Job describes himself as a scapegoat:

> He has made me a byword of the people
> and I have become a public Tophet.
>
> (17:6 author's trans.)[1]

But immediately Job describes the beneficial effect produced by the example that his punishment constitutes for those making him a scapegoat. This is absolutely striking, for it is a matter of a religious and moral benefit that the persecutors derive from their persecution but that Job plainly refuses to take seriously.

> The upright are appalled[2] at this,
>   and the innocent stir themselves up against the godless.
> Yet the righteous hold to their way,
>   and they that have clean hands grow stronger and stronger.
>
> (17:8-9 NRSV)

The text is ironic. The suffering of innocent victims is a principle of moral and religious edification in the theology of the friends; it is a factor of good behavior for human beings, a miraculous tonic for the entire social body. It is the principle of religion in primitive societies as I was led to define it in *Violence and the Sacred*. It is this principle that is perpetuated in all sorts of institutions and phenomena that are no longer sacrificial in the strict sense, but that remain so in a broad sense, for example Greek tragedy, whose beneficial effect Aristotle defined as *katharsis,* sacrificial purification. This purification operates by the feelings of fear and pity that the victim inspires in the spectators, the victim who cannot *not* be justly struck by fate and who is abandoned by the spectators, even if they previously identify themselves with the victim. In the speeches of Job, to the contrary, there is no question that evils come from people and from the formidable aggravation of natural disasters combined with the effect of human wickedness. The members of the community need to make of Job a victim in order to feel good, in order to live more harmoniously with one another, in order to feel established in their faith. They are even ready to make of him, after his death, a semi-divine figure, and this is doubtless why we have the text of Job, whose initial form had to present a plague-ridden person who is shown to be guilty and finally divinized. But in Job's manner of speaking here, openly and ironically, there is something prodigious that relates to us the essence of a religion founded upon humanity and the social order, and that protests against it.

One may find a confirmation of this in a text of incredible audacity, where Job presents his friends as kinds of doctors, priests, manipulators of sacrifice. He treats them as grotesque shamans:

> As for you, you are only charlatans,
>   physicians in your own estimation.
>
> (13:4 JB)

And in a passage of closely related meaning he says:

> You would even cast lots over the fatherless,
> and bargain over your friend.
>
> (6:27 RSV)

In other words, the orphan and the friend are literally chosen as sacrificial victims. The psalms do much the same thing, but with much less audacity. The penitential psalms show us the righteous one surrounded by a circle of enemies dedicated to his downfall. These enemies are presented as monsters satiated with blood, as veritable beasts of prey, as bulls, as dogs. The power and formidable audacity of Job are that this vision of enemies is above all that of the three friends, who are intellectuals, the wise, the scholars, the theologians. Now they are perfectly in accord, Job tells us, with the pack of lynchers; their theology is of one piece with the violent unanimity of the persecuting pack.

We have texts where Job presents himself as condemned by God, other texts where he speaks of being condemned by God and humans, and finally others where he sees himself as condemned by human beings only. Among the latter are some extremely precious texts where he says, "I don't know what is happening to me." There are therefore, beside passages completely original, some hesitations, some oscillations from one point of view to another, and even some strange combinations of the two. I think that this is one of the reasons why the text is occasionally so bad. The copyists and the modern scholars have not truly understood what they had told of. But everything becomes clear enough if one takes hold of the primary thread, which is the theology of the scapegoat and the immense biblical movement toward the refusal of victimary religion.

Then the obscure passages become the most revealing—those passages where Job asks himself where he is, whether he is truly innocent or guilty. He vacillates in the certitude of his innocence; he is endangered by the acquiescence of the tragic hero—for example, the acquiescence of Oedipus who in the end acknowledges himself guilty of parricide and incest. This is a type of acquiescence that is reminiscent of what one today calls the brainwashing practiced by totalitarian societies.

> Though I am innocent, my own mouth would condemn me;
>   though I am blameless, he would prove me perverse.
> I am blameless; I do not know myself;
>   I loathe my life.
>
> I say, "I will forget my complaint;
>   I will put off my sad countenance and be of good cheer,"
> I become afraid of all my suffering,
>   for I know you will not hold me innocent.
> I shall be condemned;
>   why then do I labor in vain?
>
>   (9:20-21, 27-29 NRSV)

It is remarkable that the text of Job conveys to us a hesitation between theologies radically different. In contrast to Oedipus and modern victims of totalitarian processes, Job resists the all-powerful mimetic contagion that generally holds sway over the victims themselves, even if his language sometimes vacillates. The work of the text in the book of Job is somewhat comparable to that of the text of Oedipus, but it is much more explicit. In Oedipus the murder of Laos, of which Oedipus is accused, is presented initially and repeatedly as if it were a collective act, done by a number of people. And at the moment the shepherd arrives who is going to reveal the so-called guilt of Oedipus, Oedipus is still persuaded that there were many murderers and that he could not be guilty. "One man alone cannot take the place of all." In other words, he cannot be the scapegoat for all. He does not remember, the unfortunate man, that at the beginning of the play he said, "I suffer much more than you," because the king as representative of all the people suffers for all. Without a doubt Sophocles is ironic here, but he is ironic in a fashion almost esoteric. As a consequence, this question of multiple murderers is never posed again. Now this cannot be accidental. Sophocles tries to suggest, in a remote fashion, something analogous to that which the text of Job states explicitly, but he cannot really do it, for the Greek tradition does not permit him. The tragic victim finally resigns himself to the fate that befalls him; he or she never puts directly the question of the persecutors' system of representation.

But in the book of Job there is a fourth person who is less primitive, Elihu, who arrives to the rescue of traditional theology. Hebraists think the Elihu text is a later addition. They are probably right. The style is too different for it to be the product of the author of the dialogues. On the other hand, the youth of Elihu is even more significant inasmuch as the three friends present themselves as settled, even old, and above all persons who always appeal to the past, to the tradition of the ancestors, which is necessarily venerable and even indisputable because it is ancient and has always been followed. Bildad counsels Job to turn to the past (8:8-10). Eliphaz's counsel is similar (15:9-10, 17-19). It is evident that if the scapegoat system works well, one never sees a just person persecuted. Consequently, the friends are right; they have never seen the scandal of injustice, since wherever somebody is beset with misfortune, that person is guilty, and whenever somebody is guilty, that person is beset with misfortune.

So Elihu comes to the rescue and makes a claim on behalf of his youth. He rejects the past and the traditional theology, but he does not express anything else but traditional theology. In his discourse it is traditional theology that tries to renew itself. In reading a version of the book of Job that did not include a fourth friend, certain readers were scandalized by the arrogance of Job and added the personage of Elihu, a "new" theologian. He says exactly the same thing, but less well, as his three predecessors. He dwells on the function of testing that suffering can play, but his predecessors have already spoken of that.

This function of testing played by suffering is certainly not illusory, but only the individual who is subjected to suffering has the right to attribute this role to it. We do not have the right to make suffering a weapon against the neighbor. To make of this function of testing a justification of the suffering of others is to put oneself once again in the place of a savage God; it is to confound what is only a human judgment with a judgment of God.[3]

If I am right, if Elihu is a reinforcement for the traditional theology, there would thus be a mirror effect between the content of the text of Job and the elaboration of this same text. That is to say, the text must have been elaborated in the train of theological struggles that the content of the book of Job reflects.

Another battle is Job's struggle with himself. Now he says to himself, "If God treats me this way, how could I be innocent?" Then to the contrary, he dares follow the thread of his own thought to the end, that is, to deny completely the link between the fate of humans upon this earth and the fate the deity reserves for them. He will therefore denounce the principle of earthly retribution—of misfortune as sign of malediction and success as sign of election:

Why do the wicked live on,
    reach old age, and grow mighty in power?
Their children are established in their presence,
    and their offspring before their eyes.
Their houses are safe from fear,
    and no rod of God is upon them.
Their bull breeds without fail;
    their cow calves and never miscarries.
They send out their little ones like a flock,
    and their children dance around.
They sing to the tambourine and the lyre,
    and rejoice to the sound of the pipe.

> They spend their days in prosperity,
> and in peace they go down to Sheol.
>
> (21:7-13 NRSV)

It is this genre of discourse that is perceived as scandalous by the old theological guard, and it is the same discourse that makes of Job a sympathetic person in the eyes of a modernity seeking in him the prefiguration of its own atheism, of its own revolt against the evil or supposed indifference of any deity. Modernity remains faithful to the old theological guard in that it scarcely does more than invert its arguments.

The essential question is to know whether the deity confirms human judgments, whether God is only a machine registering the unanimous accord against victims. A God like that is literally satanic. In Jewish thought Satan is the adversary, the one who is an obstacle to us and accuses us. This term is borrowed, it seems, from juridical language. It does not seem originally to have designated a supernatural being. Psalm 109:6 designates as "satan" (Hebrew, śāṭān) the human antagonist, the implacable adversary of the one who speaks in the text and complains of being falsely accused. In this Psalm God is called as witness, but it is a matter of a purely human quarrel, perhaps a dialogue between two adversaries, perhaps a monologue—it doesn't matter. From the text it comes out clearly that the satan is the persecuting accuser who makes a man appear to be evil in order to ruin him in the eyes of everyone, including God himself:

> They say, "Appoint a wicked man against him;
> let an accuser stand on his right.
> When he is tried, let him be found guilty;
> let his prayer be counted as sin."
>
> (Ps. 109:6-7 NRSV)

There is no persecution, no violence, without the process of accusation, and without the success of this process the scapegoating vision does not triumph.

In the prologue of the book of Job the satan is sacralized, has become one of the sons of God, but he still plays strictly his role as accuser. He takes upon himself the role of Job's accuser before God, first in accusing Job of not fearing God and of not keeping himself from evil except for reasons of self-interest. He predicts that Job will turn against God and curse him, initially if he loses his possessions and subsequently if he becomes ill, if he is struck in his bones and flesh.

But the most satanic are the friends of Job. They do not understand their satanic role, their role as accusers; they do not understand that their religion is founded upon the hidden scapegoat, like all mythic religion, that is, all human religion. They see only guilty victims and punished criminals. Their system functions without missing a beat and is never belied by experience. Without any fear of deceiving himself Eliphaz cries out:

> Think now, who that was innocent ever perished?
>   Or where were the upright cut off?
> As I have seen, those who plow iniquity
>   and sow trouble reap the same.
> By the breath of God they perish,
>   and by the blast of his anger they are consumed.
>
> (4:7-9 NRSV)

They see a perfect correlation between pain and guilt, and nothing can disabuse them of this. They cannot see someone distressed, struck down, without thinking he is like that in all justice. When they attack their victim, they never have the least doubt that this victim is guilty. They do nothing else than apply that universal magic causality so well defined by the ethnologists. They transpose on the level of human thought something still fairly close to animal life, where one cannot see a fellow creature injured, sick, or handicapped in some way or the other without attacking it, in order to rid the species of it. As in certain primitive tribes, when a death or a sickness strikes, a search begins for the one who is guilty, and of course the guilty party is discovered. One lives then in a world without sick persons, without infirm people, without sufferers, and above all without innocent people wrongly condemned—which is still somewhat like the perfection of animal life.

The friends of Job believe that their God punishes only the

wicked because they do not understand the victimary mechanism of which they are the tools. Job understands it because he is the victim of this mechanism, but in contrast to so many other victims, he does not accept the verdict that condemns him. Something in his mind surges up against this extraordinary alliance made up of the misfortune that strikes him from the external world, presumed to be the hand of God, and the universal tendency to consider this misfortune as merited.

Job is thus alone against all the others; he has need of an ally, a defender. Will he search for one among humans who do not hold against him the prejudices of his friends, of his wife, of everyone in his circle? Since he has God against him, so it seems, will he turn more than ever toward other humans? No. He understands that he can obtain nothing from men. Men are all on the side of the God who exacts vengeance. They are satanic because they play the role of advocates of God as the accuser of humans (13:7-8).

Unable to find a defender among human beings, Job has no choice but to address himself to God. It is there that the Judaic religious genius shows through so brilliantly: Job addresses God against every probability, so it seems, for everyone agrees in saying that God himself punishes him, that God himself puts him on trial. Very often he bends before it, and the appeal that he launches is so contrary to good sense (even he himself thinks) that it sounds almost ridiculous:

> Even now, in fact, my witness is in heaven,
>   and he that vouches for me is on high.
> My friends scorn me;
>   my eye pours out tears to God,
> that he would maintain the right of a mortal with God,
>   as one does for a neighbor.
>
> (16:19-21 NRSV)

In other words, God, another God, a defender God of victims, would assume the defense of humans against God. Alongside the God who hears only the satans, the human or supernatural accusers, there must be a God capable of understanding Job's defense. Since he does not respond to Job and since there is no one in human society who willingly takes up the defense of the innocent one unjustly overwhelmed, it is necessary that God himself take charge and play a role contrary to the one imposed on him by the friends. He must become the defender. If God could make himself human, in other words, he would defend Job rather than prosecuting him.

In a parallel passage (19:25) the word *gō'ēl* appears, usually rendered "redeemer." This is a technical term of Israelite law (cf. Num. 35:19). It is often applied to the Messiah in rabbinic Judaism. Initially, it designated the defender of the oppressed, a sort of advocate.

In a certain sense, this could not be God since it is precisely God who accuses Job, yet the defender could be none other than God. We see the text hesitate between two conceptions of God, one that comes from the immemorial sacrificial base and one that will vanish in the Gospels. And I think that the notion of the Paraclete (*paraklētos* in Greek means "the advocate," "the defender"), the idea of the Spirit-Paraclete in the Gospel of John that is always present with the disciples or with all victims unjustly accused, constitutes the development of what is found in seminal form in the book of Job. The Spirit is what basically prevents us from mythologizing victims and from believing the argument of the three friends who confront Job. It is the Spirit that continues the work of the text of Job.

The conclusion of the book of Job is not at the high level of these texts where Job affirms that he has a defender. The conclusion does not betray them, but it does not succeed in defining the God in question and speaking of him as the Gospels will speak. It takes refuge in the unfathomable and incomprehensible character of the deity. But there is all the same that extraordinary passage where God says that Job has spoken well and not his friends. But much more than that, for the believer the response of God to Job is a response that the end of the book does not succeed in giving. For God gives satisfaction to Job by dying on the cross, that is, by saying to him in effect, "I am really on the side of the victims; I suffer everything that you suffer, and I suffer it in such a manner and in such a public way that I will eventually deprive all the false friends of the theological arguments that have served them so well until now. I am breaking their marvelously circular mechanism of self-satisfaction, which permits them to feel perfectly justified in the midst of the worst horrors of which they themselves are accomplices, if not the perpetrators. This sign of the cross will reveal all the disorder and horror of the world and perhaps even temporarily contribute to it, where order was reigning in appearance only. The true human adventure is this: With the discovery of a God completely other, the defender of victims, the Paraclete, I am establishing humanity.''

Job spoke well in announcing this ''new'' God, while his friends spoke badly in having defended the sinister old theological rubbish.

Finally, I return to the traditional interpretations of Job. The problem of Job has always been posed as if it was a matter of explicating the enigma of unjust suffering or of resolving the problem of evil. This approach to defining the subject of the book perpetuates the error of the three friends, and of all those who ostracize Job. As already noted, this is also partially the error of Job himself. This way of stating the problem of evil in general leads to not distinguishing two types of evil that the book of Job requires us to distinguish: evil that comes directly from human beings (the ostracism Job suffers) and evil that does not come directly from human beings and may thus come from God (the loss of children, the accidental loss of goods, the skin disease). The book of Job speaks almost exclusively of the evils that come from humans and that are the evils par excellence for the victim. To speak of evil in general is to render inseparable and insurmountable the two types of evil: God is not only seen as the human acceptance of misfortunes befalling one's neighbors, but also as the one who contributes to their miseries.

So the usual interpretation remains faithful to the theology of the three friends, and the indictment of it must be even more radical, for modern history abundantly confirms what the text already tells us: The evils due to human agency are the most terrible and must engage our attention more than the evils produced by nature.

This confirmation comes from modern science. Science would never have developed if humans had persevered in the belief of Job's friends, if they had continued to persecute victims each time someone suffered misfortune among them or each time they themselves suffered misfortune. They would never have caught a glimpse of the great modern projects, the modern will to improve the human lot by all sorts of developments—scientific, technical, judicial, political, social, etcetera. These developments demand that magical causality be renounced. They would never have invented medicine, for example, if, faced with the sores of Job, they had persevered in the idea that he was justly punished and that it would thwart God to try to heal him.

The Gospels not only plainly reveal the religious fabrication of the victimary mechanism but also disconnect the two types of evil more radically than does the book of Job. In this way they permit the world to undertake the type of project which from that point on is truly its own. All the effort of human beings must bear upon their relations with their neighbors. The Gospels formally deny the idea that illnesses or infirmities are the divine punishment of a sin committed by the sick person or by his or her parents. The Gospels explicitly deny that accidents, the collapse of a tower, for instance, that produce numerous victims are divine punishments.

The Gospels do not establish humans in enterprises, economic, scientific, or whatever. They have other concerns. But they cannot do what they do for victims and against magical thought without removing the obstacles that until then impeded this type of development. And if these developments have not improved the life of all as much as they could have if they had been controlled by the gospel outlook, it still is not any less evident that we owe these developments, first of all, to what I call the "gospel way-clearing."

Today we are more than ever in a position to understand the extent to which the evils that come from humankind are the most terrible. It suffices, indeed, that the savage blindness of the scapegoat process is weakening thanks to the Bible and to the gospel, so that we may succeed in eliminating or attenuating evils that previously appeared to be without remedy in as much as we imagined them as the work of some cruel deity or, amounting to the same thing, of some implacable nature. We are learning more and more to master these evils. We are healing the sores of Job.

It has surely required long centuries to obtain this result. I know well that very great evils have simultaneously come upon the scene, but they witness by the same token to a new liberty among human beings. The Bible and the Gospels are not responsible for the human abuse of what they have given to the world. In other words, both the increase in evils afflicting us and their diminution vindicates God in revealing the purely human origin of these evils, for these evils are always susceptible to being eliminated by humans. Once they escape the theology of the three friends, human beings master the necessary means if they only have the will to do so.

To pose the question of evil as though evil were in every case a matter of one problem, that is, anything that affects my own precious self, making it suffer, or simply irritating me, is not to pose the question of Job. This self-concern is rather what I would call the metaphysics of the tourist, who conceives that his or her presence in this world is essentially like a deluxe voyage. He or she happily admires the lovely terrains and sunsets, is moved by the monuments left by past civilizations. He or she deplores modern ugliness and complains of the general insipidness, because now everything resembles everything else and there are no more differences. He or she becomes noisily indignant about the poverty encountered, is perpetually engaged in head-shaking, like Job's friends. But above all this tourist complains about the organization of the voyage and is going to transmit a complaint to the management. He or she is always ready to return his or her ticket, and the expression ''return one's ticket'' is typical of those who travel for their own pleasure or who go to a spectacle. This mentality of the frustrated tourist produces vehement curses concerning what is called the problem of evil. If God exists, how can he tolerate the evil present in the world? If God exists, he can be only the supercop, and in his mode of being as supercop he could at least protect us against the many disagreeable incidents of our passage through the world.

One might counter that this is an easy irony that forgets the principal evil. For even if this tourist mentality disappeared and if human beings cooperated, if they even renounced their quarrels in order to work together for the building of a better world—still in all, they would be mortal. Death is the insurmountable wall over which human beings cannot pass; the ameliorations of which I have spoken, whether already achieved or yet to come, are still but little beside this terrible, this irremediable evil, this supreme evil that is death. Even the happiest of humans, those who do not scratch their sores on Job's ashheap, exist in fear of death. Science will never conquer death, and no humanism will protect us from it.

But what does Christianity say on this subject? It says that death is conquered by the Christ. It says that the Christ was resurrected three days after the Passion and that we too can rise again thanks to him. It says, in sum, that those who are capable of refusing sacrifices and their violence completely enough, perfectly enough, to die like the Christ, escape from all conceivable evils, even from the worst evil, which is death. Christianity tells us perhaps that humans die only because they kill. Satan is the inventor of death because he is the inventor of murder.

It is evident, of course, that this belief cannot be deduced in a rigorous scientific fashion from what we have just said about the refutation of the theology of the three friends. There is an absolute rupture here. But at the same time one sees how the understanding of the vicious cycle of violence, the immemorial prison of humanity, and the hope of leaving this cycle can and must open the way to the idea that the gospel of Christ involves a total rupture with all forms of violence, including the most terrible—death itself. It seems to me, starting with Job, that the idea of eternal life in this Christian sense comes from this rupture with violence, and that it holds nothing in common with a hypothetical effort to elude the consequences of our present finitude. To the contrary, this belief holds that everything that is mortal in the human condition stems from the human propensity to commit murder.

This idea is not unrelated, I believe, to the marvels and terrors of modern science, to the world, unmasterable perhaps, yet admirable, that human beings have constructed in our time. And according to whether one regards this world with or without faith, the contradictory sayings of the Christ about the world to come, that is, about the world where the gospel is spread—our world—become all equally true, even if they contradict one another. Without the eyes of faith, our world is indeed one where there are multiplied signs and wonders so grand that they could lead even the elect astray. With eyes of faith this same world is one where the disciples, according to the Christ, will perform signs and miracles much more astonishing than his own. In the world where the vicious cycle that imprisoned Job is opened up, everything becomes allusion to the Resurrection!

CHAPTER 13

JOB AND THE GOD OF VICTIMS

James G. Williams

The most recent tendency in biblical scholarship has been to "save the text" of the book of Job by viewing the speeches of God (chapters 38–41) as integral to the original work.[1] One interpreter, Robert Gordis, has argued that the Elihu speeches were composed by the poet at a later stage in his life in a manner similar to Goethe's writing of the second part of *Faust*. I myself have argued for the literary unity of Job.[2]

I still hold to the literary unity of Job, but I now think it is a mistake to "save the appearances," or save the text in this case, by struggling to find a vision, message, or understanding in the God-speeches that both responds adequately to Job's predicament and is acceptable to modern or postmodern theological rationales. What I will argue in this paper is that in the dialogues Job's "sociological" commentary on his experience as a sufferer is accompanied by occasional visions of a God of victims who would stand with and for him and, by implication, redeem the sorry state of humankind if human beings and their societies could be transformed by coming to know this God. However, this glimpse of an adequate theology, a theology of the God of victims that would not base itself on sacrifice and scapegoating but on a divine-human community of justice and love, is not carried forward in the theophany. In God's speeches he seems to ignore or evade the question of justice that Job poses. Contrary to the drift of recent Job interpretation, I would call this poor theology.

My argument is informed by René Girard's theory of religion and culture and his application of this theory to the book of Job. The limits imposed on this paper do not permit a full discussion of his theory. However, I will give a capsule summary of its main lineaments in order to alert the reader to the type of interpretive analysis that is forthcoming.[3]

The key terms are *mimetic desire, mimetic rivalry, victim, sacrifice,* and *scapegoat.* Girard argues that human violence has its roots in *mimetic desire.* Contrary to Freud, Girard holds that there is *not* an inherent drive to possess the parent of the opposite sex. What *is* inherent as the structure of the human creature's brain and total system is the drive to imitate and to acquire what is imitated (acquisitive mimesis). Where sexual rivalry with a parent or adult model does arise, it is a function of the desire to imitate a feared and respected model. This desire puts the subject in a double-bind. The mandate of the model is "imitate me"; yet since this sort of desire is *acquisitive,* if one were to imitate the model completely one would be and have what the model is and has. In other words, the radical realization of mimesis would entail displacing or eliminating the model/rival.

So it is that mimetic desire always carries with it the potential of *mimetic rivalry,* which operates in a nonconscious manner. One's chief model is always the chief rival, and of course there may be any number of other rivals who likewise seek the object of the model's desire as it is known or imagined. The flip side of this is that one's rival is always a model in some sense.

Mimetic rivalry would result in a mimetic crisis, complete social chaos, without some means of breaking out of it and regulating it. The universal tendency of human groups has been to regulate it by engaging in spontaneous or ritualized violence against a *victim,* a person or animal to which the community imputes its ills. By the collective action of all against one, mimetic conflict is, in principle, gathered up and delivered over in the sins that are placed upon the victim. As we shall see in Job, *unanimity* is one of the key structural features of the generative process of violence and sacrifice. The community is without full awareness of what is happening, for such awareness would undercut the justificatory myth and its ritual base.

Since human communities maintain their order through a system of differences, this established way of differentiating everything important is at the rock bottom of any language and culture. The system is threatened by violence within the group that arises from mimetic desire and rivalry. As already noted, the *sacrifice* of a human or an animal victim is one of the two primary ways of controlling a momentary reversion to the chaos of violence and maintaining the system of differences. The other primary way is through finding a *scapegoat,* known to the Greeks as the *pharmakos.* The scapegoat, taken here in a broad sense not restricted to the text in Leviticus 16, refers to a human or animal victim to whom is ascribed potential or actual disasters befalling the community. The two, sacrifice and scapegoat, converge in the situation of an expulsion followed by a lynching.

Prohibitions are the interdictions whose function is to prevent the repetition of the mimetic crisis. Ritual is a mock mimetic crisis; it undoes the prohibition by representing the crisis, and then it reaffirms the prohibition through resolution in sacrifice. Thus in a partially concealed fashion ritual and sacrifice perpetuate the event of victimage that overcame the social crisis in the first place. Myths and theologies are typically rationalizations of an initial act of violence that has become ritualized. Prohibition, ritual, and myth function to enable the group to camouflage the violence from itself. In fact, it is quite common for the victim to be apotheosized as a god.

The foregoing gives the essentials, at least, for understanding how and why Girard reads the book of Job as he does in *Job: The Victim of His People.* We shall now see how my version of Girard's theory works out in interpreting Job. I will first survey some key elements in the dialogues and God-speeches, then I will sketch some theological implications of the argument.

Job, Friends, and God

The Dialogues

The ambiguity of Job's protest resides in his own ambivalence: God is the divine enemy who persecutes him, yet also the witness who will defend him.

Job had been respected, even venerated. As Girard has indicated, the text presents him as a kind of idol. Others waited for him to speak as they wait for the autumn rain. They even watched his face for a reading of his emotions:

> I smiled on them when they had no confidence;
> and the light of my countenance they did not extinguish.
>
> (29:24 NRSV)

He has been, in other words, a model for others—wealthy, influential, respected for his piety. Others desired what he desired, for as one who "sat as chief," who "lived like a king" (29:25), what he wanted and intended was what others wanted and intended.

Now everything is changed. Job is like a king, and his fate is comparable to that of sacred kings in tribal settings and in various royal rites.[4] His fortunes have been reversed, and he sits on the ashheap as an object of the community's derision and scorn. Who and what has brought about this disastrous change? In an apparent cause-and-effect statement, Job attributes his condition to God's action and then speaks of his outcast status:

> Because he [presumably God] has loosed my cord
>   and afflicted me,
> they have cast off restraint in my presence.
> On my right hand the rabble rise up,
>   they expel me [Hebrew, "my feet"],
>   and they cast up against me their ways of destruction.
>
> (30:11-12 author's trans.)

Likewise in chapter 19 there is an apparent causal connection between divine action (vv. 6-12) and the response of his family and community (vv. 13-22).

The assumption that there is a divinely established network of retributive violence separating the righteous and the wicked is one Job shares with the friends. Eliphaz contends that evildoers perish by the breath of God (4:9), and the wicked "writhe in pain all their days" (15:20 NRSV), with "terrifying sounds" in their ears (15:21 NRSV). Indeed, they "wander abroad for bread" (15:23 NRSV), for "they have stretched forth their hand against God" (15:25 NRSV). Bildad offers a graphic description of the terrors that beset the wicked, who "are torn from the tent in which they trusted, and are brought to the king of terrors" (18:14 NRSV), that is, the lord of the underworld. This is the fate of "the dwellings of the ungodly, such is the place of those who do not know God" (18:21 NRSV).

Job, through the mimetic process, draws the conclusion that the friends (i.e., his community, the tradition) are right about the way the world actually operates. And insofar as it operates in this way, God is responsible for it and must be unjust, for he, Job, is innocent. Even if he could have a trial, or at least a hearing, he doesn't believe it would proceed fairly. God, the judge, would "[crush] me with a tempest" (9:17 NRSV).

> Though I am innocent, my own mouth would condemn me;
>   though I am blameless, he would prove me perverse.
> I am [innocent]; I do not know myself;
>   I loathe my life.
>
> (9:20-21 NRSV)

With this sort of protest Job separates himself from the social unanimity that the social order demands (and that is never far below the surface, even in supposedly enlightened democratic societies). Girard quotes a passage from Aeschylus's *Eumenides* where the Erinyes say,

> May joy be exchanged for joy
> in a common love
> and may we hate with a single soul;
> for this is man's great remedy.[5]

The common human remedy is that we join "in a common love" and especially that "we hate with a single soul." The Bible by and large does not accept accommodation to the order of generative violence, but the friends, even though they speak for an advanced wisdom tradition, reflect an uneasiness that shows the principle of sacrificial violence is not far below the surface. Does Job possess the divine wisdom of Adam (15:7-8)? No, he does away with the piety, the fear of God (15:4) that undergirds the sacred order of things. He keeps "to the old way that the wicked have trod" (22:15 NRSV).

Job, like Oedipus the king, is seen by his social order as taking the ancient way of the wicked that leads to a sacrificial death. Oedipus, however, "is a *successful* scapegoat because he is never recognized as such,"[6] and he concurs in the judgment upon himself. This is what the social order seeks to inculcate, for the unanimity of the generative mechanism will ideally include even the victim's own complicity in the judgment made. If the sacrificial pattern is submerged and rationalized in totalitarian ideology, as in the modern period, then victims will not only concur with the judgment but confess their sin publicly.[7] In this regard, Oedipus is an ancient mythopoetic archetype of the confession in a modern totalitarian trial. But Job, as a *failed* scapegoat, "derails the mythology that is meant to envelop him, by maintaining his own point of view" rather than acceding to the unanimity that the friends wish to impose upon him.[8]

The theology of the friends, whose assumptions Job accepts and whose conclusions he deplores, is viewed by Girard as a projection of the social order that is maintained through the generative process of the sacrificial mechanism and its operations. That is to say, the God of the friends and the God Job accuses of injustice is really the socially transcendent symbol of the generative structure that operates, as I have briefly indicated, in the dynamics of mimesis, victimization, sacrifice, and scapegoating. When dealing with such a generative structure, we would not expect the text to spell it out in our own terms, but there are some definite signs of the connection of God and social order.

One sign is Job's sarcastic reply after Zophar has spoken for the first time, "No doubt you are the people, and wisdom will die with you" (12:2 NRSV). This is clearly a statement of the principle *vox populi vox Dei*. Continuing in an ironic vein, Job conflates in two sentences the legitimation of the arguments of the friends:

> Wisdom is with the aged,
>   and understanding in length of days.
> With God are wisdom and might;
>   he has counsel and understanding.

> (12:12-13 RSV)

The elders and God, the elders—including undoubtedly the sages—representing God: This is the bulwark of the social order. Job then goes on to describe the putative wisdom of God as really arbitrary, tyrannical power that is just as prone to create disorder as order (12:14-25). This is the dark side of the generative order—

perpetual conflict and violence. The way of controlling it is also, of course, given by this God, given through the wisdom of the elders.

The second sign has to do with the kind of metaphors used for the enemies that Job says God has sent against him, enemies that from the friends' standpoint are cohorts that torment the wicked. When Eliphaz asserts that "the destroyer will come upon" the wicked (15:21 NRSV), he probably has in mind a human agent, another unscrupulous one who follows the ancient path of the wicked. When Zophar speaks of God's fierce anger, whose result is that "the possessions of his house will be carried away" (20:28 RSV), attacks by human groups or armies are meant. This is probably an allusion to what happened to Job when the Sabeans and Chaldeans attacked. In other instances, mythical allusions to celestial armies of God are made. Job speaks of being struck by the "arrows of the Almighty" (6:4 NRSV) and cries out that "his archers surround me . . . He bursts upon me again and again; he rushes at me like a warrior" (16:13*a*, 14 NRSV). In chapter 16 the imagery of divine armies is intermingled with attacks by Job's own people:

> They have gaped at me with their mouths;
> > they have struck me insolently on the cheek,
> > they mass themselves together against me.
> God gives me up to the ungodly,
> > and casts me into the hands of the wicked.
>
> > > (16:10-11 NRSV)

"They mass themselves together against me": This is what is happening to Job. He is the object of collective violence, and the rather fluid movement between the image of human mobs and divine gendarmes, which are thugs from Job's point of view, is a tip-off that the movement of the social order against the scapegoat and God's action against the wicked are two ways of talking about the same thing. The God persona of the theophany seems to confirm this connection in sarcastically instructing Job to deal with the wicked as God does if he is up to it, namely, humble, trample, and bury them (40:11-13; see below, under "The God Speeches").

In these passages depicting attacks on Job, attacks that come only upon evildoers according to the friends, the implied model for the multiplicity of enemies is the human mob. ''The seething crowd is the perfect vehicle for the divine vengeance. It hurls itself at the victim and tears him to pieces; all the participants share the same terrible appetite for violence.''[9] An example of this appetite for violence is the Dionysiac *diasparagmos* or ritual dismemberment, as seen, for example, in the murder of Pentheus in *The Bacchae* of Euripides.

The model of a crowd lynching a victim, portrayed so starkly in *The Bacchae* and avoided in Sophocles' *Oedipus Rex* by Oedipus's own complicity in his victimization, may also inform the speeches of the friends. In the dialogues their so-called comfort takes the form of instruction and dispute that erupts increasingly into sarcastic attacks, until finally, in the third cycle of speeches, Eliphaz makes the accusation that has been in their minds all along: ''Is not your wickedness great?'' (22:5 NRSV). He follows this charge with a list of specific iniquities (22:6-9). Recognizing this verbal equivalent of lynching, Job cries out:

> How long will you torment me,
>   and break me in pieces with words?
>
> (19:2 NRSV)

''Break me in pieces'' (*tĕdakkĕ'ûnanî*) is a form of a verb used a number of times in Job. In fact, Eliphaz will use it later in accusing Job of crushing the arms of the fatherless (22:9), and he employed it earlier in an impersonal plural form as he described the short, miserable, ignorant existence of human beings, who ''are crushed like a moth'' (4:19 NRSV). And although a different verb is used at 9:17, the same metaphorical configuration is evidently involved in Job's contention that God ''crushes me with a tempest'' (NRSV). In any case, with their speeches the friends justify the violence—they sacralize it. ''The insults and meanness are metamorphosed into the grandiose accomplishments of a supernatural mission.''[10]

God as the social order, the sacred community, is what Job presupposes but cannot accept. He protests against it, and in some lucid moments he distinguishes God from society. This is when Job affirms the God of victims who will vindicate him. There are

moments when Job remembers the God of creation and reminds
him, "You have granted me life and steadfast love, and your care
has preserved my spirit" (10:12 NRSV), but he immediately falls
into the accusatory complaint that "bold as a lion you hunt
me . . . You renew your witnesses against me" (10:16*a*, 17*a*
NRSV). In keeping with the judicial metaphors of chapter 9, he
wishes for an arbiter (9:33). Later, in one of his most bitter and
graphic descriptions of the way God and man attack him, he pours
out a cry for vengeance that really turns into a momentary
affirmation of faith:

> O earth, do not cover my blood,
>   let my outcry find no resting place.
> Even now, in fact, my witness is in heaven,
>   and he that vouches for me is on high.
> My friends scorn me;
>   my eye pours out tears to God,
> that he would maintain the right of a mortal with God,
>   and that of humans with their neighbors [author's trans. of
>   v. 21*b*]
> For when a few years have come
>   I shall go the way from which I shall not return.
>
>   (16:18-22 NRSV)

Verse 21 has posed difficulties for translators, but the sense of the
Hebrew text seems clear enough to me. The Hebrew, if literally
rendered, "The right of a man with God" and "[of] a man [with
respect], to his neighbor," simply refers to the totality of
relationships in which God maintains compassionate justice and
stands on the side of the victim.

The passage nonetheless betrays a certain duality of God, as
Girard points out.[11] Job's blood on the earth is a sign that his divine
and human persecutors have done their work. Now the God of
victims is ranged against the God of the persecutors. However, a
second text does not bear the same ambiguity of God's duality:

> But as for me, I know that my Vindicator [*gō'ălî*] lives,
>   and afterwards he will arise upon the earth.
> And after my skin is thus destroyed,
>   then [even] without my flesh I shall see God.

> And the one whom I myself see taking my part,
>   my eyes will see not as an alien.
> My heart fails within me!
>
> (19:25-27 author's trans.)

My own view is that verses 26 and 27 have been difficult for commentators because of theological controversies, not because of the condition of the text. Without one word, *zot* in verse 26*a*, everything else would be intelligible and grammatically correct. I have resorted to the old solution of Buttenweiser's in changing *wĕʾaḥar ʿôrî niqqĕpû-zōʾt* to *niqqāp zōʾt*, "and after my skin is destroyed in this manner" (or thus). As problematic as that might be, I would simply emphasize that everything else falls into place nicely—*unless* one feels compelled to deny any hint of resurrection from the dead (so many Jewish and Christian biblical critics) or to deny any christological import of the passage (so most Jewish and many Christian critics). Doctrinal and ideological interests have preoccupied many exegetes. Although other translations than mine are certainly possible, I would prefer to leave these other issues open and note Job's note of hope in looking to the God who is *gōʾēl*, vindicator or avenger of the rights of the oppressed.

Girard says these two passages are a high point to which Job does not return. This is not the case. In his longing to find God and make his case before him, Job again affirms the justice of the God of victims:

> I would learn what he would answer me,
>   and understand what he would say to me.
> Would he contend with me in the greatness of his power?
>   No; but he would give heed to me.
> There an upright person could reason with him,
>   and I should be acquitted forever by my judge.
>
> (23:5-7 NRSV)

This passage is particularly important for its indication of the "good mimesis" of the God of victims. Acquisitive mimesis involves a network of power relations in which the subject, imitating the imagined desire of the model of authority, seeks to possess what the model/rival has. The ultimate result, if carried to its conclusion, is the elimination of the model/rival or of the subject's self-identity— or *both* if the conflict takes the form of savage revolt or revolution. In this moment of lucidity Job turns momentarily from bitter complaint to envisage how God would not be concerned with exercising his power but would listen to his case and give heed to him (*hû' yāśim bî*, "he himself would place [his heart or mind] with me").

So these three texts, 16:18-22, 19:25-27, and 23:5-7, go beyond Job's protestations of suffering and innocence to give a glimpse of a God of victims. As such, these brief tableaus hold the potential of subverting the mimetic certainties of the scapegoat mechanism, but they are not sustained.

The God-Speeches

Girard views the God-speeches as an addition to the work that simply represents a God of persecutors taking refuge in nature. This God does not deal with the question of Job's innocence or Job's relations with his community—"the best way of neutralizing the subversive force of Job's speech."[12] The God of chapters 38–41 avoids the dilemma of human and divine-human relationships by taking refuge in the natural world, lecturing Job at length on the wonders of the cosmos.

> This God demonstrates his strength so as not to have to use it. He is no longer the God of the friends, who was openly exercising his terror against scapegoats [this clause my trans. of the French]. He no longer brandishes the celestial armies against the rebel.
>
> He resorts to cunning and wins his case.[13]

Contrary to Girard, I think the same author wrote both the dialogues and the theophany. This position now commands a consensus in biblical scholarship.[14] Perhaps Girard's powerful case concerning the God of the God-speeches should and will induce us to reexamine this consensus. In any case, certain stylistic features have led me to view chapters 38–41 as integral to the book of Job. Recently, in my 1984 article, I discussed two matters that are pertinent to this question. The first is the aesthetic argument of Robert Alter's essay on Job that chapter 38 is deliberately constructed as a contrast to Job's lament.[15] As I put Alter's conclusion, in my own words, "God's pulsating, expansive, life-affirming display of wild cosmic wonders stands in marked opposition to Job's wish to turn inward to the narrow and safe confines of death's darkness."[16] The second is the use of the narrative dialogue formula, "and he answered . . . and he said," used consistently in both dialogues and God-speeches (in the latter, 38:1; 40:1, 3, 6; 42:1). This textual fact is a small matter, and in any case a redactor could have added it, although this hypothetical redactor would have been consistent to a fault. This consideration touches at the least upon another: If the concluding chapters of Job were added to the dialogues, the work was done with great skill.

In an essay that appeared over a decade ago, I discussed six points of connection between the theophany and the dialogues:[17] God's coming in a tempest (9:17/38:1), God as hunter of prey and the image of the lion (10:16; 16:12/38:39), God's strength and the image of the horse (9:12/39:22), the Behemoth and Job (10:8/40:15), hedging Job about and establishing order (3:23; 7:12/38:8), and an implied comparison of Job and the wild ass (6:5/39:5). To these we may add God's command to the "man" (*geber*) who curses the time of his birth (3:3) to gird up his loins and answer some questions like a *geber* (38:3).

In short, from a stylistic standpoint there is almost nothing to prevent seeing the two segments of the book as a unity and much to argue for it. The perspective and content of the speeches are another matter. Here I would agree with Girard about the answer of God from the whirlwind, but I think the author took a "wrong turn"; he was attempting to find the "excluded middle" between the God of persecutors and the God of victims, but he was unable to manage it. This excluded middle would have been an encounter showing Job to be implicated in his society's quest for victims, which is necessary for the perpetuation of the scapegoat mechanism, while also affirming Job's integrity. This encounter that I imagine would not save the text but the Job of the text, the victim who has cried out to God and his friends.

The God of the theophany is different from the God of the dialogues—the friends or community writ large—in two respects. One is that his concern with the cosmos shows that humankind is not "originally" in the picture. Job (humankind) sees and identifies himself through hearing and responding to God, and to that extent there is an ancient Israelite dialogical element in the God-speeches that could become the basis of a new revelation, a disclosure of a new being of God, man, and language. However, this dialogical element is undercut by the *rivalry* of God with Job. Job had better get the message: "Whoever confronts me I requite, / For everything under the heavens is mine" (41:11 Habel's trans.[18]). Let him who is able draw near to Behemoth with his sword (40:19)—for of course only God is able!

The second way in which the God speaking to Job is different from the God of the friends is that he does not condemn Job and account him as one of the wicked—though wicked there are, who must be eliminated. Thus the poem takes away with one hand what it gives with the other. God does not exonerate Job and demands that he confess his ignorance, but God allows him to be exonerated and confirms him in the end. Nonetheless, God demands of Job that he eliminate the wicked as—of course!—only God can.

In a passage often cited as proof that the theophany does not omit questions of justice and morality, God actually reverts to the old sacred tradition that the friends represent.

> Deck yourself with majesty and dignity;
>   clothe yourself with glory and splendor.
> Pour out the overflowings of your anger,
>   and look on all who are proud, and abase them.
> Look on all who are proud, and bring them low;
>   and [crush][19] the wicked where they stand.
> Hide them all in the dust together;
>   bind their faces in the world below [or in the hidden place].
>   (40:10-12 NRSV)

Habel has commented that "Yahweh's second speech opens with a challenge for Job to demonstrate that he has the power to govern the earth with an arm as glorious and mighty as El's" (40:7-14). He goes on to say that "Job is to exhibit the capacities of El by unleashing his wrath (*'ap*), abasing the proud and crushing the wicked."[20] He points out that "the 'furies' . . . and 'wrath/ anger' . . . of God are associated with his day of judgment on the wicked (Job 20:28, 21:30)." Job is called upon to "demonstrate his capacity to complete the punitive process and deliver the wicked as captives to the underworld according to the principles Job was advocating."[21]

Now the question I would ask is this: What is it that really distinguishes God in this passage from the friends and their God in the dialogue? Zophar has already described "the wicked's portion from God":

> To fill their belly to the full
>   God will send his fierce anger into them,
>   and rain it upon them [into their flesh]
> They will flee from an iron weapon;
>   a bronze arrow will strike them through.
> It is drawn forth and comes out of their body,
>   and the glittering point comes out of their gall;
>   terrors come upon them.
>   (20:23-25 NRSV; v. 23*c* author's trans.)

The God of justice who judges the righteous and the wicked, dividing them into those to be rewarded and those to be punished, is a belief that may be seen as an advance on more primitive notions of the sacred, especially if it validates a tradition of law and wisdom. However, it was easy to turn that very belief against Job by making him one of those who "keep to the old way which wicked men have trod." Moreover, the God of the theophany exhibits a certain relish in describing what the one to be identified as El does to the wicked. The literary style is a good example of what Robert Alter has described as "intensification" in poetic parallelism.[22] Not only will the El-figure look on the proud and abase them, he will crush them where they stand. And not only will he crush them where they stand, he will hide their bodies in the ground where they cannot be found. A good job, done with great gusto!

A good job, but beside the point. The God who is willing to acknowledge to Job that if he really were able to perform as the great divine judge and warrior, "your own right hand will give you victory" (40:14)—this God does not hear Job's cry for the God of victims, the God of compassionate justice, the God who vindicates the rights of the oppressed, the God who listens to the petitioner. This is rather the God that delights in describing what he will do to the wicked.

So I read the theology of the God-speeches as poor theology. It is a definite but very ambiguous attempt to respond to the good sociology of the dialogues—to the awareness of the human condition that Job articulates and to the few occasions of insight when Job cries out to a God that is not identical with the sacred, is not the social order as transcendent reality. Openness to a new disorder, a new reality of God, human beings, and language, is undercut by the rampant rivalry with which God confronts Job. God does not declare Job guilty, but it is as though he wishes to convince Job and make him a kind of human partner in crushing and eliminating the wicked. The God of the theophany loves the animals who are beautiful in their wildness, but his underlying savagery is great.

Theological Implications

The Importance of Girard's Theory for
Biblical Studies and Theology

Girard's theory of religion and culture may turn out to be the most important explanation of the human condition since the work of Freud, who in many respects is Girard's own model and rival. And his hermeneutics of biblical and literary texts may turn out to be the single most important influence since the contribution of Rudolph Bultmann. In many ways, I think, his hermeneutics surpasses the work of Bultmann, for it is grounded in a theory of the human condition that carries with it both insight into human behavior and an impulse to social action.

Of course, his theory is controversial in a number of ways. First, there is the question of an "original" event at the origin of language and culture. Second, there is the issue of a methodology that attempts a global explanation of human behavior. These first two sources of controversy have to do with the current disfavor for attempts to "explain" anything at a meta-level and achieve some sort of "closure" in terms of theory and methodology. Two other issues have to do more directly with Girard's message or counter-vision to the human condition that he delineates: language's instability and entrapment, and the possibility of liberation through the biblical revelation of the God of victims, and in particular through the Logos that is the defender of victims (contrary to Heidegger's analysis of the Logos); and the central position of the Gospels in both his culture criticism and his biblical hermeneutics.

Whether or not one agrees or disagrees totally with Girard, his work will have to be taken into account. Yes, there is the voice that says biblical critics have "more and other work to do,"[23] but if that means that critics have the vocation of reducing the biblical canon to its putative historical circumstances, or of relativizing it completely because they know of no real religious and theoretical center in their scholarship and hermeneutics, then this "more and other work" will simply leave the field for the fundamentalists and their opposite number, these "postmodernists" who find in every text a sacrifice to be offered to its own contradictions.

This is not the place to offer an extended discussion of what Girard's contribution to theology might be. To put it as concisely as possible, I think the general contribution of Girard's theory is a hypothesis and method of culture criticism that does not undercut—I would say, unknowingly slay and sacrifice—what is most precious in the texts that are foundational in the Western religious traditions. Although his theory and biblical hermeneutics are vulnerable to criticism and possible revision, his is a powerful interpretive vision. As Mark Wallace has summarized:

> Like Ricoeur and some others, he argues against the Derridean suspension of the text's referential capacities by showing, through the dynamics of unchecked mimesis, how the biblical narratives do make a claim to truth, a claim about reality, insofar as they unmask the hidden desires at the base of our loftiest cultural and religious aspirations. This is the challenge of Girard's antiviolent hermeneutic.[24]

For Jewish theology it offers an entrée into a core element of Israel's uniqueness as the people of revelation who were the first to

begin consciously to counteract the victimage mechanism. For
Christian theology it offers the significance of the Logos that is the
decisive revelation of the innocent victim and the God of victims, a
disclosure that is rooted in the Jewish heritage and Jesus of
Nazareth.

Job and the Canon

With the next three implications we turn more specifically to the
book of Job. I have neither cut the text of Job into fragments or
putative redactions, nor have I agreed with the text, which I assume
represents the Job poet's work and point of view. Nonetheless, I
have argued strenuously to save not the text but the Job of the text,
the victim who has cried out to God and his friends. This Job now
needs defenders, in my estimation. The first obligation of the
interpreter who stands in service to the biblical tradition of the
disclosure of the innocent victim and the God of victims is not to the
text as such but to the victim and to the God of love and justice. As
Girard has argued, this obligation is a moral demand requiring a
"transformative reading,"[25] which is in effect a deliberate
misreading. Faced with certain choices—for example, the denial of
persecution of victims as a text's reference—"one must either do
violence to the text or let the text forever do violence to innocent
victims."[26]

But can this enterprise, which receives its impulse from the work
of Girard, really affirm the biblical canon? In the arena of
postmodern critical theory the very concept of canon is besieged
from every side (see below, under "The Book of Job As
Scapegoat"). My own intention, however, is to take it very
seriously. We must also take seriously, even if we cannot accept as
normative, the questions and concerns arising out of diverse
intellectual and sociohistorical settings: (1) the charge by women
and minorities that dominant religious and literary canons have
functioned to exclude them, that is, to victimize them intellectually,
spiritually, economically, etcetera; (2) a "postmodern" intellectual
and cultural situation that, whether or not it is partially an artificial
construct of intellectuals, is widely validated and employed as
validation for philosophical and theological positions (an extreme
side of this development in theology has moved from the "death

of God'' to the radicalization of the consequences of this divine demise in thinking about every kind of authority, including canonical texts); and (3) the conservative, as well as evangelical and fundamentalist, reaction in American religious life—which is very much a part of certain political currents—to the voiding of canon, authority, and conventional moral standards (criteria of differentiation), a state of affairs that is perceived as chaotic. The total state of affairs represented in this interpretive situation could be called, in Girardian terms, a ''mimetic crisis.''

In this interpretive situation characterized by extreme reactions that are symptoms of a mimetic crisis, I prefer to find a way that has been excluded, the ''excluded middle,'' or as it is called in French, *le tiers exclu*.[27] With respect to the biblical canon (and here I'm referring to the Protestant and Roman Catholic canons) this means to view it as an integral whole, to look to it as the touchstone of theology and religious life, but at the same time to view it as a treasury of questions that ''authorize'' us to question the canon itself and argue with it. In taking this standpoint I have been influenced by the Jewish tradition. This tradition includes the ''Promethean element in biblical prayer'' (e.g., the intercessory debates of Abraham, Moses, Jeremiah, Job, and some of the psalmists with God). The phrase was used by my late teacher, Sheldon Blank of Hebrew Union College-Jewish Institute of Religion. Also important for me are the tradition of rabbinic debate on the meaning of Scripture passages and the ongoing contest with God in the writings of Elie Wiesel.

I see the book of Job as the paradigm instance of the canonical basis for raising questions, a basis that cannot shield the book of Job or the canon itself. Another one of my teachers, Matitiahu Tsevat, cites at the end of his thought-provoking essay on Job the words of *Pesiqta Rabbati,* ''Had he [Job] not clamored so—as it is now the practice to say in prayer 'God of Abraham, God of Isaac, and God of Jacob,' so one would say 'and God of Job.' ''[28] But this position in the Midrash is one that must finally save text, canon, and tradition at the price of Job's challenge, which is his cry to and for the God of victims. And so in articulating a positive view of canon I think we should always have in mind ''God of Job,'' the God and the Job of that challenge, even if ''God of Job'' does not appear in the canonical text or in our prayers.

Job's Vindicator and the Christ

I think that my reading of the book of Job and its place in a view of the canon offers a new and positive linkage of Job's cry for a vindicator and the Jesus of the New Testament Gospels. The Jesus of the Gospels becomes, for the Christian tradition, the *decisive* event revealing the reality and meaning of the God of victims, of the God, the Logos, by which the world is created and constituted and who takes the side of the poor, the needy, the oppressed. What Job calls for, the Gospels focus on. What Job expresses in a few moments of anguished lucidity, the Gospels illuminate in the story of the Passion. In this sense, I think Christian theology should look firmly and unashamedly at Job as an adumbration of Jesus as the crucified.

Girard devotes a chapter of his book on Job to the relation of Job to the Gospels. His position has influenced my own, but mine is somewhat different from his. Allow me to quote at length two of his key statements:

> In a world of violence, divinity purified of every act of violence must be revealed by means of the event that already provides the sacrificial religion with its generative mechanism. The epiphany of the God of victims follows the same "ancient trail" and goes through the exact same phrases as all the epiphanies of the sacred of the persecutors. As a result, *from the perspective of violence, there is absolutely no distinction between the God of victims and the God of persecutors.* Our pseudoscience of religions is based entirely on the conviction that there is no essential difference between the different religions. . . .
>
> This central event [of the sacrifice or scapegoating of a victim] . . . is also present in the Gospels, but on this occasion it does not just appear in transit: it is not only clearly described, but named. It is called the Passion. Jesus is the perfect victim, because he has always spoken and behaved in accordance with the Logos of the God of victims. He provides the only perfect image of the event which is at the root of all our myths and religions.[29]

Now it is not accurate to say that scholars of religion, as a whole, see no essential difference between the different religions, although it *is* probably the case that most would avow that in principle one should not pronounce on the soundness of their truth claims or on the religious and moral values they espouse. This latter "impartiality" or "disinterestedness" is, I take it, what Girard is talking about, and he has certainly put his finger on a problem. When this point of view "goes to seed," becoming a sort of pan-religiosity or pan-mythology, then it has a great public reception because it makes it easy to relegate human problems and differences to a transcendent private sphere removed from historical situations and social and political crises. Witness the popularity of Joseph Campbell's mythography as he presented it in the Bill Moyers interviews. In the interviews Campbell even stated in one anecdote that violence and misery occurring before one's very eyes should be affirmed as an expression of the violence of the Logos. *"From the perspective of violence, there is absolutely no distinction between the God of victims and the God of persecutors."*

Two more serious questions about Girard's hermeneutics are his approach to the Gospels and Christian supersedure of the Jewish tradition. His approach to the Gospels seems literalistic at times, although he picks and chooses passages that suit his points without worrying about consistency or harmonizing the texts (see, e.g., his approach to the parable of the wicked tenants).[30] But he is not a literalist or fundamentalist in reading the Gospels. He believes that a revelation occurred whose light shines through the Gospels, and he doesn't worry about the history of the Gospels', formation. I think, however, that a Girardian approach to the Gospels will have to come to grips with the history of criticism and sociohistorical questions about Jesus and the early Jesus movement.[31] The challenge will be to find that *via media,* or the excluded middle, that will avoid the Scylla of reactionary retreat into a precritical position and the Carybdis of historical reductionism and various postmodern deconstructions.

The question that has priority for me is that of Christian claims to superiority over Judaism. Of course, for Christians their view of their own tradition and its relevatory center will presumably take precedence in any sort of interpretive activity. Some of Girard's statements, however, seem to go beyond this *pro nos* position, giving the impression of asserting an absolute truth that only the

Christian tradition—and note well, this means above all the Gospels for Girard—knows with certainty. It should be noted in his defense, however, that Girard doesn't claim that this ''only perfect image of the event'' that demythologizes the scapegoat mechanism is a *Christian* event. No, it is an event that fulfills the Jewish tradition of revelation, and its personal bearer is the Jew Jesus. It is true that the subsequent Christian tradition has transmitted the meaning of this event through the Gospels—sometimes contradicting itself in that Christianity became, by and large, another sacrificial religion and, among other things, did violence to its own texts by persecuting the Jews.

However, I do think that any language implying the inherent superiority of Christianity or the Gospels should be avoided. The primary thing, with which I know Girard agrees, is the revelation of the truth of the God of victims. The witness of Christian faith is based on the Gospels and the Christ-event as making a decisive difference for us. Concomitantly, I think Christian theology should take a new look at texts like those describing the Servant of the Lord in Isaiah 52:13–53:12. Contrary to Girard, I think it is no more and no less ambiguous than the Gospels in its disclosure of the God of victims.

One further note. One implication of this discussion of Job and the Christ is that the Jewish tradition of interpretation has—or should have—a great deal of interest in explication of the victimage mechanism as part and parcel of its distinctive religious heritage.

The Book of Job As Scapegoat

Scapegoating and victimage is a difficult subject, in great part because it is easy to see it in the enemy or outsider but not in ourselves. The problem is exacerbated by the popularity of the idea of claiming to be a victim as a way of victimizing one's enemies. This tendency is probably due to Judeo-Christian influence on Western thought and institutions, but of course like any way of seeing things it can be vulgarized and used for crass ideological purposes.

Thus the theory of the victimage mechanism operative in human societies is simple at one level, but it is a very complex matter to unravel its workings and to be sufficiently aware of one's own motives.

With respect to Job, that complexity may be seen in the fact that my own argument may be turned against me in this way: You take the Girardian path of locating the core of Job in the text's insights into persecution of the scapegoat and Job's occasional lucid affirmations of a God of victims, but you execute your hermeneutics at the expense of the God-speeches and the epilogue. Aren't you simply pitting one view against another and seeking to detract from interpreters whose hermeneutical discourse is quite different from yours?

My response is that undoubtedly I have sinned, probably in more ways than I could be aware of. I ask for forgiveness, and then I would ask to be allowed to impose just two strictures concerning the problem of scapegoating the text and those who hold different positions. One is that the approach to the text shall not disregard any part of it, even if one does not like it. In this context I have not had opportunity to deal with the prologue, the epilogue, Elihu's speeches, or the ode to wisdom. One would have to deal with all of them and take them seriously—not exclude them or scapegoat them. This serious treatment is what I have undertaken to achieve with the dialogues and the God-speeches, which I think are the most important parts of Job, but which must certainly be related to the rest of the book, just as the book must be related to the rest of the canon. Engagement with the canonical text, questioning it and being questioned by it, is the necessary condition of an adequate doctrine of canon, as I indicated in "Job and the Canon." Yes, maybe I missed something in the theophany. Maybe I haven't done the poet justice. Well, the canon will still be there tomorrow for new questions and new comprehension. It is much more important than we are as critics.

By the way, Girard views all other parts of Job as additions to the dialogue and "additions to the additions."[32] I don't agree with him on this. However, even if they are additions, they offer us a challenge, a set of voices from the tradition that must be heard. If nothing else, they may enable us to highlight what is truly distinctive about Job. Girard holds, of course, that in some cases it is necessary to "do violence" to a text (see in "Job and the Canon" and the second stricture immediately below). However, I don't think he means by that to "scapegoat" it by expelling it, in effect, from the canon because it is secondary or tertiary to some original text or event. Such, at least, is not my intention.

The other stricture is that Job the victim and the God he discloses shall not be sacrificed to any God or to any interpretation, whether it be the sacred social order of the friends with their God of violence or some transcendental "amorality" that Job the New Man in his enlightened state is supposed to see.

Most of the students and colleagues I converse and consort with don't wish to take the side of the friends, nor do they espouse a conservative or fundamentalist point of view. Therefore, I will take up another tendency to victimize Job, which poses at least as great a threat as a conservative or reactionary position affirming the God of the sacred social order. The transcendental amorality or new "higher morality" is a powerful current in modern intellectual history and has had, I think, quite an effect on Job interpretation. Nietzsche's theme of *ressentiment,* which he views as the detestable slave morality of Judaism and Christianity, is countered by his vision of the *Uebermensch,* whose god is Dionysus and who affirms the eternal return of all things. What Nietzsche did not understand was that his archetype of the authoritarian imposer of slave morality, the Christian God, was really his model-obstacle, and that in trying to eliminate and transcend resentment in the idea of the Overman, he was really enthroning resentment in a new mode. The eternal return is the eternal cycle of violence, of revenge. "Life itself," he says in *The Will to Power,* "its eternal fruitfulness and recurrence, creates torment, destruction, the will to annihilation."[33]

Heidegger was evidently much influenced by Nietzsche in understanding the Logos as that structure of being that violently brings together opposites. In the tradition of Hegel, Marx, Nietzsche, and Freud, he sees the biblical concept of the relation of God and human beings as that of master and slave (although Hegel did not extend this image to the New Testament). He argues that the tradition of the Logos represented in the Gospel of John is a form of combat and violence visited upon humans understood as slaves, whereas the Logos of the Greek tradition is a violence perceived and committed by free men. Girard points out that what Heidegger fails to see is that a structure of violent mastery always requires slavery, for it depends on the model-rival or the model as obstacle.[34] When the model of reality and of human existence is conceived in this way, you will simply get Nietzche's eternal return all over again—and it is a very dull round of things. The options are basically four: Submit slavishly to the master (model), get rid of the master, break away in revolt (which may also result in eliminating the master), or get rid of yourself—suicide. So it is the same old thing over and over again: submit, submit, submit . . . ; or kill, kill, kill . . . ; or rebel, rebel, rebel . . ; or kill yourself, kill yourself, kill yourself . . . Another way to put it is that all of this is *revenge:* With options 1 and 4, submission and suicide, it is internalized and directed against oneself.

So it is that when I read or hear interpretations of Job that contend Job is to see that justice is not rooted in the divine order of things, or that the divine presence itself is enough, or that creation is a grand mystery, or that suffering is simply a perspective on things, or that God and world are a mystery beyond good and evil, I would ask some questions in return: (1) Granted that God and the world are wonderfully and beautifully mysterious, are all understandings of truth and justice equally meritorious or unmeritorious? (2) Is the round of human violence to be justified by divine violence—that is, by the sacred, by the transcendent social order? (3) Is what happens to the victim unimportant? A positive response to any one of these questions means that Job is being scapegoated again.

Jewish theology, in the name of the God of Abraham, the God of Isaac, and the God of Jacob, must say resoundingly to all these questions, "No!"

Christian theology, in the name of the God of Jesus Christ, must say resoundingly to all these questions, "No!"

And if Jewish and Christian theology say no, then the God of *Job* will be in no danger of an imminent demise. Nietzsche of course, in Aphorism 125 of *The Gay Science,* has his Madman announce not just that God is dead, but that "we have killed him"—a textual fact widely ignored or suppressed. But the God of Job is not a God that must slay or be slain.

NOTES

1. In Defense of God the Sage

1. In addition to the major commentaries note V. Kubina, *Die Gottesreden im Buche Hiob* (Freiburger Theologische Studien 115; Freiburg: Herder, 1977); H. Rowold, "The Theology of Creation in the Yahweh Speeches of the Book of Job" Ph.D. dissertation, Concordia Seminary in exile, 1977; S. Terrien, "The Yahweh Speeches and Job's Response," *RevExp* 58 (1971) 497-509; M. Tsevat, "The Meaning of the Book of Job," *HUCA* 37 (1966) 73-106; A. Brenner, "God's Answer to Job," *VT* 31 (1981) 129-37; R. A. F. McKenzie, "The Purpose of the Yahweh Speeches in the Book of Job," *Bib* 40 (1959) 435-45.

2. N. Habel, "The Symbolism of Wisdom in the Book of Proverbs," *Int* 26 (1972) 131-57.

3. J. W. Kleinig, *The Getting of Wisdom* (M.Ph. thesis, Cambridge University, 1981).

4. J. L. Crenshaw, *Old Testament Wisdom: An Introduction* (London: SCM Press, 1981), 21.

5. G. von Rad, *Wisdom in Israel* (Nashville: Abingdon, 1972), speaks of wisdom as "world reason," ch. 9; cf. R. N. Whybray, *Wisdom in Proverbs* (London: SCM Press, 1965).

6. I proposed an earlier version of this translation in "The Symbolism of Wisdom in the Book of Proverbs," 154-55. By reading the *mē'az* at the end of v. 22 as the opening word of v. 23, we have two lines in 3:3 meter. The inner parallelism of v. 23 then becomes apparent, and the logic of reading *darkô* ("his way") with the second half of v. 22 seems obvious.

7. B. Vawter, "Prov. 8.22: Wisdom and Creation," *JBL* 99 (1980) 205-16. Admittedly the LXX renders *qny* as "create," but Aquila, Symmachus, and Theodotion clearly read "acquire." The *qōnēh* of Gen. 14, 19, and 22, usually rendered "creator," can just as readily mean "lord" or "master" as in 1QapGen. The title *qynt ilm* used of Asherah in Ugaritic texts means either "mistress of the gods" or "mother of the gods." Gods do not usually "create" other gods! Apart from the rendering of the LXX, which as Vawter demonstrates is dubious, there is no reason to translate *qny* by "create." Perhaps, as Berhard Lang suggests, wisdom, in one tradition, was originally a goddess, the teacher

whom God "begat" or "acquired' to become the first sage. See his recent book, *Wisdom and the Book of Proverbs: The Israelite Goddess Redefined* (New York: Pilgrim, 1986). The verb *hôlālĕtî* in Prov. 8:24 would tend to support this position. In the present form of the text, however, wisdom is acquired as the *derek*, the way to create a cosmos. Yahweh, like other sages, "acquires" wisdom first!

8. Cf. F. Cross, *Canaanite Myth and Hebrew Epic* (Cambridge: Harvard University Press, 1973), especially his treatment of Exodus 15.

9. See my commentary *The Book of Job* (Philadelphia: Westminster, 1985), 391-93. All translations of the book of Job are taken from this commentary.

10. N. Habel, "Only the Jackal is My Friend: Of Friends and Redeemers in Job," *Int* 31 (1977) 227-36.

11. Even if one does not take Job 28 as the "poet's personal reflection in the debate thus far," as I suggest in *The Book of Job,* 302, the thematic development of God as the first sage in this passage obtains.

12. S. L. Harris, "Wisdom or Creation," *VT* 23 (1983) 419-27, argues that the feminine suffixes of 28:27 do not refer to wisdom but to the "verbal content of the preceding sentence as a whole," which is tantamount to "creation" in general. However, the feminine suffix in v. 23 clearly refers to wisdom, and the verbs in v. 27 make good sense if we recognize the characterization here of God as the first sage discerning wisdom in creation.

13. Harris, ibid., illustrates that these verbs are also significant in creation contexts.

14. Compare the discussion in *The Book of Job,* 391-93.

15. See note 1 above; cf. also D. Robertson, *The Old Testament and the Literary Critic* (Philadelphia: Fortress, 1977), 50-54, where he regards the book of Job as a comedy and God as the butt of the joke.

16. Rowold, in *The Theology of Creation in the Yahweh Speeches of the Book of Job,* delineates the features of the challenge question form in detail. While challenge questions are designed to acclaim God as the only one who has achieved such great things and to expose the impotence of all rivals, including Job, these questions also reveal riddles and realities of the universe that tantalize and invite the listener to explore.

17. The portrait of the sea being contained by God anticipates the elaborate portrait of how the force of chaos represented by Behemoth and Leviathan is kept under control. See *The Book of Job,* 550ff., for a detailed discussion.

2. The God of Job: Avenger, Tyrant, or Victor?

1. When I use terms like "dualism" or "monism," I refer to tendencies in these directions. I am well aware that the terms are encumbered with philosophical connotations that may make them less well suited in discussions of OT materials. Just as there is hardly a monotheism in the OT that can be described as philosophically reflective, there is hardly a theoretically reflected kind of monism or dualism (although Job may be a book where the chances of finding more thorough reflection on these matters are unusually good). Under all circumstances the terms may help us to categorize certain tendencies in the material.

2. With this formulation, I cover both the possibility of a God who controls evil and the possibility of a God who is the ultimate origin of evil.

3. R. Gordis, *The Book of God and Man* (Chicago: University of Chicago Press, 1978), 191; and *The Book of Job* (New York: Jewish Theological Seminary, 1978), 560.

4. M. Tsevat, "The Meaning of the Book of Job," *HUCA* 37 (1966) 98; 97-106. "He Who speaks to man in the Book of Job is neither a just nor an unjust god but God" (p. 105).

5. Ibid., 98.

6. H. D. Preuss, "Jahwes Antwort an Hiob und die sogenannte Hiobliteratur des alten Vorderen Orients," *Beiträge zur alttestamentlichen Theologie* (ed. H. Donner et al.; Göttingen: Vandenhoeck & Ruprecht, 1977), 304-43.

7. N. C. Habel, *The Book of Job* (London: SCM Press, 1985), 65-66, 564; J. van Oorschot, *Gott als Grenze* (BZAW 170; Berlin: W. de Gruyter, 1987), 209. Unless otherwise indicated, all subsequent quotations from Job follow Habel's translation in his commentary.

8. O. Keel, *Jahwes Entgegnung an Ijob* (FRLANT 121; Göttingen: Vandenhoeck & Ruprecht, 1978); F. Lindström, *God and the Origin of Evil* (ConB 21; Lund: Gleerup, 1983), 137-57; T. Mettinger, "In Search of the Hidden Structure: YHWH as King in Isaiah 40–55," *SEÅ* 51-52 (1987) 148-57; J. C. L. Gibson, "On Evil in the Book of Job," *Biblical and Other Studies in Memory of P. C. Craigie* (JSOTSup 67; Sheffield: JSOT Press, 1988), 399-419. Slightly different is J. Day, *God's Conflict with the Dragon and the Sea* (Cambridge: Cambridge University Press, 1985), 62-87.

9. A. Brenner, "God's Answer to Job," *VT* 31 (1981) 131-32.

10. Habel, *The Book of Job*, 68-69; cf. p. 66. Cf. J. E. Hartley, *The Book of Job* (Grand Rapids: Eerdmans), 534. "By questioning Job about the primordial monsters Behemoth and Leviathan, Yahweh is trying to persuade Job that he is Master of all powers in the world, both earthly and cosmic. Certainly then he is lord of all powers, earthly and cosmic, that brought on Job's afflictions."

11. See above, note 8. Cf. Mettinger, "In Search of the Hidden Structure," 199.

12. Preuss, "Jahwes Antwort an Hiob," 342.

13. D. J. A. Clines, "The Arguments of Job's Three Friends," *Art and Meaning* (JSOTSup 19; Sheffield: JSOT Press, 1982), 199-214.

14. The use of an accented character here to introduce the *accusative* is also found in verse 2. I therefore view Habel's interpretation (*The Book of Job*, 131-33) with some skepticism. Cf. J. Léveque, *Job et Son Dieu* (Ebib; Paris: Garabalda, 1970), 247-48.

15. My translation of v. 24. I am not inclined to make any textual emendations in 24*b*. Cf. Job 24:25 and Gen. 43:11.

16. Notably Job 34:10-30, esp. vv. 12, 17; see also 19:6-7; 27:2, 7; and 40:8.

17. M. Pope, *Job* (AB; 3rd ed.; Garden City, N.Y.: Doubleday, 1974) 99.

18. M. Fishbane, "Jeremiah IV 23-26 and Job III 3-13. A Recovered Use of the Creation Pattern," *VT* 21 (1971) 153.

19. On this verse cf. D. A. Diewert, "Job 7:12. *Yam, Tannin* and the Surveillance of Job," *JBL* 106 (1987) 203-15; and J. G. Janzen, "Another Look at God's Watch over Job (7:12)," *JBL* 108 (1989) 109-14.

20. *Enuma Elish* tabl. IV; Exod. 15:8, 10; Pss. 18:16; 48:8.

21. Translation after Gordis, *The Book of Job*, 98.

22. Num. 16:32; Isa. 5:14; Hab. 2:5; Prov. 1:12; Job 18:13.

23. V. Kubina, *Die Gottesreden im Buche Hiob* (Freiburger Theologische Studien 115; Freiburger: Herder, 1979), 115-23; cf. 124-43.

24. Cf. Exod. 22:8; Deut. 25:1; Prov. 17:15.

25. See 38:4, 5, 18, 20; 39:26; and cf. 42:2-3. Léveque, *Job et Son Dieu*, 518-19.

26. Keel, *Jahwes Entgegnung an Ijob*, 86-125.

27. To these formulations on God's arm cf. Isa. 51:9, where "YHWH's arm" appears

in a chaos battle context, on which see Mettinger, "In Search of the Hidden Structure." On Job 40:9-14 see especially Keel, *Jahwes Entgegnung an Ijob,* 126-27.

28. Brenner, "God's Answer to Job," 133.

29. E. Ruprecht, "Das Nilpferd im Hiobbuch," *VT* 21 (1971) 209-31; Keel, *Jahwes Entgegnung an Ijob,* 126-55; and Kubina, *Die Gottesreden im Buche Hiob,* 68-75.

30. ANET, 14-17; M. Lichtheim, *Ancient Egyptian Literature,* vol. 2 (Berkeley: University of California Press, 1976), 214-23.

31. See Keel, *Jahwes Entgegnung an Ijob,* 139n.378, for references; E. Chassinat, *Le temple d'Edfou* 3 (Cairo, 1928) fig. 82.

32. B. Lang, "Job XL 18 and the 'Bones of Seth,' " *VT* 30 (1980) 360-61.

33. Habel, *The Book of Job,* 551, 553-54.

34. H. Rowold, *"Mî hû? Lî hû!"* *BL* 105 (1986) 104-9. Following the lead of Rowold (and for v. 4 cf. also Habel, *The Book of Job*), I translate 41:2-4 as follows: "Isn't he fierce when he is aroused? / Who is he that can stand against me? / Who is he to confront me so that I must sue for peace? / Under the whole of heaven, he is mine. / Did I not silence his boasting, / his mighty word and his persuasive case?"

35. J. G. Gammie, "Behemoth and Leviathan: On the Didactic and Theological Significance of Job 40:15–41:26," *Israelite Wisdom* (ed. J. G. Gammie et al.; Missoula, Mont.: Scholars Press, 1978), 217-31; Habel, *The Book of Job,* 558-59, 561-62, 564, 571.

36. J. Ziegler, "Die Hilfe Gottes am Morgen," *Alttestamentliche Studien* (BBB 1; Bonn: Peter Hanstein, 1950), 281-88.

37. B. Janowski, *Rettungsgewissheit und Epiphanie des Heils* 1 (WMANT 59; Neukirchen: Neukirchener Verlag, 1989).

38. For judgment at dawn within the "civil" sphere see 2 Sam. 15:2; Jer. 21:12; Ps. 101:8. For God's help "at dawn" see also Isa. 17:14; Pss. 46:6; 88:14; 90:14; 143:8.

39. Lindström, *God and the Origin of Evil,* 137-57. Notably, Brenner, "God's Answer to Job," 131-32, refers to Job 9:4-10. Habel (*The Book of Job,* 66-69) refers to Job 1:21 and 2:10: "God is indeed the 'source' of the evil that Job suffered (2:10), just as he is the Creator who controls chaos" (66); "Job finally understood that 'the Lord gives and the Lord takes away' (1:21)."

40. Paul Ricoeur, *The Symbolism of Evil* (Boston: Beacon, 1969) 171-74, 175-91.

41. J. D. Levenson, *Creation and the Persistence of Evil* (San Francisco: Harper, 1988), 15.

42. To some theologians dualistic tendencies always have a smell of gnosticism. It should then be remembered that monistic tendencies with ideas of divine pancausality are also encumbered with theological difficulties. What meaning is left to the proclamation of salvation in the NT if we presuppose that all events are *a priori* subject to the power and will of God, asks Lindström. He continues: "In my opinion the judgment prophecies of the Old Testament prophets present a similar contradiction to the notion of divine pancausality" (*God and the Origin of Evil,* 118).

43. One should perhaps also take into closer consideration the fact that the hippopotamus and the crocodile are *metaphorical* representations of ultimate evil. Since the descriptions of these animals in Job are hardly allegories, it follows that every single formulation does not necessarily operate as part of the symbolic message of the author. As zoological specimens these two animals are of course created. But does such a statement regarding creation constitute a statement on the origin of evil?

44. Note the following cases: (1) Gen. 1:3 (let there be light)—Job 3:4; (2) Gen. 1:21—Job 40:15; (3) Gen. 2:7 and 3:19 (man formed of dust and returning to dust)—Job 1:21; 4:19; 10:9; (4) Gen. 2:7 (breath of life)—Job 27:3; 32:7-8; 33:4; (5) Gen. 2:21-24 (the rib)—Job 18:12 ("rib" stands for "wife"; see Gordis, *The Book of Job*, 191-92); and Genesis 3 (fall of man)—Job 31:33 ("Did I conceal my sins like Adam?").

45. I would like to thank Michael S. Cheney, Th.M., who checked my English, and Dr. Fredrik Lindström, who submitted my draft to a critical reading.

3. The Problem of Evil in the Book of Job

1. Because the deity in the Hebrew text of Job is masculine by verb forms, pronouns, and adjectives, I will use the male designation of him. He is also, let it be said, quintessentially masculinist—at least I see not the remotest tinge of feminism in him.

2. I am not sure that the term applies. Though the deity in the Hebrew Bible is extremely powerful, it seems to me less clear that he is conceived as *all*-powerful, because that philosophical category is not self-evidently present in the Bible itself. It is, of course, present in the tradition to which we are heir, but that should inculcate caution in claiming it for other cultures.

3. As in my book, *In Turns of Tempest: A Reading of Job with a Translation* (Stanford, Calif.: Stanford University Press, 1990), I prefer the lower-case term with the definite article to the capitalized God. The latter permits the reader to apply whatever concept of deity she now holds, which is no doubt conditioned by the Jewish-Christian tradition of monotheism, among other ideas. To say "the god" is not intended by itself to change anyone's concept, but it may help the reader to suspend judgment about it for purposes of thinking about Job. My view is that the book of Job is not clearly monotheistic.

4. A. MacLeish, *J.B.* (Boston: Houghton Mifflin, 1958), 14.

5. Throughout this article I use my own translation, published and annotated in *Tempest,* 48-173. This sentence is discussed on pp. 200-201.

6. For this interpretation of *haśśāṭān* ("the satan"), see *Tempest,* 22, 50, and below.

7. As the entire argument of *Tempest* shows, I am reading Job deconstructively. It seems well to say so out loud, lest I be taxed with inadvertent deconstruction.

8. The word is *brk,* which ordinarily means to "bless." Throughout Job 1-2, the verb sometimes seems to mean "bless" and sometimes "curse." See *Tempest,* 50, 193, 195-96.

9. See *Tempest,* 23, 194-95.

10. The best treatment of curse that I have found is Sheldon Blank, "The Curse, Blasphemy, the Spell, and the Oath," *HUCA* 23 (1950/51) 73-95. See also Georg Grisen, *Die Wurzel [śbʿ] "Schwören"* (Bonn: Peter Hanstein, 1981); Johannes Pederson, *Der Eid bei den Semiten* (Strasbourg: K. J. Trhuhner, 1914); Willy Schottrof, *Der Altisraelitische Fluchspruch* (Neukirchen-Vluyn: Neukirchener Verlag, 1969).

11. I have heard it argued that this is not a curse formula, but I have not seen an alternative rhetorical identification of it. The conditional clause "If a," with no result clause to complete the sentence is well known as a curse (see Blank, "The Curse"), but I know no clear evidence that such a conditional clause without a result clause is

also something else. I should be happy for such evidence, because multiple meaning is always more interesting than univocality.

12. The wager has, I think, been imported into the argument from later Western culture. I have never come across the quotation of an ancient Near Eastern wager, though it would be surprising if those cultures did not gamble.

13. That proviso may or may not be important. *B. Baba Batra* 16b quotes Raba: " 'With his lips' he did not sin, but in his heart he sinned" (M. Weiss, *The Story of Job's Beginning* [Jerusalem: Magnes Press, 1983], 71).

14. In the chapter on Job in *Irony of the Old Testament* (2nd ed.; Sheffield: JSOT Press, 1982), I was troubled by the presence of magic. I have come to think that the magical—the production of a result by one's formulaic action or words, with no other intervening causality—is, despite many theoretical protests to the contrary, intrinsic to religion, and its presence no longer bothers me.

15. I treat the book as the unity it now is, rather than distinguishing the ideas in the separate parts that we may analyze as stages in its composition. The latter enterprise is perfectly legitimate, but it has too often pretended to be the only legitimate way of interpreting, and I resist that historiographic imperialism.

16. Unless we read the fascinating variant from LXX, Syriac, and a few Hebrew MSS, *lū yēš*, "Would that there were." For comment, see *Tempest*, 74.

17. This is especially true in the second cycle, where Job and the friends talk past one another more than in the first. In the third cycle, Eliphaz leaps upon Job with completely false accusations (ch. 22), some of which he may implicitly answer in ch. 31; Bildad lamely reverts to Eliphaz's opening point (4:17-21) about the divine moral transcendence (ch. 25), and Zophar says nothing at all. The notion that Zophar's speech either can be or needs to be reconstructed from Job's surrounding speeches is irrelevant to my purposes, and in any case, I find Zophar's silence dramatically interesting and Job's speeches as they stand profoundly and ironically alienated.

18. I use this term not because I find any concept of a heaven as a place where the divine dwells but simply as a surrogate for the idea that the divine holds court somewhere, and Job's "witness" is there. The word is *šāmayim*.

19. The witness? The sentence might also be taken as a jussive: "That he may decide . . .''

20. Repointing *ûbēn 'ādām* from MT *ûben-'ādām*.

21. Cf. Pope, *Job*.

22. One is reminded of Gilgamesh, who wanders in search of life in the face of death, having sought early in the epic to achieve immortal fame. The end of the epic seems to reflect a kind of resignation in the face of failure, but at the beginning of Tablet I are these lines (from Maureen Gallery Kovacs, trans., *The Epic of Gilgamesh* [Stanford, Calif.: Stanford University Press, 1989] 3-4): "Find the copper tablet box, / open the . . . of its lock of bronze / undo the fastening of its secret opening. / Take and read out from the lapis lazuli tablet / how Gilgamesh went through every hardship." By the fact that we can read about the adventures, Gilgamesh has his wish for immortal fame.

23. For a "translation" that seems to me more intelligible than the Hebrew, see *Tempest*, 100, 102.

24. "Wretch" is *rā'*, an "evil" person.

25. An interesting implicate of this view, suggested recently in a seminar by Mr. David Magerman, involves Yahweh's original boast about Job to the Prosecutor: "There's no one like him on earth" (1:8). He suggested that Yahweh may call the Prosecutor's attention to Job precisely with the underhanded intention of setting Job up

for destruction—punishing the righteous for being righteous. The idea had not occurred to me before, nor have I seen it in the literature. And it has come so recently that I have not had time to ponder it thoroughly.

26. See, however, N. Habel, *The Book of Job* (Philadelphia: Westminster, 1985), especially p. 431, arguing that ch. 31 is Job's testimony in the trial.

27. By the time *Tempest* was finished, I had not worked through the one that suggests that the deity will deal disaster to himself, so that possibility appears only in passing (p. 316).

28. This is not because Elihu was interpolated into the book, though I suspect he was. Elihu takes the issue of evil in no new direction, so far as I can see, and I would rather not waste space on it.

29. R. Carstensen, *Job: Defense of Honor* (Nashville: Abingdon Press, 1963), 91.

30. L. Steiger, "Die Wirklichkeit Gottes in unser Verkündigung," in *Festschrift H. Diem* (Munich, 1965) 160, quoted by O. Keel, *Jahwes Entgegnung an Ijob* (Göttingen: Vandenhoeck & Ruprecht, 1978), 11: "dürftig und leer . . . drei Stunden Naturkunde."

31. See *Tempest,* 18-20.

32. See *Tempest,* 370-78.

33. That blandly passes up a number of problems in 42:2-5. The most interesting to me is the problem of Qere-Ketib in v. 2. The text has *yd't.* The Qere points "I know [*yāda'tî*] that you can do everything." The Ketib implies *yāda'at,* "you [masculine singular] know." The many possibilities of the Ketib reading are most intriguing.

34. See *Tempest,* 25-26, 170, 375-77.

35. At least of the kind of religion that entails that kind of understanding of guilt.

4. Wounded Hero on a Shaman's Quest

1. E. Dhorme, *A Commentary on the Book of Job* (Nashville: Thomas Nelson, 1967), clxxv.

2. Marvin Pope, *Job* (AB, 15; 3rd ed.; New York: Doubleday, 1973), xxxii-xl.

3. G. Guttiérrez, *On Job: God-talk and the Suffering of the Innocent* (Maryknoll, N.Y.: Orbis, 1987).

4. R. Girard, *Job: The Victim of His People* (Stanford, Calif.: Stanford University Press, 1987).

5. B. S. Childs, *Introduction to the Old Testament as Scripture* (Philadelphia: Fortress, 1978), 526-44.

6. C. Fontaine, "Folktale Structure in the Book of Job: A Formalist Reading," *Directions in Biblical Hebrew Poetry* (ed. Elaine Follis; JSOTSup 40; Sheffield: Almond, 1987), 205-32.

7. V. Propp, *Morphology of the Folktale* (2nd ed.; Austin, Tex.: University of Texas Press, 1968).

8. N. Sarna, "Epic Substratum in the Prose of Job," *JBL* 76 (1957) 13-25; W. J. Urbock, "Oral Antecedents to Job: A Survey of Formulas and Formulaic Systems," *Semeia* 5 (1976) 111-37.

9. P. J. Milne, *Vladimir Propp and the Study of Structure in Hebrew Biblical Narrative* (Bible and Literature 13; Sheffield: Almond, 1988), 122.

10. M. Lüthi, "Aspects of the Märchen and Legend," *Genre* 2 (1969) 162-65.

11. M. Lüthi, *Once Upon a Time: On the Nature of Fairy Tales* (trans. Lee Chedeayne and Paul Gottwald; Bloomington, Ind.: Indiana University Press, 1976), 70.

12. Ibid., 115.

13. Ibid., 135.

14. C. Lévi-Strauss, "Structure and Form: Reflections on a Work by Vladimir Propp," *Structural Anthropology,* vol. 2 (trans. M. Layton; New York: Basic Books, 1976), 115-45.

15. Fontaine, "Folktale Structure," 226-27.

16. J. Blenkinsopp, "The Search for the Prickly Plant: Structure and Function in the Gilgamesh Epic," *Soundings* 58 (1975); B. Alster, "Paradoxical Proverbs and Satire in Sumerian Literature," *JCS* 27 (1975).

17. L. Dégh, "Folk Narrative," *Folklore and Folklife* (ed. Richard Dorson; Chicago: University of Chicago Press, 1972); Lüthi, "Aspects of the Märchen and Legend' '; E. Meletinsky et al., "Problems of the Structural Analysis of Folktales," *Soviet Structural Folkloristic,* vol. 1 (ed. P. Maranda, Approaches to Semiotics, 43; The Hague: Mouton, 1974).

18. Propp, *Morphology of the Folktale,* 21.

19. R. Dorson, "Foreword," in Hasan M. El-Shamy, *Folktales of Egypt* (Chicago: University of Chicago Press, 1980), ix-xxxix.

20. J. B. Pritchard, ed., *Ancient Near Eastern Texts Relating to the Old Testament* (3rd ed. with supplement; Princeton, N.J.: Princeton University Press, 1969), 127-28.

21. Ibid., 12-14.

22. Meletinsky et al., "Problems of the Structural Analysis of Folktales," 97.

23. W. K. Simpson, ed., *The Literature of Ancient Egypt: An Anthology of Stories, Instructions and Poetry* (rev. ed.; New Haven, Conn.: Yale University Press, 1973), 92-107.

24. D. Wolkstein and S. N. Kramer, *Inanna, Queen of Heaven and Earth: Her Stories and Hymns from Sumer* (New York: Harper & Row, 1983).

25. W. W. Hallo and J. J. A. Van Dijk, *The Exaltation of Inanna* (YNER 3; New Haven, Conn.: Yale University Press, 1969).

26. J. G. Gammie, "Behemoth and Leviathan: On the Didactic and Theological Significance of Job 40:15–41:26," *Israelite Wisdom: Theological and Literary Essays in Honor of Samuel Terrien* (ed. J. G. Gammie et al.; New York: Union Theological Seminary, 1978), 222.

27. Fontaine, "Folktale Structure," 220.

28. Ibid., 222.

29. Dégh, "Folk Narrative," 60-62.

30. Meletinsky et al., "Problems of the Structural Analysis of Folktales," 78, 134-39.

31. Simpson, *The Literature of Ancient Egypt,* 31-49.

32. Fontaine, "Folktale Structure," 218.

33. Lüthi, "Aspects of the Märchen and Legend."

34. J. Dow, "Universal Aspects of Symbolic Healing: A Theoretical Synthesis," *American Anthropologist* 88 (1986) 58.

35. B. G. Myerhoff, "Shamanic Equilibrium: Balance and Mediation in Known and Unknown Worlds," *American Folk Medicine: A Symposium* (ed. W. Hand; Berkeley: University of California Press, 1976), 99.

36. A. Porterfield, "Shamanism: A Psychosocial Definition," *JAAR* (1987) 725.

37. Dow, "Universal Aspects of Symbolic Healing," 57-59.

38. J. Achterberg, *Imagery in Healing: Shamanism and Modern Medicine* (Boston: Shambala New Science Library, 1985), 111-41.

39. J. G. Janzen, *Job* (IBC; Atlanta: John Knox, 1985), 70-71.

40. Dow, "Universal Aspects of Symbolic Healing," 59-62.

41. Porterfield, "Shamanism: A Psychosocial Definition," 726; ibid., 61.

42. Achterberg, *Imagery in Healing,* 19-20.

43. So with Janzen, *Job,* 251-52.

44. I. Paulson, "The Animal Guardian: A Synthetic Review," *HR* 3 (1964) 208-9.

45. A. S. Kapelrud, "Shamanistic Features in the Old Testament," *Studies in Shamanism* (ed. C. M. Edsman; Stockholm: Almquist & Wiksell, 1967), 91.

46. See Gammie, "Behemoth and Leviathan," 1978, however.

47. I would like to thank Jeffrey Pulis, Claudia Camp, Deborah Vickers, Marie Sugrue, Paige Besse, and Sheila Lloyd for their help in the preparation of this manuscript.

5. The Book of Job and Inner-biblical Discourse

1. A notable recent exception is the work of J. Gerald Janzen, *Job* (IBC; Atlanta: John Knox, 1985). Among earlier studies, R. Gordis, *The Book of God and Man* (Chicago: University of Chicago Press, 1965), was attentive to Joban language, style, and allusion (especially chs. 12–14). See also his *The Book of Job: A Commentary* (New York: Jewish Theological Seminary, 1978), passim.

2. All Scripture translations in this chapter are the author's.

3. Job's use of this mythic thematic has various reverberations. See, for example, my remarks in "Jeremiah IV.23-26 and Job III.3-13: A Recovered Use of the Creation Pattern," *VT* 21 (1971) 151-67.

4. Another intriguing employment of *mâ* as a rhetorical centerpiece can be found in Micah 6:2-8 (six times).

5. The link was already noted by Rashi.

6. Cf. Jer. 23:20, where *mĕzimmâh,* as "purpose" or "plan," is applied to God.

7. For this device, see L. Jacobs, "The *Qal Va-homer* Argument in the Old Testament," *BSO(A)S* 35 (1972) 221-27, and my further observations in *Biblical Interpretation in Ancient Israel* (Oxford: Clarendon, 1985), 420, 526n. 2.

6. Rabbinic Interpretations of Job

1. Rabbinic Judaism emerged and developed in the first six centuries of the Common Era as the normative form of Jewish practice up to the modern era. Its founders, careful readers and interpreters of the Hebrew Bible, were known as rabbis (teachers). On the rabbis and the rabbinic period, see Judah Goldin, "The Period of the Talmud (135 B.C.E.–1035 C.E.)," in *The Jews: Their History* (ed. Louis Finkelstein; New York: Schocken, 1970), 119-224.

For a full study of the range of rabbinic comments on the figure of Job, see Judith R. Baskin, *Pharaoh's Counsellors. Job, Jethro, and Balaam in Rabbinic and Patristic Tradition* (BJS 47; Chico, Calif.: Scholars Press, 1983). For rabbinic commentary on the book of Job as a whole, see Herman Ezekiel Kaufmann, *Die Anwendung das Buches Hiob in der Rabbinischen Agadah* (Frankfurt a.M., 1893), and Solomon Buber, ed., *Majan-Gannim. Commentary on Job of Rabbi Samuel ben Nissim Masnuth* (Berlin, 1889).

The following abbreviations are used in the essay and notes: *m.* (*Mishnah*), *b.* (*Babylonian Talmud*), and *j.* (*Jerusalem Talmud*). English translations of talmudic passages in this essay are generally based upon those in *The Babylonian Talmud* (trans. and ed. I. Epstein; 18 vols.; London: Soncino, 1935), while English translations from *Genesis, Exodus,* and *Deuteronomy Rabbah* are based upon *Midrash Rabbah* (trans. and ed. H. Freedman and Maurice Simon; 10 vols.; London: Soncino, 1938.)

2. Marvin Pope, *Job. A New Translation and Commentary* (AB; Garden City, N.Y.: Doubleday, 1973), xxiii-xxx, notes that scholars agree that there are at least two distinct elements in the biblical book, probably of separate origin. A prologue and epilogue (Job 1, 2, and 42:7-17), apparently the remnants of an ancient folktale describing a righteous sufferer who maintained his faith despite unwarranted torments, differ in style and content from the main body of the text, the poetic dialogues between Job and his companions, a far more sophisticated and complex literary achievement.

3. Nahum Glatzer, "The Book of Job and Its Interpreters," *Biblical Motifs. Origins and Transformations* (ed. Alexander Altmann; Cambridge: Harvard University Press, 1966), 197-220, suggests that "the figure of Job, more so than others in the Bible, lent itself to a considerable diversity of interpretations" as a consequence of the "variety of views reposed in the book itself, its position in the biblical canon," and because of the multiplicity of "motifs employed in the Talmudic-Midrashic literature in its presentation of Job" (197). See also, his *The Dimensions of Job. A Study and Selected Readings* (New York: Schocken, 1969).

4. *Deuteronomy Rabbah* 2:4.

5. On rabbinic views of Gentiles see Baskin, *Pharaoh's Counsellors*, 7-9; and Moshe Greenberg, "Mankind, Israel and the Nations in the Hebraic Heritage," *No Man Is Alien. Essays on the Unity of Mankind* (ed. J. Robert Nelson; Leiden: Brill, 1971), 15-40. Despite biblical and mishnaic testimonies to the common descent of all human beings, and promises of equal reward for righteousness (see, i.e., *m. 'Abot* 3:14), the possibility of Gentile merit and reward apparently remained a matter of rabbinic debate, although *b. Sanhedrin* 105a does state affirmatively that the righteous among the nations will have a place in the world to come.

6. *J. Sota* 20c.

7. *B. Baba Batra* 15b.

8. Ibid.

9. Possibilities also include the time of Jacob, the time of Moses, the time of servitude in Egypt, the days of the judges, the time of the kingdom of Sheba, the time of the kingdom of the Chaldeans, and the time of the return of the exiles from Babylon. See Baskin, *Pharaoh's Counsellors,* 10ff. In *b. Baba Batra* 15a it is even suggested that Job never existed at all and that his story is no more than a parable to teach the virtue of resignation. See *Pharaoh's Counsellors,* 132n.23 (i).

10. The pseudepigraphical *Testament of Job* also preserves the tradition that Job married Dinah. See below, n. 18, and Baskin, *Pharaoh's Counsellors,* 29-32.

11. This assertion is given substance by the similarities of two verses: "O that my words were now written, would that they were inscribed [ויחקו]" (Job 19:23), and "He chose the first part for himself, for a portion of a ruler [מחקק] [or "inscriber"] was reserved" (Deut. 33:21). Since Job asked that his words be inscribed, and Moses is called an inscriber, the rabbis assume that Moses must have lived in the time of Job and written his story.

12. See *b. Baba Batra* 15b, and *Seder 'Olam Rabbah* 21.

13. Rabbinic sources that record this tradition include *b. Soṭa* 11a, *b. Sanhedrin* 106a, and *Exodus Rabbah* 27:3. It is clear that each of Pharaoh's counselors came to epitomize for the rabbis a particular aspect of the Gentile world: Job is the righteous Gentile who acknowledges God and lives a meritorious life beyond the boundaries of Israel; Jethro is the Gentile who goes a step further, forsaking his former life to become a Jewish proselyte; while Balaam becomes paradigmatic of Israel's enemies. The rabbis see him as wicked and blasphemous, committed to the constant oppression and eventual destruction of the Jewish people.

14. The belief in unswerving divine justice is a basic assumption of rabbinic theology. The *Melkilta* at *Be'Shallaḥ* 6 records that the sage Pappias (fl. 80–110 C.E.) once expressed views implying a certain arbitrariness on the part of God on the authority of "But He is at one with Himself, and who can turn Him? / And what His soul desires, even that he does" (Job 23:13). He was severely rebuked by R. Akiba (fl. 110–135 C.E.), who said, "There is nothing to answer the words of Him by whose word the world was called into existence, for He judges all in truth and everything in judgment." A later rabbi is quoted in the talmudic tractate *b. Baba Qamma* 50a: "He who says the Holy One, blessed be He, is lax in dealing out justice, let his life disintegrate. He is longsuffering but collects his debt in the end." Similarly, the rabbis held the view that no man suffers gratuitously, although the reasons for such suffering may be beyond human comprehension. As one sage admitted (*m. 'Abot* 4:15), "It is beyond our power to understand why the wicked are at ease, or why the righteous suffer."

15. This tradition is found in *Exodus Rabbah* 21:7; similar versions are found in *Genesis Rabbah* 57:4 and *j. Soṭa* 20d.

16. *B. Baba Batra* 16a.

17. Some of the rabbis do attempt to mitigate these harsh judgments, for as Gordis, *Book of Man*, 222, points out, "Regardless of what Job may have said in his anger and suffering, in the end he is humbled by the display of God's omnipotence and admits his own ignorance and presumption." The rabbis did not overlook this; Raba himself admits in *b. Baba Batra* 16a that Job's impotent ranting teaches that a man is not held responsible for what he says in distress, while *Exodus Rabbah* 14:11 teaches that Job finally came to his senses and recognized that divine greatness and power are indeed beyond human imagining.

18. On the *Testament of Job,* see Robert A. Kraft, *The Testament of Job* (TextsT 5; Pseudepigrapha Series 4; SBL; Missoula, Mont.: Scholars Press, 1974), which contains Greek text and English translation and an annotated chronological bibliography; and Baskin, *Pharaoh's Counsellors*, 29-32. On the *Life of Job* by Aristeas, see Robert Doran, "Aristeas the Exegete," in *The Old Testament Pseudepigrapha* (ed. J. H. Charlesworth; vol. 2; New York: Doubleday, 1985), 855-60.

19. *'Abot de Rabbi Nathan* 2. Gordis, *Book of Man*, 224, explains this tendency as a fear that Job's righteousness might place the patriarchs and other Jewish luminaries in the shade. And even more important, he maintains, was the need to justify Job's sufferings. Thus all of his faults and shortcomings were exaggerated. Marcel Simon, "Melchisédech dans la polémique entre Juifs et Chrétiens et dans la legende," *RHPR* 17 (1937) 58-93, shows a similar process at work in rabbinic remarks about Melchizedek and comments particularly, 66, on a rabbinic preoccupation with removing honors from Melchizedek and adding them to Abraham. On the superlative qualities

attributed to Abraham in Amoraic times, see Alexander Altmann, *"Homo Imago Dei* in Jewish and Christian Theology," *JR* 48 (1968) 235-59, who observes, 251, that in this period "Abraham assumes the role which Christian theology assigned to Jesus."

20. This midrash appears in *Genesis Rabbah* 73:9 and *b. Baba Batra* 15b.

21. See Baskin, *Pharaoh's Counsellors,* 80-86.

22. *B. Baba Batra* 15b.

23. For examples of such polemics, see A. Lukyn Williams, *Adversus Judaeos: A Bird's Eye View of Christian Apologiae until the Renaissance* (Cambridge: Cambridge University Press, 1935). On Jerome, in particular, see Marcel Simon, *Verus Israel. Etude sur les relations entre Chrétiens et Juifs dans l'Empire Romain 135–425* (Paris, 1948), 212. On Jewish-Christian exegetical contact, see Judith R. Baskin, "Rabbinic-Patristic Exegetical Contacts in Late Antiquity: A Bibliographical Reappraisal," in W. S. Green, *Approaches to Ancient Judaism* 5 (BJS; Chico, Calif.: Scholars Press, 1985), 53-80.

24. For patristic interpretations of the figure of Job, see Baskin, *Pharaoh's Counsellors,* 32-43.

25. Louis Ginzberg, *Legends of the Jews,* vol. 5 (Philadelphia: Jewish Publication Society, 1925), 381-82n. 3.

26. *B. Baba Batra* 15b and *j. Soṭa* 20c.

27. Reuven Kimelman, "Rabbi Yohanan and Origen on the Song of Songs: A Third Century Jewish-Christian Disputation," *HTR* 73 (1980) 567-95. Origen's knowledge and use of Jewish traditions are well known. See N.R.M. de Lange, *Origen and the Jews: Studies in Jewish-Christian Relations in Third-Century Palestine* (Cambridge: Cambridge University Press, 1975).

28. Origen, *Libelus de Oratione* 30 (*PG* 11, col. 547).

29. Jerome, *Letter* 73 *(PL* 22, col. 677).

30. Jerome, *Preface to Job* (*NPNF*, ser. ii. 6, 491).

7. Providence in Medieval Aristotelianism

1. Maimonides, *Guide of the Perplexed* III.22-23. All references to Maimonides, unless otherwise noted, will refer to these chapters. I rely on the translation by S. Pines (Chicago: University of Chicago Press, 1963).
All Scripture quotations are also from the Pines translation unless otherwise identified.

2. I rely on the text of the *Expositio super Job ad litteram* in vol. 26 of the Leonine edition of Aquinas's *Opera Omnia* (Roma: Sancta Sabina, 1965); cf. Thomas Aquinas, *The Literal Exposition on Job* (trans. A. Damico; interpretive essay by M. D. Yaffe; Atlanta: Scholars Press, 1989) (referred to below as Damico-Yaffe). All references to Aquinas, unless otherwise noted, refer to his comments ad loc. on the biblical text cited.

3. For my "protreptic" reading of Aristotle, see "Myth and 'Science' in Aristotle's Theology," *Man and World* 12 (1979) 70-88. Cf., in general, Martin D. Yaffe, "Interpretive Essay" in Aquinas, *Exposition,* 1-65.

4. Yaffe, "Myth and 'Science' in Aristotle's Theology," 72ff.

5. To establish this claim in full is of course beyond the scope of the present essay. The claim rests on the continual recurrence of Aristotle's protreptic analogies with the arts in both Maimonides' and Aquinas's writings, as well as of Aristotelian philosophical or

"scientific" terminology itself, which is decisively modeled on those analogies. In the Maimonidean text under consideration here, a protreptic analogy with the arts is the *sine qua non* of Maimonides' purported solution to Job's problem (see under "The Speech of God"). For the *prima facie* plausibility of this claim with respect to Aquinas's treatment of providence, at any rate, consider Aquinas's own numerous Aristotelian references to the arts in his articles on providence in *Summa Theologiae* I.22 (especially a.2, which refers also to I.14.8), as well as *Summa Contra Gentiles* III.64-113 (especially his general comparisons of art and nature in 64-66, but also the details of his appeals to specific arts throughout).

6. Cf. Aquinas' remark in the prologue to his *Exposition* that it is by merely plausible arguments (*per probabiles rationes*) that the book of Job arrives at the conclusion that human beings are ruled by divine providence.

7. Cf. Marvin Pope's introduction to his AB translation of Job (3rd ed.; Garden City, N.Y.: Doubleday, 1973), xv-lxxiv.

8. Cf. Pope, AB, on Job 19:26.

9. In *Guide* III.22 (*in princ.*), Maimonides cites the controversy in the Babylonian Talmud, *B. Batra* 15a. On the other hand, Aquinas, despite his acquaintance with Maimonides' opinion in the *Guide*, takes the opposite viewpoint, sc., that the story of Job is historical; see Aquinas, *Exposition*, prologue (*in fin.*), and 68-69 and 71 on 1:1.

10. For the following, cf. Leo Strauss, "How to Begin to Study *The Guide of the Perplexed*," in the Pines translation, xi-lvi; also Strauss, *Persecution and the Art of Writing* (Glencoe, Ill.: Free Press, 1952), 38-94.

11. Maimonides' Jewish-Aristotelian predecessor Saadiah Gaon (882–942 C.E.) interprets the book of Job as a whole in terms of the view here ascribed to Eliphaz. See *The Book of Theodicy: Translation and Commentary on the Book of Job by Saadiah ben Joseph al-Fayyumi* (trans.; with a philosophic commentary by L. E. Goodman; New Haven, Conn.: Yale University Press, 1988), 126.

12. For the following, cf. especially Otto Bird, "How to Read an Article of the *Summa*," *New Scholasticism* XXVII (1953) 129-59; also Yaffe, "Interpretive Essay," in Aquinas, *Exposition*, especially 25ff.

13. *Ad eruditionem incipientium* (*Summa Theologiae* I, Prologue).

14. Cf. Aristotle, *Nicomachean Ethics* 1141b4ff., with Aquinas, *Commentary on the Nicomachean Ethics*, sec. 1191-92; Aquinas, *Summa Theologiae* I-II.58.5.

15. Aquinas, *Exposition*, 285. The Vulgate, on which Aquinas relies, translates Job 21:21 as "For what difference does it make what happens to his house after him . . . ?"

16. Cf. Maimonides, *Guide* I.71, with Aristotle, *De anima* 427b14ff., 413b2-4, 432a10f., 433a9-12, b27-30, 434b6ff.; Strauss, *Persecution and the Art of Writing*, 40-41.

17. Cf., for the following, Aquinas, *Exposition*, 215-16, on 13:10.

18. Cf. Yaffe, "Interpretive Essay" in Aquinas, *Exposition*, 2 n. 9.

19. Aquinas, *Exposition*, 68.

20. Aquinas, *Exposition*, 374, on 33:13. Cf. also 99, 153-54, 300 on 3:1, 7:18, 23:4, respectively.

21. Maimonides, *Guide* III.23 (Pines, 496).

22. Aquinas, *Exposition*, 423, 425, 426, 428, 428-29, 429-30, 441, on 38:17, 21, 25, 33, 34, 36; and 39:31, respectively. Cf. 448, 452, 454, and 465 on 40:10, 14, 20; and 41:16, respectively.

23. Aquinas, *Exposition*, 441-42, on 39:33-35.

24. Aquinas, *Exposition*, 452, on 40:14.

8. "Why Do the Wicked Live?"

1. Calvin probably did not know Thomas's commentary directly but rather through such later commentators as Nicholas of Lyra or Denis the Carthusian. The works of both Lyra and Denis were collected by the Geneva Library.

2. Ambrose, *De interpellatione Iob et Devid, Corpus scriptorum ecclesiasticorum latinorum* 32/1.; ET "The Prayer of Job and David," trans. Michael P. McHugh (FC 65; Washington, D.C.: Catholic University of America Press, 1971), 320-420.

3. Ambrose, *De interpellatione* III.5. Cf. III.1.1.

4. Ambrose, *De interpellatione* II.2.3.

5. Ambrose, *De interpellatione* I.2.4.

6. Ambrose, *De interpellatione* II.1.2. Cf. 3.7-3.8.

7. Ambrose, *De interpellatione* II.2.3.

8. Ambrose, *De interpellatione* III.2.3.

9. Ambrose, *De interpellatione* III.3.9. Cf. Gregory the Great, *Moralia in Ioa* 25.30.51. Gregory's text can be found in S. Gregorii Magni, *Moralia in Ioa* cura et studio Marci Adriaen (CC 143, 143A; Turnhout, Belgium: Typographi Brepols Editores Pontifici, 1979); ET can be found in Library of Church Fathers (Oxford: John Henry Parker, 1844–50). Cited by book, section, and paragraph numbers.

10. Ambrose, *De interpellatione* II.1.2-2.4, II.4.13 (citing 1 Cor. 2:14).

11. Ambrose, *De interpellatione* II.4.11.

12. Ambrose, *De interpellatione* III.2.3.

13. Ambrose, *De interpellatione* II.4.16. Repeatedly Ambrose interprets the insights of Job and David in terms of Paul's exemplary suffering by citing or paraphrasing 1 Cor. 2:14-15, Rom. 11:33, and Phil. 1:21. See I.4.3, I.4.16, IV.2.6.

14. Ambrose, *De interpellatione* III.3.8 (citing Prov. 3:12). Cf. II.4.15, II.5.17.

15. Ambrose, *De interpellatione* I.9.30, IV.5.19.

16. Gregory, *Moralia* 3.9.15, 5.1.1, 6.23.40, 6.25.42, 7.5.39, 8.54.92, 23.24.27-48, 24.9.23, 26.13.21, 26.34.62, 26.45.82, 29.17.31, 33.19.35.

17. Gregory, *Moralia* 5.1.1.

18. St. Thomae de Aquino, *Expositio super Ioa ad litteram* (cura et studio Fratrum Praedicaetrum, *opera Omnia* 26 Rome: ad Sanctae Sabinae, 1965); ET: Thomas Aquinas, *The Literal Exposition on Job,* trans. Anthony Damico, with introduction and notes by Martin D. Yaffe (Atlanta: Scholars Press, 1989). Cited by chapter and verse: 2:11; 5:18; 8:2; 10:22; 17:13; 18:18-20. In 20:1ff. Thomas discerns some progress in Job's debate with his friends as he sees that Zophar conceded the possibility of a future life, although he still thought that the adversities and the prosperity of the present life were the result of sin or merit. It should be noted that precritical Joban exegetes, including Gregory, Thomas, and Calvin, separate Elihu from the other friends, largely because the divine rebuke in 42:6 refers to Eliphaz and his "two friends." Thomas argues that although Elihu was reproved by God in 38:2, nonetheless he *did* believe in immortality (32:2 and 37:24). Nevertheless, he too argued that the happiness or the misfortunes of the present life come about because of sins (37:24).

19. Thomas, *Expositio,* prologue, *in princ.*

20. Thomas, *Expositio,* 2:11; 4:7-12; 8:2; 9:25 (Job speaking); 3:4 (Job); 22:2-5; 11:15-30; 27:2; 27:8-17 (Job).

21. Thomas, *Expositio,* 21:26-27.

22. Thomas, *Expositio,* 3:3ff., 19:6-8, 21:3-21. Cf. chs. 14 and 17.

23. Thomas, *Expositio,* 24:24-25, 25, *in princ.*, 27:7-8, 29, *in princ.*

24. See Calvin, *Ioannis Calvini Opera Quae Supersunt Omnia* (CO) 33:686-696;

CO 34:61, 129-130, 149, 222, 259, 264, 302, 307; CO 35:494. Calvin admits that Job's sorrow did, at times, throw him into a "disordered passion" that made him question the resurrection (CO 33:155-156, 515; CO 34: 223-224). Nonetheless, hope in the afterlife was imprinted on his heart (CO 33: 156, 517). Moreover, Calvin sometimes admits that Job had only a "small spark" of knowledge about the resurrection (CO 34:131). Nevertheless, he does insist that in 14:14 Job defended the resurrection (CO 33:687). Throughout the sermons, Calvin argues that Job's hope for the future life provided him with a correct doctrine of providence.

25. CO 35: 494. Cf. CO 33:135, 406-407, 609; CO 34:253-254, 301-302, 305-307, 444-445, 462; CO 35:1-3, 28-29. Because he excludes Elihu from the divine rebuke, Calvin uses Elihu to correct Bildad, Zophar, Eliphaz—and Job. Space limitations prevent me from discussing Calvin's reading of Elihu's speeches; unless otherwise noted, the references to Job's friends include only Zophar, Bildad, and Eliphaz.

26. CO 33:221, 241, 277-278, 442, 451, 463, 477, 653; CO 34:52, 241, 254, 341, 369-373, 606-607, 64; CO 35:93, 247, 264, 360, 397, 455, 458-459. On the hiddenness of God in Calvin's thought see B. A. Gerrish, "To the Unknown God," in *The Old Protestantism and the New* (Chicago: University of Chicago Press, 1984) 131-49; and Heinrich Berger, *Calvins Geschichtsauffassung* (Studien zur Dogmengeschichte und systematischen Theologie 6; Zürich: Zwingli-Verlag, 1955) 51-55, 224-26, 237ff. On Calvin's view of providence and history see also Josef Bohatec, "Gott und Geschichte nach Calvin," in *Philosophia reformata* (1936):129-61; and "Calvins Vorsehungslehre" in *Calvinstudien* (1909):434-41.

27. Thomas, *Expositio,* 16:17-18; 17:11. Cf. 30:16-17. See also *Summa Theologiae* (S.T.), I.II.37-39.

28. CO 34:350, 586.

29. CO 33:85, 286-287, 439, 625; CO 34:62, 97, 135, 602, 607, 610. In several of these passages, Calvin also joins Job and David to Abraham, although he does not frequently cite from Genesis. See CO 33:82-83 for Calvin's recognition that the suffering of the just is the biblical norm.

30. CO 33:138, 166-167, 222, 267-259, 285, 288-289, 375, 510; CO 34:92-93, 277-278, 280, 291, 350, 589-590, 619; CO 35:114, 145, 199-200, 270-272, 285-287.

31. CO 33:269. Calvin may actually be referring to Ps. 119:71: "It has been good for me that I was afflicted . . . "

32. CO 33:666; CO 34:277-278, 350; CO 35:114, 199-200. Also compare references in n. 28.

33. CO 33:660-666.

34. CO 33:109, 385-388.

35. CO 33:104-116, 372, 437-438, 649-650, 565; CO 35:169. Repeatedly Calvin assures his hearers that the phrase "without cause" or "without reason" in Job 1:3 should not be taken as referring to God's action but only to human perception.

36. CO 34:135. See also CO 33:135; CO 34:59, 534.

37. CO 33:85, 120-121, 123, 135, 153, 190-191, 286, 294, 302, 341-342, 432-435, 686-687, 740; CO 34:10-11, 52-53, 100, 124, 258-260, 605, 610,; CO 35:140-223. Cf. 33:513-514, 681, 692; CO 34:263.

38. CO 33:120-124.

39. CO 33:122-124, 140, 223, 283, 287, 341, 357, 432-436, 477, 513-514, 612, 681, 684-687; CO 34:5, 11-12, 52, 57, 65, 101, 258, 292, 587-588, 605-608, 611, 624.

40. CO 33:685.

41. CO 34:610.

42. See Calvin's comments on Pss. 69:14 and 73:18 in CO 31:644, 683. See also those on Pss. 9:18; 10:12; 13:4; 37:12; and 73:28 in CO 31:105-106, 115-116, 133, 372-373, 689-690. Cf. ˜CO34:242, 405; CO35:459. In the Job sermons, Calvin commends

David for his confidence in God; unlike Job, David sang in the midst of his sadness (CO 33:152-153). See also CO 33:286. This topic is explored more thoroughly in Barbara Pitkin's University of Chicago dissertation, "What Pure Eyes Can See."

43. On Job's more radical question of divine justice and Calvin's references to "absolute power," see Martin D. Yaffe, "Double Justice and Exegesis in Calvin's Sermons on Job," *CH* 58 (1989) 322-338.

44. CO 33:371-372; CO 34:36, 175, 222, 336, 360, 362; CO 35:58-60, 131-132, 153-154, 206, 315, 369, 454, 479-480.

45. CO 34:68-70.

46. CO 35:382, 383, 406, 412, 444, 474.

47. CO 35:380-381, 387-388, 396-399, 403-404, 435.

48. CO 33:205ff., 371-372, 373, 440, 543, 586, 590, 602, 633, 643-648; CO 34:98, 232, 347, 362; CO 35:174-176, 260, 263, 300-302.

49. CO 35:367-369, 374-375, 380-381, 387-388, 396, 403, 420.

50. CO 33:683.

51. Cf. Robert Bellah et al., *Habits of the Heart* (San Francisco: Harper & Row, 1985): "A genuine community of memory will also tell painful stories of shared suffering that sometimes creates deeper identities than success" (153).

52. CO 33:82, 105, 117, 122, 385, 514; CO 34:139. Both Job and David are seen as models for imitation and instruction: CO 33:83, 93, 111, 120, 132, 151, 164; CO 34:59, 114. For the portrayal of David in the Reformation see Edward A. Gosselin, *The King's Progress to Jerusalem: Some Interpretations of David during the Reformation Period and Their Patristic and Medieval Background* (Malibu, Calif.: Undena Publication, 1976).

9. Job and His Friends in the Modern World

1. M. Susman, "Das Hiob-Problem bei Franz Kafka," *Der Morgen* 5 (1929) 49. M. Brod also discusses Kafka's work in terms of "the primeval Job-question" (*Über Franz Kafka* [Frankfurt a.M.: Fischer, 1966] 155).

2. N. Frye, *Anatomy of Criticism: Four Essays* (Princeton, N.J.: Princeton University Press, 1957), 42.

3. See N. Glatzer, *The Dimensions of Job: A Study and Selected Readings* (New York: Schocken, 1969), 48.

4. G. Scholem, *Walter Benjamin—die Geschichte einer Freundschaft* (Frankfurt a.M.: Suhrkamp, 1975), 212-13.

5. F. Rosenzweig, quoted in N. Glatzer, *Franz Rosenzweig* (New York: Schocken, 1953), 160.

6. N. Frye, *The Great Code: The Bible and Literature* (New York: Harcourt, 1983), 195. Cf. H. Fisch: "*The Trial* is surely very Jobian" (*A Remembered Future: A Study in Literary Mythology* [Bloomington, Ind.: Indiana University Press, 1984], 166). Critics like D. M. Kartiganer ("Job and Joseph K.: Myth in Kafka's *The Trial*," *Modern Fiction Studies* 8 [1962] 31) and R. St. Leon ("Religious Motives in Kafka's 'Der Prozess': Some Textual Notes," *Journal of the Australasian Universities Language and Literature Association* 19 [1963] 29-33) suggest that Kafka was consciously influenced by Job when he wrote his novel, even though Kafka never mentioned this biblical book in his diaries, notebooks, or extant letters (see Glatzer, *Dimensions,* 48). Such claims of affinity and

influence are muted in R. Suter's study (*Kafkas' 'Prozess' im Lichte des 'Buches Hiob'* [Frankfurt a.M.: Lang, 1965]), which is considerably more cautious than the chapter on Job and *The Trial* in the more recent book by M. Wilk (*Jewish Presence in T. S. Eliot and Franz Kafka* [Atlanta: Scholars Press, 1986], 133-67).

7. See, e.g., M. Weinfeld, *Deuteronomy and the Deuteronomic School* (Oxford: Clarendon, 1972), 265-77, 288.

8. On Job's concern about attitudes that cannot be controlled legally, see G. Fohrer, "The Righteous Man in Job 31," *Essays in Old Testament Ethics* (ed. J. L. Crenshaw and J. T. Willis; New York: Ktav, 1974), 13-17. On the relationship between Job 31 and the "internal dimension" of Israelite law, see M. B. Dick, "Job 31, The Oath of Innocence, and the Sage," *ZAW* 95 (1983) 48-53.

9. For a more detailed discussion of this process, see S. Lasine, "Kafka's 'Sacred Texts' and the Hebrew Bible," *Papers in Comparative Studies* 3 (1984) 121-35.

10. See the studies cited by N. C. Habel, *The Book of Job: A Commentary* (OTL; Philadelphia: Westminster, 1985) 54; and D. Cox, "The Book of Job as Bi-Polar Mašal: Structure and Interpretation," *Anton* 62 (1987) 16-20.

11. The most extensive treatment is that of L. Kirchberger (*Franz Kafka's Use of Law in Fiction: A New Interpretation of* In der Strafkolonie, Der Prozess, *and* Das Schloss [New York: Lang, 1986]). Also see R. Gray, "But Kafka Wrote in German," *The Kafka Debate: New Perspectives for Our Time* (ed. A. Flores; New York: Gordian, 1977) 244; and M. Spann, *Franz Kafka* (Boston: Twayne, 1976), 98-101.

12. Habel, *Book of Job,* 54.

13. Dick, "The Legal Metaphor in Job 31," *CBQ* 41 (1979) 50.

14. Cox, "Book of Job," 21.

15. Ibid., 15.

16. W. H. Sokel, "The Programme of K.'s Court: Oedipal and Existential Meanings of *The Trial,*" in *On Kafka: Semi-Centenary Perspectives* (ed. F. Kuna; New York: Barnes, 1976) 7.

17. E.g., I. Watt, *The Rise of the Novel: Studies in Defoe, Richardson and Fielding* (Berkeley: University of California Press, 1957) 31, 34, 57; and W. C. Booth, *The Rhetoric of Fiction* (2nd ed.; Chicago: University of Chicago Press, 1983), 69.

18. S. Mailloux, *Interpretive Conventions: The Reader in the Study of American Fiction* (Ithaca: Cornell University Press, 1982), 81, 87.

19. S. Mailloux, "Learning to Read: Interpretation and Reader-Response Criticism," *American Critics at Work: Examinations of Contemporary Literary Theories* (ed. V. A. Kramer; Troy, N.Y.: Whitston, 1984), 309-10.

20. For an interpretation of the book of Job as a drama, see L. Alonso Schökel, "Toward a Dramatic Reading of the Book of Job," *Semeia* 7 (1977) 45-59. For the theatrical in Kafka, see J. Rolleston, *Kafka's Narrative Theater* (University Park, Pa.: Pennsylvania State University Press, 1974).

21. E. Scarry, *The Body in Pain: The Making and Unmaking of the World* (New York: Oxford University Press, 1985), 298. J. B. White distinguished between readers of literary and legal texts by noting that the reader of the legal text is "its servant, seeking to make real what it directs" (*Heracles' Bow: Essays on the Rhetoric and Poetics of the Law* [Madison, Wisc.: University of Wisconsin Press, 1985], 95).

22. On this level of reading, see P. J. Rabinowitz, "Truth in Fiction: A Reexamination of Audiences," *Critical Inquiry* 4 (1977) 126-27.

23. B. de Spinoza, *A Theological-Political Treatise and a Political Treatise* (New York: Dover, 1951), 149.

24. F. Kafka, *Der Prozess* (Frankfurt a.M.: Fischer, 1950). Numbers after the abbreviation "P" are page numbers from this edition. The verb in Job 1:17 is *pāšaṭ* Kafka's word is *überfallen,* the same word used by Luther when translating *pāšaṭ* in Job 1:17.

25. See Job 16:9-14. On K. perceiving the goddess of Justice and Victory as goddess of the Hunt, and his feeling "goaded" by the Court, see the section "Victimization and Responsibility."

26. Far from being willing to declare the count of his steps to the higher authority, K. cannot even see two steps ahead, as he is told by the Court chaplain (P 254). In K.'s transfiguration dream, "Ein Traum," which Kafka chose not to incorporate into *Der Prozess,* K. had hardly taken two steps before he was already at the cemetery where his tombstone was about to be inscribed (F. Kafka, *Sämtliche Erzählungen* [ed. P. Raabe; Frankfurt a.M.: Fischer, 1970], 145). All Scripture translations in this chapter are the author's.

27. For the technical use of this term in German law, see Kirckberger, *Kafka's Use of Law,* 113n.23.

28. On Job's responsiveness to social injustice, see G. Gutiérrez, *On Job: God-talk and the Suffering of the Innocent* (Maryknoll, N.Y.: Orbis, 1987), 31-34 and passim; and S. Lasine, "Bird's-eye and Worm's-eye Views of Justice in the Book of Job," *JSOT* 42 (1988) 34-38. Ironically, a *midrash* asserts that Job was afflicted because he *failed* to intervene on behalf of helpless victims (the doomed male Israelite babies) when he was one of Pharaoh's counselors (*b. Soṭa* 11a; *Exod. Rab.* 1.9).

29. The chaplain's response to K.'s remark calls attention to K.'s motive: " 'That's correct, . . . but that's the way the guilty talk' " (P 253). For more on the way K. attempts to obscure his individual accountability by "hiding in the collective," see Lasine, "Kafka's 'Sacred Texts,' " 125-26.

30. K.'s irresponsible charges against the warders at his interrogation, which lead to their harsh punishment, immediately follow K.'s taking the role of intercessor for other, hypothetical, accused persons (and not for himself! [P 57]). This suggests that those charges may have been prompted by K.'s playing the role of advocate. K.'s behavior toward *actual* accused persons tends to be condescending, if not cruel; see n. 51, below.

31. Habel, *Book of Job,* 548-49; Cox, "Book of Job," 17-20.

32. *Num. Rab.* 20, 12. On the relevance of this dictum for the merchant Block, who strongly resembles the biblical Balaam, see S. Lasine, "Kafka's *The Trial,*" *The Explicator* 43 (1985) 34-36.

33. See further in Lasine, "Kafka's 'Sacred Texts.' " 124.

34. Girard's most complete treatment of Job is *La Route antique des hommes pervers* (Paris: Grasset, 1985). Also see his "Job and the God of Victims" in this volume.

35. R. Girard, *Des choses cachées depuis la fondation du monde* (Paris: Grasset, 1978) 154.

36. Girard, *La Route,* 192, 216.

37. Ibid., 192.

38. E.g., B. Bassoff, "The Model as Obstacle: Kafka's *The Trial,*" *To Honor René Girard* (ed. A. Juilland; Saratoga, Calif.: Anma Libri, 1986) 299-315. Bassoff explicitly applies Girard's theory to Kafka's novel, but without mentioning Girard's work on Job.

39. Girard, *La Route,* 11-12, 38, 155-61.

40. Spann, *Franz Kafka,* 102.

41. E.g., Bassoff, "Model," 305; Kirchberger, *Kafka's Use of Law*, 85; H. H. Hiebel, *Die Zeichen des Gesetzes: Recht und Macht bei Franz Kafka* (Munich: Fink, 1983), 16, 214-15.

42. E.g., E. Marson, *Kafka's Trial: The Case Against Josef K.* (St. Lucia, Queensland: University of Queensland Press, 1975), 282; and R. R. Nicolai, *Kafkas "Prozess": Motive und Gestalten* (Würzburg: Königshausen und Neumann, 1986), 208; cf. 181.

43. The pronoun "they" (*sie*) can refer to the bank or the Court (see Marson, *Kafka's Trial*, 321n. 4), if not both.

44. F. Kafka, *Beschreibung eines Kampfes: Novellen, Skizzen, Aphorismen aus dem Nachlass* (Frankfurt a.M.: Fischer, 1954), 295-96.

45. For a full exposition of the arguments sketched in this paragraph, see Lasine, "Bird's-eye," 29-47.

46. See Brod, *Über Franz Kafka*, 76; Marson, *Kafka's Trial*, 16-17; and R. Robertson, *Kafka: Judaism, Politics, and Literature* (Oxford: Clarendon, 1985), 42-44, 53, 101.

47. Robertson, *Kafka*, 53.

48. On the moral implications of a viewer's standpoint, see Lasine, "Bird's-eye," 30-38.

49. See Kafka's two-sentence-long story "Auf der Galerie" (*Sämtliche Erählungen*, 129).

50. Significantly, Kafka had used the metaphor of a theatrical whipping scene to describe human moral agency in a 1911 diary entry. He notes that if an actor goes beyond the script in his excitement and *really* whips another actor, "the spectator must become a person and intervene" (*Tagebücher 1910–1923* [Frankfurt a.M.: Fischer, 1951], 220).

51. E.g., K. automatically takes the role of the Inspector, and not the accused, when he replays the arrest scene for Fräulein Bürstner (P 39). K.'s play-acted "Aufseher" is a loud ruffian, unlike the actual Inspector. Later, he grabs an elderly, dignified, accused man and after speculating that this gentleman might take K. for a judge, gives him a violent shove (P 82). Finally, he tyrannizes the merchant Block as though the latter were a lowly person from a foreign country (P 202).

52. E.g., K. assumes that he can make Frau Grubach truly believe his lie about attacking Fräulein Bürstner, because she has borrowed a large sum of money from him (P 41). Similarly, he is confident that his mother, to whom he sends money, will always believe that he is a Manager at the Bank (P 277, 280).

53. Robertson, *Kafka*, 104-5; cf. 111.

54. Ibid., 103. For the aphorism, see n. 59, below.

55. See Lasine, "Bird's-eye," 31-35.

56. See, e.g., Prov. 20:9; 26:12, 16; 28:11; Jer. 17:9.

57. The aphorism used by Robertson actually fits the apocryphal book of 4 Ezra much better than either Job or *Der Prozess*. On the inappropriateness of the concept of original sin for an understanding of *Der Prozess*, see Sokel, "Programme," 1.

58. See Deut. 29:28; 30:14-16, 19-20. In Kafka's novel, the opportunity for a positive moral existence in illustrated by characters like Fräulein Bürstner and is implied by the life choices K.—and the man from the country—fail to make.

59. See, e.g., Deut. 30:11-14. Kafka''s aphorism, cited by Robertson, *Kafka*, concludes by noting the attempt to falsify knowledge obtained in the Fall by making "knowledge into a goal," and with this aphorism, which appears on the next page: "Knowledge we have. Whoever strives for it intensely is suspect of striving against it"

(Franz Kafka, *Hochzeitsvorbereitungen auf dem Lande und andere Prosa aus dem Nachlass* [Frankfurt a.M.: Fischer, 1953], 102-3, 104).

60. " 'ādām qārôb lĕ'aṣmô"—that is, a human being is partial to himself. See N. Leibowitz, *Studies in Vayikra* (Jerusalem: World Zionist Organization, 1983), 194. Cf. the Satan's assumption that all humans are selfish (Job 2:4), a hypothesis that is invalidated when tested on Job.

61. A. Camus, *La Chute* (Paris: Gallimard, 1956). Cf. E. Levinas: "The forgetting of self drives justice" (*Autrement qu'âtre ou audelà l'essence* [The Hague: Nijhoff, 1974], 203).

11. A Response to the Book of Job

1. Robert Gordis, *The Book of God and Man: A Study of Job* (Chicago: University of Chicago Press, 1965), v.

2. Marvin Pope, *Job* (Garden City, N.Y.: Doubleday, 1973).

3. Samuel Terrien, *Job: Poet of Existence* (Indianapolis: Bobbs-Merrill, 1957).

4. John Calvin, *Sermons from Job*, (trans. Leroy Nixon; Grand Rapids: Eerdmans, 1952). The end of each sermon is "Now we shall bow in humble reverence before the face of our God."

5. John Calvin, *Institutes of the Christian Religion* I, 16, 3 (trans. Ford Lewis Battles; ed. John T. McNeill; 2 vols.; Philadelphia: Westminster, 1955) 1:200-201.

6. Ibid., III, 7, 2, 1:691.

7. Ibid., 1:223.

8. San Francisco: Harper & Row, 1988.

9. Levenson, *Creation*, 49, quoting from Knight, "Cosmogony and Order in the Hebrew Tradition," *Cosmogony and Ethical Order* (eds. Robin Lovin and Frank Reynolds; Chicago: University of Chicago Press, 1985), 142. For Levenson on Job, see 153-56.

10. Cicero, *The Nature of the Gods* (trans. Horace C. P. McGregor; vol. 1; New York: Penguin, 1972), 70-71.

11. Levenson, *Creation*, 155, 156.

12. Terrien, *Job*, 39.

13. Ibid., 50.

14. Ibid., 239.

15. Ibid., 112.

16. For my more elaborated reasons for holding this position, see James M. Gustafson, *Ethics from a Theocentric Perspective* (2 vols.; Chicago: University of Chicago Press, 1981 and 1984).

17. Marvin Pope, *Job*, 146.

18. Terrien, *Job*, 241.

12. Job As Failed Scapegoat

1. This is the rendering of the translator in consultation with Professor Girard. The Hebrew text has *tōpet lĕpānîm*, "Tophet to the face." *Tōpet* recalls the victimization and sacrifice of children that occurred at the place called Tophet in the valley of Hinnom. See

2 Kings 23:10; Jer. 7:32; 19:11-12; evidently the same place is intended in Jer. 32:35. On the practice of child sacrifice see Lev. 18:21; 20:2-5; Deut. 12:31; 18:10; 2 Kings 16:3; 17:17; 21:6; Jer. 7:31; 19:6; Ezek. 16:20-21; 23:39. As for *lĕpânîm,* the sense of "to the face" or "before" is here construed as "before everyone."

2. A biblical expression designating the shock that the divine punishment of the guilty provokes in those who witness it.

3. With respect to suffering, Simone Weil very powerfully observed this difference between the other and me. The relation to the other, for Christianity, is at stake in this question.

13. Job and the God of Victims

1. See Leo G. Perdue, *Wisdom in Revolt: Creation Theology in the Book of Job* (Sheffield: Almond, 1991).

2. R. Gordis, *The Book of God and Man* (Chicago: University of Chicago Press, 1965), 110-12; James G. Williams, "You Have Not Spoken Truth of Me: Mystery and Irony in Job," *ZAW* 81 (1971) 231-55; "Deciphering the Unspoken: The Theophany of Job," *HUCA* 40 (1978) 59-72; "Job's Vision: The Dialectic of Person and Presence," *HAR* 8 (1984) 259-72.

3. See especially R. Girard, *Violence and the Sacred* (Baltimore: Johns Hopkins, 1977); *The Scapegoat* (Baltimore: Johns Hopkins, 1986); *Job: The Victim of His People* (Stanford, Calif.: Stanford University Press, 1987); and *Things Hidden Since the Foundation of the World* (Stanford, Calif.: Stanford University Press, 1987). See also James G. Williams, "The Innocent Victim: René Girard on Violence, Sacrifice and the Sacred," *RSR* 14 (1988) 320-26. For a full bibliography to 1986, see *To Honor René Girard* (Stanford French and Italian Studies 34; Saratoga, Calif.: Anma Libri, 1986). For an essay on Job that gives his basic argument and sharpens some of his concerns and insight in a manner not found in his book, see Girard, "Job As Failed Scapegoat," in this volume.

4. Girard, *Job,* 86-90.

5. J. Grosjean, trans., *Eumenides,* cited in Girard, *Job,* 148.

6. Girard, *Job,* 35.

7. Ibid., 111-17.

8. Ibid., 35.

9. Ibid., 25.

10. Ibid., 27.

11. Ibid., 140.

12. Ibid., 141.

13. Ibid., 141-42.

14. See Perdue, *Wisdom in Revolt.*

15. R. Alter, *The Art of Biblical Poetry.* (New York: Basic Books, 1985), ch. 4.

16. Williams, "Job's Vision," 261.

17. Williams, "Deciphering the Unspoken."

18. Norman Habel, *The Book of Job* (OTL; Philadelphia: Westminster, 1985), 551.

19. Habel's rendering, ibid.

20. Ibid., 558.

21. Ibid., 563.

22. Alter, *The Art of Biblical Poetry*, 19-21 and ch. 3; Kugel, *The Idea of Biblical Poetry* (New Haven, Conn.: Yale University Press, 1981), ch. 1.

23. Burton Mack, "The Innocent Transgressor: Jesus in Early Christian Myth and History," *Semeia* 33 (1985) 67.

24. M. Wallace, "Postmodern Biblicism: The Challenge of René Girard for Contemporary Theology," *Modern Theology* 5 (1989) 323.

25. Wallace's term, ibid., 314.

26. Girard, *The Scapegoat*, 8.

27. See Sandor Goodhart, "I Am Joseph: René Girard and the Prophetic Law," *Violence and Truth* (ed. Paul Dumouchel; Stanford, Calif.: Stanford University Press, 1988), 255n. 12, with reference to the work of Michel Serres.

28. M. Tsevat, "The Meaning of the Book of Job," *HUCA* 37 (1966) 106.

29. Girard, *Job*, 159, 160-61. Italics added.

30. Girard, *Things Hidden*, 187-88.

31. So Mack, "The Innocent Transgressor," 147-65.

32. Girard, *Job*, 143.

33. No. 1052, as quoted in Girard, "The Founding Murder," in *Violence and Truth*, 243.

34. Girard, *Things Hidden*, 266.

A SELECT BIBLIOGRAPHY

Collections of Essays on Job

Crossan, John Dominic (ed.). *The Book of Job and Ricoeur's Hermeneutics.* *Semeia* 19 (1981).

Duquoc, Christian, and Floristan, Casiano (eds.). *Job and the Silence of God.* Concilium 169. New York: Seabury, 1983.

Sanders, Paul S. (ed.). *Twentieth Century Interpretations of the Book of Job.* Englewood Cliffs, N.J.: Prentice-Hall, 1968.

Ancient Near Eastern Literature

Gordon, Edmund I. *Sumerian Proverbs: Glimpses of Everyday Life in Ancient Mesopotamia.* Philadelphia: The University Museum, University of Pennsylvania, 1959.

Gray, John. "The Book of Job in the Context of Near Eastern Literature." *ZAW* 82 (1970) 251-69.

Jacobsen, Thorkild. *The Treasures of Darkness.* New Haven: Yale. 1976.

Lambert, Wilfred G. *Babylonian Wisdom Literature.* Oxford: Clarendon, 1960.

Lichtheim, Miriam. *Ancient Egyptian Literature.* 3 vols. Berkeley/Los Angeles: University of California, 1973–80.

Preuss, H. D. "Jahwes Antwort an Hiob und die sogennante Hiobliteratur des alten Vorderen Orients." *Beiträge zur alttestamentlichen Theologie,* ed. Herbert Donner, *et al.* Göttingen: Vandenhoeck & Ruprecht, 1977, 323-345.

Pritchard, James B. *Ancient Near Eastern Texts Relating to the Old Testament.* 3rd ed. Princeton: Princeton University Press, 1969.

Williams, R. J. "Theodicy in the Ancient Near East." *CJTh* 2 (1956) 14-26.

Surveys of Joban Interpretation, Special Studies, and Commentaries

1. Surveys of Interpretations of the Book of Job

Glatzer, Nahum. "The Book of Job and Its Interpreters." *Biblical Motifs. Origins and Transformations,* ed. Alexander Altmann. Cambridge, Mass.: Harvard University Press, 1966, 197-220.

Müller, H.-P. "Altes und Neues zum Buch Hiob." *EvTh* 37 (1977) 284-304.

———. *Das Hiobproblem.* Erträge der Forschung 84. Darmstadt: Wissenschaftliche Buchgesellschaft, 1978.

2. Commentaries and Special Studies

Cox, D. *The Triumph of Impotence. Job and the Tradition of the Absurd.* Rome: Universita Gregoriana, 1978.

Crenshaw, James L. *Old Testament Wisdom.* Atlanta: John Knox, 1981.

Dhorme, E. *A Commentary on the Book of Job.* London: Nelson, 1967.

Fohrer, Georg. *Das Buch Hiob.* KAT 16. Gütersloh: Gerd Mohn, 1963.

———. *Studien zum Buche Hiob.* 2nd ed. Gütersloh: Gerd Mohn, 1982.

Glatzer, Nahum. *The Dimensions of Job. A Study and Selected Readings.* New York: Schocken, 1969.

Good, Edwin, *In Turns of Tempest: A Reading of Job with a Translation.* Stanford: Stanford University Press, 1990.

Gordis, Robert. *The Book of Job.* New York: Jewish Theological Seminary of America, 1978.

———. *The Book of God and Man.* Chicago: University of Chicago Press, 1978.

Habel, Norman. *Job.* Old Testament Library. Philadelphia: Westminster, 1985.

Janzen, J. Gerald. *Job.* Interpretation. Atlanta: John Knox, 1985.

Pope, Marvin. *Job.* 3rd ed. Anchor Bible. Garden City: Doubleday, 1974.

Rad, Gerhard von. *Wisdom in Israel.* Nashville: Abingdon, 1972.

Scott, R. B. Y. *The Way of Wisdom.* New York: Macmillan, 1971.

Terrien, Samuel. *Job: Poet of Existence.* Indianapolis: Bobbs-Merrill, 1957.

Tur-Sinai, N. H. *The Book of Job.* Jerusalem: Kiryath Sepher, 1957.

3. The Social World of the Book of Job

Gammie, John G., and Leo G. Perdue (eds.). *The Sage in Israel and the Ancient Near East.* Winona Lake, Ind.: Eisenbrauns, 1990.

Perdue, Leo G., and John G. Gammie. *Paraenesis: Act and Form. Semeia* 50 (1991).

4. The Genre of Job

Murphy, Roland. *Wisdom Literature.* FOTL 13. Grand Rapids: Eerdmans, 1981.

5. The Place of Job in Biblical Theology

Albertz, R. *Weltschöpfung und Menschenschöpfung.* Stuttgart: Calwer, 1974.
Crenshaw, James L. *Whirlpool of Torment.* Philadelphia: Fortress, 1985.
Gutiérrez, Gustavo. *On Job: God-Talk and the Suffering of the Innocent.* Maryknoll, N.Y.: Orbis, 1987.
Hermisson, Hans-Jürgen. "Observations on the Creation Theology in Wisdom." *Israelite Wisdom.* ed. John G. Gammie, *et al.,* Missoula, Mont.: Scholars Press, 1978.
Keel, Othmar. *Jahwes Entgegnung an Ijob.* FRLANT 121. Göttingen: Vandenhoeck und Ruprecht, 1978.
Knierim, Rolf. "Cosmos and History in Israel's Theology." *Werden und Wirken der Alten Testaments,* ed. Rainer Albertz, *et al.* Göttingen, Vandenhoeck und Ruprecht, 1980, 59-123.
Levenson, Jon. *Creation and the Persistence of Evil.* San Francisco: Harper & Row, 1988.
Murphy, Roland. "Wisdom and Creation." *JBL* 104 (1985) 3-11.
Perdue, Leo G. *Wisdom in Revolt, Metaphorical Theology in the Book of Job.* JSOTSup 112/Bible and Literature Series 29.
Rad, Gerhard von. *Wisdom in Israel.* Nashville: Abingdon, 1972.
Schmid, Hans Heinrich. "Creation, Righteousness, and Salvation." *Creation in the Old Testament,* ed. B. W. Anderson. Philadelphia: Fortress, 1984, 102-17.
Zimmerli, Walther. "The Place and Limit of the Wisdom in the Framework of the Old Testament Theology." *SJTh* 17 (1964) 146-58.

Literary Interpretations of the Book of Job

Fontaine, Carole. "Folktale Structure in the Book of Job: A Formalist Reading." *Directions in Biblical Hebrew Poetry,* ed. Elaine Follis. JSOTSup 40. Sheffield: Almond Press, 1987, 205-32.
Good, Edwin M. "Job and the Literary Task: A Response." *Soundings* 56 (1973) 470-84.
———. "The Narrative Art of Job: Applying the Principles of Robert Alter." *JSOT* 27 (1983) 101-11.
Perdue, Leo G. "Job's Assault on Creation." *HAR* 10 (1986) 295-315.
Robertson, David. *The Old Testament and the Literary Critic.* Philadelphia: Fortress, 1973.

Schökel, Alonzo. "Towards a Dramatic Reading of the Book of Job." *Semeia* 7 (1977) 45-61.

Tsevat, Matitiahu. "The Meaning of the Book of Job." *HUCA* 37 (1966) 73-106.

Williams, James G. "Deciphering the Unspoken: The Theophany of Job," *HUCA* 49 (1978) 59-72.

Rabbinic Interpretations of Job

Baskin, Judith. *Pharaoh's Counsellors, Job, Jethro, and Balaam in Rabbinic and Patristic Tradition.* Brown Judaic Studies 47. Chico, Calif.: Scholars Press, 1983.

Buber, Solomon, ed. *Majan-Gannim. Commentary on Job of Rabbi Samuel ben Nissim Masnuth.* Berlin: Itzkowsky, 1889.

Kaufmann, Herman Ezekiel. *Die Anwendung das Buchs Hiob in der Rabbinischen Agadah.* Frankfurt am Main: M. Slobotzky, 1983.

Christian Interpretations of Job in the Early Church, Middle Ages, and Reformation

Aquinas, Thomas. *The Literal Exposition on Job,* trans. A. Damico, Interpretive Essay by M. D. Yaffe. Atlanta: Scholars Press, 1989.

Besserman, Lawrence L. *The Legend of Job in the Middle Ages.* Cambridge, Mass.: Harvard University, 1979.

Goodman, L. E. *The Book of Theodicy. Translation and Commentary on the Book of Job by Saadiah ben Joseph al-Fayyumi.* New Haven: Yale University, 1988.

Modern Interpretations of the Book of Job

Brod, M. *Über Franz Kafka.* Frankfurt am Main: Fischer, 1966.

Frye, N. *The Great Code: the Bible and Literature.* New York: Harcourt, 1983.

Girard, René. *Job. The Victim of His People.* Stanford, Calif.: Stanford University Press, 1987.

Kartiganer, D. M. "Job and Joseph K.: Myth in Kafka's *The Trial.*" *Modern Fiction Studies* 8 (1962) 31-43.

Macleish, Archibald. *J.B.* Boston: Houghton Mifflin, 1958.

INDEX OF AUTHORS

INDEX OF JUDEO-CHRISTIAN SCRIPTURES

(All page references are in **bold** type.)